HANDBOOK OF UNIVERSITY-WIDE ENTREPRENEURSHIP EDUCATION

Handbook of University-wide Entrepreneurship Education

Edited by

G. Page West III

Wake Forest University, USA

Elizabeth J. Gatewood

Wake Forest University, USA

and

Kelly G. Shaver

College of Charleston, USA

Edward Elgar
Cheltenham, UK • Northampton, MA, USA

Published by
Edward Elgar Publishing Limited
The Lypiatts
15 Lansdown Road
Cheltenham
Glos GL50 2JA
UK

Edward Elgar Publishing, Inc.
William Pratt House
9 Dewey Court
Northampton
Massachusetts 01060
USA

A catalogue record for this book
is available from the British Library

Library of Congress Control Number: 2009925915

Mixed Sources
Product group from well-managed
forests and other controlled sources
www.fsc.org Cert no. SA-COC-1565
© 1996 Forest Stewardship Council
FSC

ISBN 978 1 84720 455 4

Printed and bound by MPG Books Group, UK

Contents

Contributors

Sophie Bacq   Teaching and Research Assistant, IAG Louvain School of Management, Université Catholique de Louvain, Louvain-la-Neuve, Belgium.

Gary D. Beckman   Visiting Assistant Professor, School of Music, University of South Carolina, Columbia, SC.

Naomi Birdthistle   Lecturer in Entrepreneurship, Department of Management and Marketing, University of Limerick, Limerick, Ireland.

Richard A. Cherwitz   Professor, Department of Communication Studies & Division of Rhetoric and Writing, University of Texas at Austin, Austin, TX.

Lynnette Claire   Assistant Professor, School of Business and Leadership, University of Puget Sound, Tacoma, Washington, DC.

Robert D'Intino   Professor, Rohrer College of Business, Rowan University, Glassboro, NJ.

Valérie Eeckhout   Institute for University Pedagogy and Multimedia, Université Catholique de Louvain, Louvain-la-Neuve, Belgium.

Alain Fayolle   Professor, EM Lyon Business School, Lyon, France.

Benoît Gailly   Professor, IAG Louvain School of Management, Université Catholique de Louvain, Louvain-la-Neuve, Belgium.

Elizabeth J. Gatewood   Director, Office of Entrepreneurship and Liberal Arts, Wake Forest University, Winston Salem, NC.

William Scott Green   Senior Vice Provost and Dean of Undergraduate Education, University of Miami, Coral Gables, FL.

Jerry Gustafson   Professor, Economics and Management, Beloit College, Beloit, WI.

Samuel M. Hines, Jr   Provost and Dean of the College, The Citadel, Charleston, SC.

Sherry Hoskinson   Director, McGuire Center for Entrepreneurship, Eller College of Management, University of Arizona, Tucson, AZ.

Jutta Huebscher   Projektstelle für Existenzgründung, Lehrstuhl für Organisation und Personalwesen, Passau University, Passau, Germany.

Briga Hynes   Lecturer in Entrepreneurship, Department of Management and Marketing, University of Limerick, Limerick, Ireland.

Frank Janssen   Professor, IAG Louvain School of Management, Université Catholique de Louvain, Louvain-la-Neuve, Belgium.

A. Daniel Johnson   Lecturer in Biology, Department of Biology, Wake Forest University, Winston Salem, NC.

Cynthia Kehoe   Associate Director for Information and Research Services, Academy for Entrepreneurial Leadership, University of Illinois at Champaign, Champaign, IL.

Norris F. Krueger, Jr   Max Planck Institute of Economics, Entrepreneurship Northwest, Boise, ID.

Christian Lendner   Professor, Department of Mechanical Engineering, University of Applied Sciences, Deggendorf, Germany.

Jed C. Macosko   Assistant Professor, Department of Physics, Wake Forest University, Winston Salem, NC.

Matthew M. Mars   McGuire Center for Entrepreneurship, Office of Technology Transfer, University of Arizona, Tucson, AZ.

Anthony Mendes   Executive Director, Academy for Entrepreneurial Leadership, University of Illinois at Champaign, Champaign, IL.

DeMond Miller   Director, Liberal Arts and Sciences Institute, Rowan University, Glassboro, NJ.

Michele O'Dwyer   Lecturer in Entrepreneurship, Department of Management and Marketing, University of Limerick, Limerick, Ireland.

Edward J. Schoen   Dean, Rohrer College of Business, Rowan University, Glassboro, NJ.

Kelly G. Shaver   Professor and Chair, Department of Management and Entrepreneurship, School of Business and Economics, College of Charleston, Charleston, SC.

K. Mark Weaver   Professor, Rucks Department of Management, Louisiana State University, Baton Rouge, LA.

G. Page West III   Professor of Strategy and Entrepreneurship, Wayne Calloway School of Business and Accountancy, Wake Forest University, Winston Salem, NC.

Sarah M. Yocum   Department of Biology, Wake Forest University, Winston Salem, NC.

Acknowledgements

We express our gratitude to the following reviewers of chapters submitted for this Handbook.

Barbara Bird, American University
Laquita Blockson, College of Charleston
Keith Brigham, Texas Tech University
Candida Brush, Babson College
Lowell Busenitz, University of Oklahoma
John E. Clarkin, College of Charleston
William Conner, Wake Forest University
Andrew Corbett, Rennselaer Polytechnic Institute
Jeffrey G. Covin, Indiana University
Amy Davis, College of Charleston
David Desplaces, College of Charleston
Pat Dickson, Wake Forest University
Paul Escott, Wake Forest University
James O. Fiet, University of Louisville
Patricia G. Green, Babson College
David Hansen, College of Charleston
Robert Hill, Texas State University
Jerome A. Katz, St Louis University
Raymond Kuhn, Wake Forest University
Benyamin Lichtenstein, University of Massachusetts at Boston
G.T. Lumpkin, Texas Tech University
J. Robert Mitchell, University of Oklahoma
Ronald K. Mitchell, Texas Tech University
Karl H. Vesper, University of Washington

1 Legitimacy *across* the university: yet another entrepreneurial challenge

G. Page West III, Elizabeth J. Gatewood and Kelly G. Shaver

Introduction

It is hard enough to build a strong entrepreneurship program within a school of business. For a quarter of a century those who pursued such programs have faced questions about legitimacy. Is the field of entrepreneurship a unique domain of teaching and research (Shane and Venkataraman, 2000; Busenitz et al., 2003)? Are the rigor, methods and cumulative nature of entrepreneurship research consistent with those observed in other academic disciplines (Aldrich and Baker, 1997; Low, 2001)? Has entrepreneurship research and teaching had real impact (Bygrave, 1994)? Is there consistent pedagogy for teaching the subject matter and is there consistent and rigorous training available to produce quality instructors (Brush et al., 2003)? Often perceived as lacking both socio-political legitimacy and cognitive legitimacy (Aldrich and Fiol, 1993), many entrepreneurship academics have been thought of as 'fools rushing in' – by others who question their wisdom in devoting time and energy to a field that does not enjoy status as a 'discipline' (Ogbor, 2000), as well as sometimes even by themselves.

Yet during this period entrepreneurship programs in business schools first blossomed, then experienced explosive growth. Entrepreneurship courses are now taught in more than 2000 universities in the US (Cone, 2008) and over 225 business schools offer majors or concentrations in the field (Katz, 2005). There are now a number of PhD programs conferring terminal degrees in entrepreneurship and many more in which entrepreneurship is a central facet of doctoral studies (Katz, 2007). The Entrepreneurship division of the Academy of Management was the fastest-growing division during the 1990s. Entrepreneurship journals have risen in impact factor ratings among peer-reviewed management journals (ISI Web of Knowledge, 2008), and the flow of manuscripts to these journals is significant.

Whether we entrepreneurship academics are simply gluttons for punishment, relish the role of the underdog, possess some masochistic need for more academic abuse, or simply – like entrepreneurs themselves – see new opportunities and want to pursue them, now there is a fledgling effort across various academic institutions to broaden entrepreneurial education beyond the walls of the business school. A number of colleges and universities in the US and other countries are currently seeking to embed entrepreneurship education in the arts, performing arts, sciences, social sciences, humanities, medicine, and in the more generalized liberal arts environment. These efforts raise whole new dimensions of the legitimacy question.

Problems and underlying issues

To understand the challenges that confront educators who seek to broaden entrepreneurship across the university, perspective is needed on the problems and issues that give rise to new legitimacy questions. The first issue anyone would encounter would be the obvious

question: why would anyone even think about trying to create an entrepreneurship curriculum for students outside the business school environment? If we can suggest some
reasons as to why this would make sense to begin with, then one subsequently encounters
issues of context that are close to the surface and on the minds of non-business educators
on a regular basis. But these issues of context are tips of an iceberg. Beneath the surface
are issues of substance that are at the heart of gaining legitimacy. We briefly explore each
of these dimensions below, as an introduction to this Handbook, in which more refined
perspectives and fuller treatment of the problems and solutions will be found.

Moving beyond the business school
The most practical argument for broadening entrepreneurship curriculum beyond the
business school environment is that entrepreneurial thinking and skills are broadly
used in the world outside academia. In the United States, over 99 percent of all business
organizations are small businesses, and they employ about half the workforce. Research
from the Global Entrepreneurship Monitor (GEM) studies finds that between 11 and
15 percent of US adults are actively working on some new business development idea
at any given time, and that 40 percent of US adults will engage in such activity at some
point during their working lives (Zacharakis et al., 1999). Some other GEM countries
exhibit an even higher percentage of individuals actively working to start a business, for
example, over 40 percent of individuals in Peru are nascent entrepreneurs. Although the
percentage of nascents varies from GEM country to country (for example, Belgium has
only 3 percent of adults actively working to start a business), in general it is estimated
that almost 9 percent of the world adult population is actively attempting to launch a
new venture at any given time (Bosma and Harding, 2006).

We also know that entrepreneurial activity within the corporate environment is
critical for generating growth through innovation and new products, and therefore for
superior economic performance. Furthermore, any number of pressures (for example,
globalization, environmental rate of change, technological discontinuities) will require
organizations of the future to be even more entrepreneurial in their ability to detect
emerging opportunities and move with facility to take advantage of them (West and
Meyer, 1997). The next wave of globalization, while not bypassing existing corporations, will be driven by individuals through entrepreneurial action as technology provides newfound power for individuals to collaborate and compete globally (Friedman,
2005). In fact as John Naisbitt argued, 'The more the economies of the world integrate,
the less important are the economies of countries and the more important are the economic contributions of individuals and individual companies' (1994: 298). Thus the
macro business environment, into which college students enter upon graduation, calls
for those who have an interest in, knowledge of, and practice in entrepreneurial thinking and skills.

Who will move into these jobs and career paths? It is not just business school students
who enter this world. Beyond going into flavors of graduate education (for example,
law, medicine, business) and education, students who major in non-business fields during
college do *something* when they graduate. They go to work in the same business environment as do business students. But whereas business graduates may find themselves
better prepared technically and with better credentials for narrow functional roles such
as investment banking analysis or marketing management, non-business graduates may

excel in roles where more holistic and integrative thinking and acting is valued. In fact, evidence abounds that entrepreneurs are not educated in business schools – 77 percent in one survey of small business owners (Schweitzer, 2007), and more than 80 percent of college-educated Inc. 500 company founders in another (Bhide, 2004).

There may be a reason for this preponderance of non-business students being more active in entrepreneurship and small business. As suggested by our opening comments on legitimacy of entrepreneurship within business schools, in that environment the corporate model reigns, where 'the operative paradigm . . . relates to larger and ongoing corporations [they] are designed to produce middle level bureaucrats [and] there is a tendency to assume that [small business] is a dwarfed version of big business' (Ray, 1990: 81). Critics note that with its functional-silo orientation, the typical business school program produces graduates who are able to manage but have little idea what to manage. No wonder that many successful entrepreneurs acknowledge their own limitations, and then hire others (probably business graduates) with superior skills in specific functional areas (for example, Brush et al., 2001) – a marvelous illustration of Stevenson and Gumpert's (1985) description of entrepreneurship as the assembly of resources beyond one's control.

Finally, we should add that there simply exists increasing demand for entrepreneurship education by students who are not majoring in business. Reflecting the marketplace dynamic, many non-business students have interesting and creative ideas for how to create value through enterprise, yet feel frustrated because they understand so little about the enterprise creation process itself. In one of our own institutions – a traditional private liberal arts university that has grown up in the shadows of tobacco, textiles, and furniture manufacturing (all in significant decline) – non-business students signed up in droves for a new entrepreneurial studies minor shortly after it was introduced. Less than two academic years into this new program, over 6 percent of the undergraduate student body registered for the minor. We understand that our experience is not unique on campuses where entrepreneurship curriculum has found its way out of the fortress of the almighty business school.

The truth is that some liberal arts professors and administrators view entrepreneurial programs as a way of enhancing a liberal arts education. They recognize the need for and value of courses that are focused purely on the phenomena of the world and the nature of our lives. However, they also believe that there is a place in the curriculum for investigating how that knowledge can be applied.

Immediate context
Having briefly made the case that there is a practical need and rationale for extending entrepreneurship to the rest of campus, one confronts certain realities in the typical university environment. Despite an expressed interest in and need for interdisciplinary teaching and research (Klein, 1990; Kleinberg, 2008), the academy – including arts, sciences, social sciences and so on – is organized by disciplines. The assumptions of scholars in a field include the philosophy, aim, central focus, methods of research and instruction, and relevant literature streams (Summer et al., 1990; Ogbor, 2000). 'These assumptions are necessary to give focus and discipline for those in the field and to draw boundaries around the field so it can be distinguished from other fields of study' (Summer et al., 1990: 370). This means that disciplines outside business, just like disciplines within

business, tend to be taught in silos, seldom if ever embracing novel content that is not discipline based or in some way very tightly oriented toward the accomplishment of the learning objectives in the discipline. Introducing new content and process of entrepreneurship into such bounded fields is problematic.

To this natural disciplinary bias we also note that knowledge in virtually every field is expanding. As more and more scholars with terminal degrees graduate, join university departments, and begin doing their own Kuhnian type of research (Kuhn, 1970), the sheer volume of published and presented work has expanded. If one of the goals of modern university education is to produce graduates who are on the cutting edge of new knowledge, this makes the intra-disciplinary challenge even greater. Not only must departmental faculty educate students in the disciplinary foundations and traditions, they must also continue to revise and update curricula to include ever greater content, as it becomes available. There is no room, no time, no staff, no budget to add non-essential extra-disciplinary content to the narrow window of 120 credits over four years.

Imagine the intense distress that would be created (has been created!) on many campuses where suggestions are made to offer business school courses to non-business students. With many of today's students (and their parents) interested in 'getting a job' after graduation, faculty across campus fear the colonial efforts of business schools to plant their flags elsewhere. Business schools are often regarded with skepticism by faculty outside the business school environment, for two reasons. First, faculty perceive that university education is a zero-sum game at the student level: if students take courses over there in business, then they will take fewer courses over here in our department. Fewer numbers of students in their classes raises issues of legitimacy for the courses and/ or department, which could affect staffing and future budgets. Second, the educational objectives are perceived as being very different between business schools and other parts of a university. This is especially true in academic environments where the liberal arts are central to the academic mission. Business schools are viewed as engaging in technical or vocational training and skills training ('how to'), whereas the focus of other disciplines is on developing critical thinking, inquiry, discovery and appreciation.

Finally we come to entrepreneurship, which has its own perception issues. Entrepreneurs and entrepreneurship are known largely, or only, through what is said about them in the news media. Although occasionally the media extol the virtues of innovation, seldom is this discussion divorced from the economics of new business development – the money required, the money to be made, wealthy individuals who have cashed out, soaring stock prices following initial public offerings, devastating financial failures from ill-conceived ventures resulting in loss of jobs and loss of investments, or illegal activities by unproductive entrepreneurs (Baumol, 1990) in the pursuit of wealth. Entrepreneurship is universally considered as a business-money thing. A guest column by one English professor in a university newspaper reflects the kind of visceral reaction that efforts to develop entrepreneurship programs across campus may engender (Hans, 2007: 7):

> [It] reflects the fundamentally self-centered, economic imperatives that are the focus of our lives today . . . forces them into the narrow grid of economic profit or loss . . . chained to the economic procedures through which money is made . . . we must change the circumstances through which they make sense of the material conditions of their lives. What better way to do that than to reduce all human endeavors to strategic thinking whose goal is the creation of economic value in a world that has long since lost sight of any larger imperatives?

Underlying institutional issues

The previous discussion presents practical concerns and challenges that cross-campus entrepreneurship efforts are likely to encounter. However, these are but symptoms of underlying institutional issues that any such efforts must address, if they are to be successful. At the core, there exists a fundamental question of what entrepreneurship really is. Entrepreneurship academics raise a similar question. Within the field it can take the form of a question about levels of analysis (for example, Gartner, 1988; Gartner et al., 1994; Davidsson and Wiklund, 2001), type of innovative work (for example, Baumol, 1993; Aldrich and Martinez, 2003), or its boundary conditions (e.g. Busenitz et al., 2003). But outside the field of entrepreneurship, the question is more fundamentally centered on whether entrepreneurship is only about making money and creating economic value. This raises the issue of broader versus narrower definition, that is, whether there is room to consider the creation of social, intellectual, and cultural value in addition to economic value. Answering affirmatively might make entrepreneurship more attractive to non-business faculty. But just as importantly, is entrepreneurship education simply about building skills so that students understand 'how to' go about creating value? Or is there something deeper about entrepreneurship education that can relate it more substantively to the educational goals of departments across the campus?

The reason why it is difficult to build a case for a broader, more-encompassing perspective on entrepreneurship that might encourage more widespread activity across campuses is that there is, as yet, no theoretical foundation for why entrepreneurship can or should be relevant and useful. Academia will resist ideas and programs if there is no cause-and-effect connection with fundamental educational goals and outcomes. In business schools we teach entrepreneurship because it is prevalent in the business world and our teaching practices are designed to make students more effective in practice. But this logic does not pass muster for non-business faculty in other departments. To encourage non-business faculty to embrace entrepreneurship education, there must be a deeper logic that connects this type of education with what they are seeking to accomplish, *and* do this in a way that is more compelling than other methods and tools they are currently using. A philosophy of education is needed that elevates entrepreneurship as a particularly and uniquely effective way of accomplishing broader learning outcomes.

Coupled to widespread poor understanding of the nature of entrepreneurship is resistance to change. Whether entrepreneurship or most other educational innovations, faculty resist change for a variety of reasons. Like an organization and its culture, a discipline influences acceptable norms, behaviors and practices for its members. Such biases relate to scholarly appreciation and recognition of contributions within the discipline, and ultimately are a major component for how its members fare in the development of their personal legitimacy within their fields, and thus on tenure and promotion. Few untenured assistant professors – faced with the pressures of too much to do and too little time in which to do it – will choose to develop new innovative courses instead of putting the time into their research. For this reason, innovation is usually discouraged; it is too risky from a professional point of view. Finally, threats to the status quo that new initiatives present usually meet stiff resistance because such initiatives can fundamentally change the flows of resources within a department or from the university administration. Change upsets the balance. People are uncomfortable with what is new because it asks them to behave differently and because flows of resources may be diverted from what they are accustomed to.

Finally, the case that can currently be made for cross-campus entrepreneurship suffers from the problem of small numbers. Although at some universities non-business faculty with an early-adopter mentality are convinced that a broader conception of entrepreneurship is warranted, and that attempting something new within their disciplines is justified because of higher-order learning goals that such efforts might accomplish, what of their more conservative colleagues? The typical response might be 'OK, but where is the evidence that this works?'. The number of universities adopting cross-campus programs is growing, but there is no published research demonstrating that this innovative approach has educational value. What evidence exists can be criticized as contextually dependent. Thus cross-campus initiatives can be attacked for failing the test of data as well as failing the test of academic philosophy.

Building legitimacy
What we have described is an institutional context in which innovative new ventures have a terribly difficult time taking hold. As Aldrich and Fiol predict, 'when entrepreneurs have few precedents for the kinds of activities they want to found . . . they are navigating, at best, in an institutional vacuum of indifferent munificence and, at worst, in a hostile environment' (1993: 645). Succeeding with innovative educational programs in higher education cannot be a matter of effectuation (Sarasvathy, 2001). Merely pursuing an aspiration, visualizing a set of actions, and engaging in some sort of learn-as-you-go approach does not and cannot overcome the types of institutional resistance we have mentioned above.

Confronted by such strong institutional forces, innovative new programs must develop legitimacy (Aldrich and Fiol, 1993; Sundin and Tillmar, 2008), and there two types of legitimacy that are critical. The first is cognitive legitimacy, which occurs when an activity is understood and has become so well known that it is taken for granted as an acceptable type. In the case of cross-campus entrepreneurship, new initiatives might be framed in a way that they are perceived as relevant to non-business faculty. Often this occurs through the use of a higher level of abstraction from actual practice, such that a more universal view of the phenomenon can be understood in a variety of ways by a variety of potential participants. For example, whereas entrepreneurship is most often perceived as the pursuit of economic or material wealth, framing the effort at a higher level of abstraction – that this is but one of many possible outcomes in a process of value creation – creates a degree of ambiguity allowing others to consider different kinds of value that can be created through educational efforts. Symbolic behaviors can also work to develop cognitive legitimacy. On one of our campuses the effort to develop a cross-campus entrepreneurship program was set up as a separate department, outside of the business school and physically located away from the business school. The message sent to the rest of campus was that this was not an effort by business types to further colonize campus. Cognitive legitimacy is also built when it can be shown that there is a consistency of approach observed in the examples of such efforts on other campuses. Where a 'dominant design' (Aldrich and Fiol, 1993) for cross-campus efforts is in evidence, then trust and confidence in the efficacy of new initiatives is built.

The second type of legitimacy is socio-political, the extent to which new efforts conform to accepted principles, rules and standards. This is a sort of catch-22. In order to conform and win broad approval of organizational stakeholders, or at least their acquiescence, innovators must use methods that are viewed as acceptable and conforming. Arguing rationally that innovative approaches are valuable is one method that would be embraced by the academy, and this is where the need for a cogent educational philosophy could be especially fruitful. When innovative new work is embraced by individuals who are also departmental or university opinion leaders, the new effort can benefit from their personal credibility and trust. And then a contagion effect (Rogers, 1983) may be experienced, as others come to believe that there must actually be something worthwhile to the new effort after all.

As we have been involved in starting up new cross-campus entrepreneurship education efforts on our campuses, we have witnessed the institutional challenges and recognized the need for the forms of legitimacy briefly described above. This Handbook is in partial response to these challenges and needs. We started our efforts with few roadmaps, sometimes stumbling as we started down the path of educational reform and sometimes winding up in the right place. A roadmap is needed, we concluded, so that others can avoid the stumblings we have experienced and have a clearer path to follow. In 2007 we issued a call to bring together in one volume a collection of essays that might describe the philosophy, planning and implementation, and examples of best practices of entrepreneurship education initiatives across the university environment. A conference was organized in late 2007 at Wake Forest University, and the chapters in this Handbook represent the best papers presented at that conference.

The contents of this Handbook
This Handbook brings together in one volume a collection of essays that explore the current state of the art of university-wide entrepreneurship education programs. Twentynine authors from different disciplines in universities in five countries discuss the opportunities and universal challenges in extending entrepreneurship education outside the business school into the sciences, performing arts, social sciences, humanities, and liberal arts environments. The three parts of the Handbook are devoted to (1) philosophy and theory that provide a legitimate intellectual foundation for the fusion or integration of entrepreneurship education with other traditional approaches across the university, (2) the politics and process of implementing entrepreneurship initiatives outside business schools, and (3) examples of fine-grained approaches to implementing entrepreneurship education in major divisions of universities outside business schools. The chapters collectively provide a path for educators to deal with the socio-political and cognitive legitimacy issues, which are central when 'few precedents exist for the kinds of activities [entrepreneurs] want to found' (Aldrich and Fiol, 1993: 645). This Handbook is therefore designed to assist educators in developing new programs and pedagogical approaches based on the previous experiences of others who have forged this exciting new path.

Part I contains chapters whose authors offer philosophical justification for entrepreneurship education as becoming part of a broader cross-campus effort. Theory on educational pedagogy further supports the role that entrepreneurship can play on a larger stage than when just considered as skills building within the business school environment. Chapter 2, by Green, is a passionate and compelling advocacy of entrepreneurship's central role in higher education. Lofty in language and ideals, its central argument is that entrepreneurship is freedom, and that its holistic nature reflects what we are seeking to do in higher education – both in terms of educational outcomes as well as understanding of the self in the world. In Chapter 3, Beckman and Cherwitz provide another view showing how entrepreneurship and the broader academy are fundamentally linked. These authors discuss how content and the traditional substance of a discipline creates meaning or value in the world outside the discipline, and how 'intellectual entrepreneurship' as an educational philosophy can embrace both the traditions and their relevance in the world into which graduates march. To answer the question, raised earlier, about how and why entrepreneurship education can provide a unique and improved approach to achieving educational outcomes in other disciplines, in Chapter 4 Krueger offers a primer of how a constructivist paradigm of education, which is at the heart of entrepreneurial learning, is broadly applicable. Finally, in Chapter 5, Gustafson muses on his years of experience in seeking greater legitimacy for entrepreneurship at Beloit College in a wry, occasionally humorous, and always pointed essay on entrepreneurship as a liberal art. Some will nod and some will cringe in reading this chapter, since Gustafson puts the microscope on the reader.

Part II is concerned with the planning and implementation process for developing entrepreneurship initiatives outside business schools. As pointed out earlier in this introduction, there are widespread misunderstandings about the nature of entrepreneurship and perceptions that entrepreneurship education does not fit established norms, behaviors, and practices of university members. Chapter 6 by Mendes and Kehoe addresses how the appropriate planning process can help to define entrepreneurship in an acceptable way for a university community, to surface challenges and suggested strategies for dealing with those challenges from stakeholders – essentially to use the planning process to achieve legitimacy from concerned stakeholders. Chapter 7, by Hynes, O'Dwyer and Birdthistle, addresses gaining legitimacy for cross-campus entrepreneurship education by designing programs that prepare graduates to work effectively in today's environments and addressing national needs for workplace skill development. The authors propose a process framework for entrepreneurship education that guides program design, development, analysis and modification.

In Chapter 8, Weaver, D'Intino, Miller and Schoen describe a case study of a university interested in gaining recognition as an 'entrepreneurial university'. The case study illustrates the role of principal influencers and champions for establishing legitimacy for the successful implementation of the desired program. The case study also details the use of project-based learning as a key component for developing students' entrepreneurial skills.

Finally, in Chapter 9 authors Macosko, Johnson and Yocum provide the basis of the appeal of entrepreneurship education to non-business faculty. We earlier argued that to encourage non-business faculty to embrace entrepreneurship education requires that this education approach must provide faculty a better method and tools for accomplishing their classroom goals and broader educational outcomes. This chapter describes the pedagogical underpinnings of active learning, details five teaching strategies that promote active learning and provides case studies of team- and project-based classes that used science-rich problems to assist students in the development of entrepreneurial skills. Essentially this chapter argues that legitimacy for cross-campus entrepreneurship programs can be gained because it produces better educational outcomes.

Part III is arranged in an order that roughly parallels the educational experience. First, Chapter 10 by Shaver outlines some of the philosophical objections and practical impediments to the entrepreneurship/liberal arts connection, but concludes on a positive note about what may be gained by each area. Next, Chapter 11 by Janssen, Eeckhout, Gailly and Bacq provides a conceptual discussion of what is meant by interdisciplinarity, especially as applied to entrepreneurship. Then at a very practical level, Claire (Chapter 12) shows how techniques more closely associated with the arts can add significant value to the students' learning about entrepreneurship. Continuing in the pedagogical vein, in Chapter 13 Lendner and Huebscher describe a short-term business simulation exercise that can be used to give students the 'feel' of an entrepreneurial venture. Then Chapter 14, by Mars and Hoskinson, shows the educational benefits that law students can offer entrepreneurship students, and vice versa. In an educational environment increasingly interested in accountability, there is always the question of how a new program should be evaluated, and that is the topic of Chapter 15 by Fayolle and Gailly. Finally, Part III concludes in Chapter 16 with Hines, who generalizes the entrepreneurial metaphor as a description of the entire liberal arts and sciences university.

Within the academy, the roots of intellectual discourse are often traced back to the ancient Greeks, whereas the intellectual underpinnings of entrepreneurship are to be found in modern times. But there is more than length of history to the tension often seen between liberal arts education and entrepreneurship education. As Shaver's chapter points out, there can be a fundamental disagreement between those who eschew mercantilism in any guise and those who would study and teach principles of business creation. In addition to a need for entrepreneurship education to confront this philosophical difference, there is a need for any new interdisciplinary endeavor to navigate its way through the bureaucracy that is the modern university.

Throughout this volume there are discussions of the interdisciplinary nature of entrepreneurship education. But what, exactly, is meant by 'interdisciplinary'? How can a truly interdisciplinary approach be distinguished, for example, from a *multi*disciplinary one? The chapter by Janssen, Eeckhout, Gailly and Bacq employs a level-of-learning conceptual model to answer this and other questions about ways in which entrepreneurship education can be delivered.

One way the entrepreneurial experience can be delivered, in a liberal arts environment, is to bring the liberal arts *to* entrepreneurship. That is the topic of the chapter by Claire, which describes a course in which students create an Entrepreneur Film Festival. After learning the rudiments of filmmaking, students shadow and interview entrepreneurs to develop story lines for their productions. The course culminates in a public film festival organized and staffed by the students.

What happens when it is not possible to offer an entire course to non-business students? The chapter by Lendner and Huebscher describes a simulation game that, in a matter of days rather than weeks, enables students to discover entrepreneurial principles and the fundamentals of business.

The chapter by Mars and Hoskinson takes the notion of interdisciplinary experiential learning a step further. Their report describes a carefully arranged set of interactions between entrepreneurship students and law students. The former have intellectual property and other business organization issues to solve, the latter have a need for clinical experience. The result is a better understanding by each, of the other. This sort of interchange will become even more important as more and more entrepreneurial companies join the 'knowledge economy.'

The chapter by Fayolle and Gailly addresses the problem of outcome assessment. In work based on the theory of planned behavior, these authors examined the effects on entrepreneurial intentions created by participation in one or another sort of entrepreneurship education program. Three studies are reported, each conducted in an engineering school. Together these studies identify methods that can assess change without having to wait until the program graduates actually create companies.

Finally, the chapter by Hines uses entrepreneurship as a metaphor for the institutional changes that must occur if the liberal arts and sciences university is to thrive in the modern era and beyond. Creativity, innovation, and clarity of vision are not merely critical for entrepreneurs. These same attributes are now required of academic officers at every level if public colleges and universities are to adapt and flourish in an environment of ever-declining governmental support.

References

Aldrich, H.E. and T. Baker (1997), 'Blinded by the cites? Has there been progress in entrepreneurship research?', in D.L. Sexton and R.W. Smilor (eds), *Entrepreneurship 2000*, Chicago, IL: Upstart Publishing, pp. 377–400.

Aldrich, H.E. and C.M. Fiol (1993), 'Fools rush in? The institutional context of industry creation', *Academy of Management Review*, **19** (4), 645–70.

Aldrich, H.E. and M.A. Martinez (2003), 'Entrepreneurship as social construction: a multi-level evolutionary approach', in Z. Acs and D.B. Audretsch (eds), *Handbook of Entrepreneurship*, New York: Kluwer, pp. 359–99.

Baumol, W.J. (1990), 'Entrepreneurship: productive, unproductive, and destructive', *Journal of Political Economy*, **98** (5), 893–921.

Baumol, W.J. (1993), 'Formal entrepreneurship theory in economics: existence and bounds', *Journal of Business Venturing*, **8** (3), 197–210.

Bhide, A.V. (2004), 'Creating new knowledge for one of America's most vital resources', in *Kauffman Thoughtbook 2004*, Kansas City, MO: Ewing Marion Kauffman Foundation, 64–8.

Bosma, N. and R. Harding (2006), *Global Entrepreneurship Monitor*, Babson Park, MA: Babson College.

Brush, C.G., I.M. Duhaine, W.B. Gartner, A. Stewart, J.A. Katz, M.A. Hitt, S.A. Alvarez, G.D. Meyer and S. Venkataraman (2003), 'Doctoral education in the field of entrepreneurship', *Journal of Management*, **29** (3), 309–31.

Brush, C.G., P.G. Greene and M.M. Hart (2001), 'From initial idea to unique advantage: the entrepreneurial challenge of constructing a resource base', *Academy of Management Executive*, **15** (1), 64–78.

Busenitz, L., G.P. West III, D.A. Shepherd, T. Nelson, G.N. Chandler and A.L. Zacharakis (2003), 'Entrepreneurship research in emergence: fifteen years of entrepreneurship research in management journals', *Journal of Management*, **29** (3), 285–308.

Bygrave, W.D. (1994), 'Doctoral students: how much have they influenced entrepreneurship education and practice', paper presented at Babson/Kauffman Entrepreneurship Research Conference, Babson Park, MA, June.

Cone, J. (2008), 'Teaching entrepreneurship in colleges and universities: how (and why) a new academic field is being built', Kansas City, MO: Ewing Marion Kauffman Foundation, www.kauffman.org/ Details.aspx? id=536, accessed January 15, 2009.

Davidsson, P. and K. Wiklund (2001), 'Levels of analysis in entrepreneurship research: current research practice and suggestions for the future', *Entrepreneurship Theory and Practice*, **25** (4), 81–100.

Friedman, T. (2005), *The World is Flat: A Brief History of the Twenty-First Century*, New York: Farrar, Straus & Giroux.

Gartner, W.B. (1988), '"Who is an entrepreneur?" is the wrong question', *American Journal of Small Business*, **13** (2), 11–32.

Gartner, W.B., K.G. Shaver, E.J. Gatewood and J.A. Katz (1994), 'Finding the entrepreneur in entrepreneurship', *Entrepreneurship Theory and Practice*, **18** (3), 5–9.

Hans, J. (2007), 'Seeking utility in ideas crushing liberal arts', *Old Gold and Black*, **7**, October, 7–8.

ISI Web of Knowledge (2008), 'Journal Citation Reports', Thomson Reuters, http://apps.isiknowledge.com, accessed June 15.

Katz, J.A. (2005), 'eWeb's List of Colleges With Majors In Entrepreneurship or Small Business', St. Louis, MO: St. Louis University, www.slu.edu/x17964.xml, accessed January 15, 2008.

Katz, J.A. (2007), 'Ph.D. Programs in Entrepreneurship', St. Louis, MO: St. Louis University, www.slu.edu/x17968.xml, accessed January 15, 2008.

Klein, J.T. (1990), *Interdisciplinarity: History, Theory, and Practice*, Detroit, MI: Wayne State University Press.

Kleinberg, E. (2008), 'Interdisciplinary studies at a crossroads', *Liberal Education*, **94** (1), 6–11.

Kuhn, T.S. (1970), *The Structure of Scientific Revolutions*, 2nd edn, Chicago, IL: University of Chicago Press.

Low, M.B. (2001), 'The adolescence of entrepreneurship research: specification and purpose', *Entrepreneurship Theory and Practice*, **25** (4), 17–25.

Naisbitt, J. (1994), *Global Paradox*, New York: William Morrow.

Ogbor, J.O. (2000), 'Mythicizing and reification in entrepreneurial discourse: ideology-critique of entrepreneurial studies', *Journal of Management Studies*, **37** (5), 605–35.

Ray, D. (1990), 'Liberal arts for entrepreneurs', *Entrepreneurship Theory and Practice*, **15** (2), 79–93.

Rogers, E.M. (1983), *Diffusion of Innovations*, New York: Free Press.

Sarasvathy, S.D. (2001), 'Causation and effectuation: toward a theoretical shift from economic inevitability to entrepreneurial contingency', *Academy of Management Review*, **26** (2), 243–63.

Schweitzer, T. (2007), 'Not only the lonely become entrepreneurs', Inc.com, www.inc.com/news/articles/200701/loners.html, accessed June 15, 2008.

Shane, S. and S. Venkataraman (2000), 'The promise of entrepreneurship as a field of research', *Academy of Management Review*, **25** (1), 217–26.

Stevenson, H.H. and D.E. Gumpert (1985), 'The heart of entrepreneurship', *Harvard Business Review*, **63** (2), 85–94.

Summer, C.E. et al. (1990), 'Doctoral education in the field of business policy and strategy', *Journal of Management*, **16** (2), 361–98.

Sundin, E. and M. Tillmar (2008), 'A nurse and a civil servant changing institutions: entrepreneurial processes in different public sector organizations', *Scandinavian Journal of Management*, **24** (2), 113–24.

West, G.P., III and G.D. Meyer (1997), 'Temporal dimensions of opportunistic change in technology-based ventures', *Entrepreneurship Theory and Practice*, **22** (2), 31–52.

Zacharakis, A., P.D. Reynolds and W.D. Bygrave (1999), *National Entrepreneurship Assessment: United States of America*, Kansas City, MO: Kauffman Center for Entrepreneurial Leadership.

PART I

PHILOSOPHY AND THEORY

2 From commerce to culture: entrepreneurship in the mainstream

*William Scott Green**

Entrepreneurship is identified almost exclusively with business. Although in medieval French 'entrepreneur' had a broader meaning – a person who has lots of energy and can get things done – in the eighteenth and nineteenth centuries, entrepreneurship became attached to commerce. As a result, American educational discourse about entrepreneurship is largely shaped by the restricted code of business and seems extraneous to a broader range of thought and action. To be sure, it would be misleading to suggest that entrepreneurship is not fundamental to contemporary business. But limiting entrepreneurship to business and business education artificially truncates its meaning and obscures important connections between commerce and culture that shape contemporary life.

Entrepreneurship is the process through which innovations become enterprises that produce value. It is how new ideas become concrete and affect people's lives. Thus, entrepreneurship cannot be reduced to innovation or management alone. It requires implementation, which transforms a new idea into something tangible from which people can benefit. And, as Carl Schramm points out, to yield benefit, the 'idea' behind a new venture must be more than merely 'great'; it must be 'actionable . . . something the market values' (2006: 65–6). Thus, entrepreneurship entails three essential components: a new idea, its implementation into an enterprise, and the market's acceptance of the enterprise. Entrepreneurship is the way a free society identifies and responds to its needs and desires and thereby advances and enriches its future.

Current entrepreneurship education often – perhaps generally – does not reflect the centrality of entrepreneurship to American progress. The conventional approach is to treat entrepreneurship as a discrete business practice, an element of a business education, rather than as a broader approach to all learning. Courses in entrepreneurship tend to cluster in economics or business curricula and concentrate on the more technical aspects of business formation. The emphasis is more likely to be on how to start a company, rather than why to start a company, or what it means to start a company. The stress is on the 'what?' of entrepreneurship, rather than the 'so what?'. A comprehensive education in entrepreneurship needs to address both.

Can entrepreneurship extend outward from a business school? Does it have a legitimate place in, for instance, the study of history, literature, psychology, sociology, religion, science, communication, music, nursing, or education – to name just a few of the subjects American undergraduates study in college? More basically, how is entrepreneurship relevant to the overarching goals of contemporary American college education?

Part of the answer lies in the elegant argument of Amartya Sen that 'enhancement of human freedom is both the main object and the primary means of [economic] development' (2000: 53):

> The usefulness of wealth lies in the things that it allows us to do – the substantive freedoms it helps to achieve. . . . For the same reason, economic growth cannot be treated as an end in itself. Development has to be more concerned with enhancing the lives we lead and the freedoms we enjoy. Expanding the freedoms that we have reason to value not only makes our lives richer and more unfettered, but also allows us to be fuller social persons, exercising our own volitions and interacting with – and influencing – the world in which we live. (Ibid.: 14–15)

For Sen, the highest expression of freedom is the ability to choose the kind of life one leads. Sen is concerned to preserve the integrity of individual difference and individual choice. As Stuart Corbridge (2002: 188) explains,

> Sen's account of development as freedom is insistently attentive to individual agency, the importance of choice as freedom in itself, and to individual human differences. . . . Sen argues that individuals must be free to choose their own accounts of the good life . . . *and* that freedom resides in such things as the right to participate in market exchange itself – it is not simply a matter of free speech. Sen further argues that the choices free agents make will necessarily be influenced by the differences that constitute us as individual human beings, or which shape our personal differences.

If development is freedom, then so too is entrepreneurship. Indeed, to conceive an idea, to give that idea sustaining life by making it into an enterprise, and then to have that enterprise yield benefit for yourself and others is a distinctive type of freedom. Entrepreneurship is a basic expression of individual insight, ingenuity, initiative, and volition that, by fusing the visionary and the pragmatic, produces substantive enhancements to our lives. It is no accident that in American popular discourse in an array of areas, the term 'entrepreneurship' now virtually denotes action that generates beneficial change.[1] By improving our goods, services, and institutions, entrepreneurship both manifests and enables freedom.

Entrepreneurship is a mode of self-actualization. Joseph Schumpeter stressed the role of individual creativity and practicality in entrepreneurial achievement.[2] And although the desire for profit certainly plays a role in economic entrepreneurship, it is not necessarily the sole or most powerful motive. Schumpeter (2000: 70) himself insisted that, beyond profit, which is one measure of entrepreneurial success,

> . . . there is the joy of creating, of getting things done, or simply of exercising one's energy and ingenuity. This is akin to a ubiquitous motive, but nowhere else does it stand out as an independent factor of behavior with anything like the clearness with which it obtrudes in our case [of entrepreneurship]. Our type [the entrepreneur] seeks out difficulties, changes in order to change, delights in ventures.

On this argument, in conceiving an idea and externalizing it into the world, every entrepreneur brings herself or himself into being, so to speak.

But entrepreneurship does not and cannot end at the border of the self. It is not about enriching the entrepreneur alone. Rather, it necessarily includes responding to others. This engagement occurs as the enterprise works its way through its 'market', broadly construed. From the perspective of entrepreneurship as freedom, the 'market' is not an institution of greed and exploitation. Rather, it is the theater in which a free society expresses its desiderata – some trivial and some urgent and consequential. Entrepreneurship therefore entails not only individual initiative but also an understanding of the collective.

Whatever else one can say about the market, it is the ultimate test of an enterprise. In a free market, what matters is neither privilege nor lineage, but whether or not the enterprise meets needs, informs desires, changes lives, and responds to things that people are prepared to value. The market is a forum of relentless assessment. No entrepreneur can misread it and succeed.

Entrepreneurship not only responds to the demands of the market, it also shapes them through successful attention to society's need and desire for the ever-improved product or service. One of Schumpeter's most arresting concepts is the notion of 'creative destruction', in which some new insight, some new product or process, eliminates an established way of doing business or solving a problem. He also observed that entrepreneurship changes markets from within, independent of external pressures such as demographics or finances (Schumpeter, 1962). Entrepreneurship has an energy that resists mechanization.

We can see entrepreneurship's integrative capacity in another way. In her celebration of the 100th year of Max Weber's *The Protestant Ethic and the Spirit of Capitalism*, Elizabeth Kolbert (2004: 154) recalled Weber's rumination that, 'the modern economic border is now bound to the technical and economic conditions of machine production, which today determine the lives of all the individuals who are born into this mechanism with irresistible force'. Building on that citation, she observed:

> For all of his insistence on the importance of abstract ideas in the inception of capitalism, Weber follows Marx in viewing alienation as the essential consequence of the modern economic order. In certain respects, Weber's critique is the more thoroughgoing. By his account, all of us – the wealthy and the poor, the owners and the workers – lead economic lives of quiet desperation. And while Marx imagines a liberating crisis at the end of history, Weber pictures a future that is apt to be as unsatisfactory as the present. Materialism has become, in his words, 'an iron cage' . . . (Ibid.: 160)

Against this background, entrepreneurship can serve as a counter-force, one possible antidote, to the alienation that both Marx and Weber saw as the ineluctable trait of capitalist modernity. Entrepreneurship is about linkages rather than separations. The entrepreneur surely is at one with the enterprise of her or his devising and also must be aware of others to create an enterprise that responds to their needs. Because it is a self-actualizing and self-generating activity, entrepreneurship also may work as a corrective to the mechanistic materialism that worried Weber and Marx.

Thus, entrepreneurship emerges as a particularly comprehensive form of freedom – a freedom that circles back and completes itself. Through the interplay of individual inventiveness, risk, drive, practicality, responsiveness to others, and the reaction of the market, entrepreneurship distinctively connects the individual to society. In turn, the market's reaction to entrepreneurial initiative gives society knowledge of itself and creates new opportunities for initiative. Because of the distinctive way entrepreneurship both enables and expresses freedom, perhaps it is reasonable to conceive it as a basic kind of human agency, a fundamental freedom.

No freedom becomes real on its own. It requires supporting structures. Entrepreneurship is not a detached phenomenon. Rather, a scaffolding of cultural, legal, economic, educational, and governmental practices constitutes and sustains an environment in which it is routine for people to earn a living and construct a life by creating new enterprises.

Entrepreneurship may well be a core value of American society and economy, but it hardly is distributed equally across nations, societies, even neighborhoods. That is no accident. Rather, there are prerequisites that must be present to allow substantive entrepreneurial activity to happen at all, whether inside or outside of business. The general study of entrepreneurship examines entrepreneurship's preconditions, the relationship among them, the forces that threaten them, and the means to defend against those threats. Among other obstacles, restrictive and cumbersome business practices, closed markets, stultifying education, and the suppression of individual creativity and initiative, in any combination, diminish entrepreneurial activity. Education in entrepreneurship must engage these realities.

This understanding of entrepreneurship shows how its study can contribute to an American college education. I have had the privilege to collaborate on a basic course in entrepreneurship at the University of Rochester (NY) and the University of Miami (Coral Gables, FL) with exceptional colleagues: David M. Primo and Thomas H. Jackson at Rochester; Steven Ullmann, Susan Wills Amat, and Trae Williamson at Miami. Entitled 'The Nature and Foundations of Entrepreneurship', the course studies the structures that make the creation of new enterprises routine in American society. It begins by reviewing the definitions of entrepreneurship proposed by major theorists, such as Joseph Schumpeter, Israel Kirzner, Ludwig von Mises, Peter Drucker, William Baumol, Robert Litan, and Carl Schramm to learn how their varied perspectives illuminate entrepreneurship's characteristic traits. The course explores how American property law, copyright law, and bankruptcy law create – and can obstruct – legal structures conducive to enterprise-creation. It probes beneath these legal structures to examine the cultural notions of self, ownership, individualism, freedom, and opportunity that necessarily undergird them and therefore are fundamental to entrepreneurial activity. The course also considers the relationships among political and economic systems – particularly democracy and capitalism – and their effect on enterprise creation. And it asks students to chart the interconnections among religion, human rights, and economic policies and practices as these affect the creation of new enterprises. One goal of the course is to identify the core values that stand behind and animate entrepreneurship and the economic and political practices that make it possible. The course concludes with students' presentations of their own projects – which range from theoretical research to case studies of entrepreneurs to creative business plans – all demonstrations of their own intellectual initiative and ownership and educational self-efficacy. With a slight enhancement, the course began to include comparative data from other nations, to help students see how entrepreneurship fares under different political and economic systems and cultural values and to help sharpen their sense of the particularities of the American system.

This kind of course – and there surely are multiple variations on how it can be constructed and taught – shows how entrepreneurship conjoins subjects conventionally treated in isolation. It allows students to experience how discrete academic disciplines must interact to make a phenomenon comprehensible. Equally important, the course bridges the divide between so-called 'professional' (or 'preprofessional') and 'liberal' education. Because the work of the course always returns to the practical realm of creating firms and enterprises and engagement with the market, it underscores for students how much of the world we humans make – and must make – for ourselves and how little of our world is random or accidental. The entrepreneurial focus helps them see – and learn to ask – how some human being (or beings) imagined, invented, conceived, built, advanced, assessed, discarded, and improved the institutions, products, and services that shape our collective life.

In university learning, entrepreneurship can extend beyond the business curriculum to become a way of thinking. It can be an approach to problems, a habit of mind, a framework for interpretation, and a viewpoint for discernment. We can look at any human activity and ask how entrepreneurial it is. What is the idea, the innovation? Where is the transformation? Where is the enterprise? Where is the benefit to others? Where is the value? In short, we in universities can use entrepreneurship as a basic category of understanding and analysis. No program of education in entrepreneurship can or should promise to make everybody into an entrepreneur. Entrepreneurship would be a fraud if everyone could do it. The point, rather, is to employ entrepreneurship as one primary approach to analyzing and apprehending human experience, to use it as a stimulus, a way of asking questions, and a mode of learning.

The stakes in this endeavor are real and consequential. Higher education is supposed to help prepare students to manage and improve the world they will inherit. Broad-based exposure to and knowledge of entrepreneurship is essential if the United States is to have an educated public able to appreciate the importance of entrepreneurship for economic and cultural development and progress. Many Americans viewed the congressional vote to stop funding the US Superconducting Super Collider (SSC) in Texas at least in part as a failure of American elected representatives to appreciate the value of pure research, to understand how unfettered investigation ultimately rather than immediately improves our lives. If so, such an inability cannot but reflect flaws in an educational system. In a different way, entrepreneurship faces similar risks. It is a distinctive but fragile freedom, and shifts in cultural values or government policy can easily undo it. A rigid educational association of entrepreneurship with business marginalizes and constrains entrepreneurship and may make it harder to develop good public policy to support it. Democracies depend on an educated public with the capacity to take the long view of matters. That educated public is substantially the product of universities. Thus, the stakes in widening the scope of entrepreneurship are high. The broad study of entrepreneurship builds an educational bridge from commerce to culture and thereby legitimates a place for entrepreneurship in the mainstream of American college learning.

Notes

*   Much of this chapter presupposes and builds upon 'Entrepreneurship in American Higher Education: A Report from the Ewing Marion Kauffman Panel on Entrepreneurship Curriculum in American Higher Education', Ewing Marion Kauffman Foundation, Kansas City, MO, 2008. See www.kauffman.org/uploadedfiles/entrep_high_ed_report.pdf. I am grateful to the Kauffman Foundation and its president, Carl Schramm, for the opportunity to serve on the panel and to learn from its members. I thank David Primo for useful improvements to this chapter, and I owe a debt to Page West for exemplary and patient editing.

1.   For example, the *New York Times Magazine* entitled a recent article 'Faces of Social Entrepreneurship' (March 9, 2008). In such instances, it is the adjective, not the noun, that requires explanation.

2.   Carl Schramm observes that, 'in seeing the importance of the individual pursuing his or her dreams in the realm of commerce . . . Schumpeter became the most human of economic theorists. He restored the individual not only to economics, but also to political theory', Carl J. Schramm, 'Economics and the entrepreneur', *Claremont Review of Books*, **VIII** (2), Spring, 2008, Special Excerpt, pp. 1–7, p. 7.

References

Corbridge, S. (2002), 'Development as freedom: the spaces of Amartya Sen', *Progress in Development Studies*, **2** (3), 183–217.

Kolbert, E. (2004), 'Why work', *The New Yorker*, **80** (37), 154–60.

Schramm, C. (2006), *The Entrepreneurial Imperative*, New York: Collins.

Schumpeter, J.A. (1962), *Capitalism, Socialism, and Democracy*, New York: Harper & Row.

Schumpeter, J.A. (2000), 'Entrepreneurship as innovation', in R. Swedburg (ed.), *Entrepreneurship: The Social Science View*, New York: Oxford, pp. 51–75. Reprinted from Schumpeter's (1911), *The Theory of Economic Development*.

Sen, A. (2000), *Development as Freedom*, New York: Anchor.

3   Advancing the authentic: intellectual entrepreneurship and the role of the business school in fine arts entrepreneurship curriculum design*

Gary D. Beckman and Richard A. Cherwitz

Introduction

The growing interest in transforming the academy to meet the realities of a modern world while simultaneously preserving and celebrating the noble traditions that have comprised the education of prior generations is both palpable and tangible. Although this is a laudable and long overdue venture, the mechanisms for accomplishing this transformation are varied and reflect institutional micro-cultures. Cross-disciplinary entrepreneurship education is emerging as a leading method to respond to these needs; it provides an opportunity to reposition the academy as a vital part of American life by embedding change within a rich liberal arts tradition. For all the criticisms and challenges American higher education has confronted over the past century, transforming the university is occurring at an almost breakneck pace; as this book and its contributors document, entrepreneurship is the theme and empowerment is the goal.[1]

Institutional change, however, is a sustained proposition; it requires more than good ideas and innovative programs. There are a myriad of topics to be considered before these endeavors can be implemented and successfully mainstreamed within the academic culture. Campus-wide efforts to transform academe via entrepreneurship share certain commonalities: garnering faculty support, visionary leadership and innovative curriculum certainly lead the list. However, many universities find that defining entrepreneurship is a vital part of their campus-wide initiatives; they discover that defining the term in a manner unique to their intended goals and institutional culture is critical to implementation and sustainability.

It is understandable that the academy is uneasy with entrepreneurship defined exclusively as the creation of material wealth. The humanist ideals that are the bedrock of higher learning, some might surmise, simply cannot be sacrificed for the expediencies of a term perceived by many as antithetical to the liberal arts tradition. There is a fundamental disconnect that these educators, perhaps intuitively, understand: our relationship with the traditions and purpose of a humanist education appears at odds with the career environment most students inhabit after graduation.

Unique definitions and conceptions of entrepreneurship can address this disconnect. Yet defining entrepreneurship by faculty committee reflects a moment in time; it is for many, an act of compromise rather than consensus among educational communities. Attempting to merge philosophical ideals into a single term is a worthy goal and, in some cases, will yield the desired results. In other cases, these efforts will fail due to the lack of a rigorous intellectual and philosophical grounding upon which campus-wide entrepreneurship education can be built.

The premise of this chapter is that what will distinguish successful cross-campus entrepreneurship initiatives in the long run will partially be based on how a supporting philosophical structure can serve as an ethos for these initiatives. Sustaining efforts that bring entrepreneurial thinking to the arts and sciences, we contend, requires a solution intrinsic to and issuing from academe's best humanist traditions – one that can inspire students and faculty to reach and exceed their goals for the benefit of themselves and society at large. We believe that defining entrepreneurship operationally (program by program from one institution to the next) and in the absence of a rigorous philosophical foundation limits the success of cross-campus programs precisely because they will not be authentic to the ideals of a liberal arts education. One can define entrepreneurship by committee and channel resources to that end, but in an environment that seeks institutional relevance in a new millennium, such an approach may cause us to squander an opportunity for leveraging our core educational traditions that empowers students and faculty alike.

Intellectual entrepreneurship as change agent

We suggest that 'intellectual entrepreneurship' (IE) provides an intellectually authentic and philosophical foundation capable of sustaining cross-campus entrepreneurship. Based in classical rhetoric, IE is a philosophy and vision of education viewing academics as innovators and 'agents of change'. It focuses on creating cross-disciplinary and multi-institutional collaborations designed to produce intellectual advancements with a capacity to provide real solutions to society's problems and needs.[2]

IE is premised on the belief that intellect is not limited to the academy and entrepreneurship is not restricted to or synonymous with business. While the creation of material wealth is one expression of entrepreneurship, at a more profound level inside and outside universities, intellectual entrepreneurs take risks and seize opportunities, discover and create knowledge, innovate, collaborate and solve problems in any number of social realms: corporate, non-profit, government, and education.[3]

IE aims to educate and nurture 'citizen-scholars' throughout the university. (Cherwitz and Darwin 2005, pp. 59–68). IE leverages the knowledge assets contained within the university's walls, empowering faculty and students to become agents of change – both internally and externally (Cherwitz and Hartelius 2007, p. 278). By recognizing the rich humanist traditions upon which the university is based, IE harnesses the core philosophy of western education to transform the master–apprentice–entitlement paradigm into one of discovery, accountability, collaboration and action (ibid., p. 283). Re-examining and re-embracing our humanist traditions through these four core concepts, we claim, can inform current efforts to bring entrepreneurial thinking to the many corners of academic institutions; these traditions can guide the creation of institutional change and, most importantly, help realize an academically engaged and socially relevant university through cross-campus entrepreneurship efforts.

Overview: the core pillars of IE

Discovery is a privilege shared by the university community. The IE ethos charges faculty and students with realizing new value in their study-objects. As knowledge increases, discovering innovative ways to apply and make relevant new findings licenses faculty and students to create change on both micro and macro levels. IE empowers individuals to 'contemplate who they are' and apply that vision to systems of culture and society by using new discoveries to advance individual and community imperatives (Cherwitz and Sullivan 2002, pp. 22–6). The IE conception of discovery goes further than innovative and socially significant outcomes, however. By discovering new value through the mechanisms of learning and research, the authentic purpose of the university is realized; the ivory tower is transformed from its perceived self-imposed isolationism into a wellspring of idea generation available to communities worldwide.

IE challenges learning communities to become accountable for their discoveries. Both faculty and students *earn* their degrees – a privilege often taken for granted. The motive for pursuing a degree is individually based, no doubt, but envisioning the impact of education beyond the individual strikes to the core function of education in a social context.[4] IE implores degree holders to devise new applications of an advanced degree beyond salaried employment that can transform society. Students and faculty recognize opportunities by surveying environments suitable for positive change that will benefit because of – not despite – their degree. This sense of empowerment helps to create the change agents who realize the potential of their education and recognize the value and reward of personal accountability.

Creativity, change and innovation do not occur in a vacuum. Collaboration, therefore, is crucial to the IE ethos. However, the benefits of collaborative efforts exceed the potential for overcoming obstacles. Incubators or synergy groups initiated at the inception of any effort can become the creative engine that drives an innovative cross-campus effort (ibid., p. 27). Working and creating in groups fulfills the promise of interdisciplinarity beyond its academic justification as a method of scholarly inquiry.

New ideas, produced by methodical intellectual discovery and an accountable mindset, have little impact unless they are acted upon. Perhaps the most important part of the IE ethos is bringing a discovered idea – one which is owned by an individual or group – to a community that will benefit from this innovation. Action goes hand in hand with becoming accountable for one's intellectual gifts. By empowering an individual to manifest an idea, one participates in a society where acting for the common good becomes the norm, not the exception. As Demosthenes knew, speech (scholarship) without action is empty and idle.

Seeking the authentic

As educators charge themselves to empower students as engaged citizens through campus-wide entrepreneurship, program developers inevitably confront the authenticity of what they design. The IE ethos encourages the larger ideal of collaboration, consensus and ownership by stakeholders as an authentic vision of cross-campus entrepreneurship initiatives. Philosophies such as this can fortify and inform the mechanisms of student empowerment and responsible citizenship. It is, then, a matter of re-discovering the root purpose of a humanist education that holds so much promise for these efforts. When students are authentically guided and nurtured through their college years, they discover and become accountable for their education while seeking to act collaboratively within communities as empowered, entrepreneurial citizens. IE, as a critical part of any university-wide initiative, provides a philosophical foundation by reflecting the authentic humanist ideal upon which our centuries-long traditions of higher education are based.

When speaking about the authentic in this context, we are not advocating a neo-conservative view of education past. Instead, it is the re-discovery of how a humanist education can prepare citizens to participate and contribute to society. As Gary Tomlinson has written, the search for authentic meaning:

> is the meaning we come to believe in the course of our historical interpretations its creators invested in it – yields fresh ideas by side-stepping the snare of objectivism. It highlights our own role in *constructing* [italics mine] authentic meanings and frees us from the presupposition that a single, true meaning is waiting to be found. (Tomlinson 1989, p. 117)

Tomlinson's insight offers a realistic interpretation of the authentic and highlights how IE and the humanist tradition *authentically* interact. That is, as educators observe the humanist traditions of higher education, it is not a singular, historical authenticity that emerges but a view of the *authentic spirit* and *intent* of humanist education. This has significant implications for cross-campus initiatives. Specifically, by dispelling a singular 'authentic meaning' of the liberal arts ideal, IE can leverage and embrace the uncertainty of the authentic by understanding the spirit and intent of higher education and applying it uniquely.[5] In this sense, IE emerges as a seamless, integrated and intrinsic philosophy that is authentic to the purpose of creating citizens who better and advance society.

John Campbell links Tomlinson's ideas to higher education by drawing upon our most genuine academic traditions:

> Intellectual entrepreneurship seeks to reclaim for the contemporary world the oldest strain in our common intellectual tradition: the need for thought and reflection in the midst of the world of action. As the experiment of the original Greek teachers of practical affairs demonstrated, and as Plato demonstrated through his reflections on these very themes, some of the deepest problems of thought emerge from the affairs of practical life. When one brings together the demands for action and the equally unrelenting demands for reflection characteristic of the new electronic and global marketplace, the term 'intellectual entrepreneur' describes a new form of union between the academy and the world and between the academy and its own deepest traditions. (Cherwitz and Sullivan 2002, p. 27)

Campbell demonstrates how IE's relevance to the larger world is wedded to its academic mission. That is, higher education is a crucial part of society's development and should be considered integrated, not segregated. As Campbell suggests, the IE ethos should permeate and infuse the academy with the promise of solving social problems by capitalizing on humanist traditions. Perhaps most important is Campbell's recognition that IE possesses relevance in a world that has seen dramatic change. IE exists as a dynamic and authentic philosophy that can engage academe, equipping students and educators with the tools and mindset needed to discover the social good both now and in the future – something that historically has been a hallmark of humanist thinking and liberal arts education.

The desire to return to the authentic in higher education has, in part, been a negotiation of context between the German university model of education and the responsibility of the university to society and the individual. Jose Ortega y Gasset (1883–1955), the famed Spanish essayist and philosopher wrote of:

the historic importance of restoring to the university its cardinal function of 'enlightenment,' the task of imparting the full culture of the time and revealing to mankind, with clarity and truthfulness, that gigantic world of today in which the life of the individual must be articulated, if it is to be authentic. (Gasset 1944, p. 75)

Gasset's articulation of the authentic focuses on the university's mission of individual enlightenment as a mechanism of personal empowerment. Conceived in this manner, cross-campus entrepreneurship efforts that impart higher education's authentic task, places students in the context of the present – the 'full culture of the time'. As higher education responds to a changing world and seeks to remain relevant, it need not radicalize a solution. Instead, by re-envisioning our humanist tradition in this 'time', cross-campus initiatives can draw upon IE as the authentic ethos that informs through tradition, not destructs through hyper-intellectualism or commercialization. Thus, IE can guide the manner in which all educational endeavors (teaching, learning, research, service) are not only conducted but conceived – realizing the transformation of the apprentice–certification–entitlement model to an empowered and fully realized 'citizen-scholar'.

Given the broader philosophical ideals that IE advocates, it can serve as the engine with which to realize a more authentic university through modest efforts, instead of a radical and immediate reconfiguration of academic culture. In fact, the IE ethos can become a catalyst to achieve a greater understanding of authentic disciplinary micro-cultures and aesthetics. By leveraging IE in this manner, the much-maligned 'silo-mentality' is eschewed and in its place, emerges the realization of Gasset's ideals.

IE, authenticity and arts entrepreneurship: a case study in curricular philosophy

Arts entrepreneurship education is emerging as the most popular method to assist fine arts students in starting entrepreneurial careers. New programs begin each year and by all anecdotal accounts, these efforts are succeeding.[6] A portion of this success can be attributed to the relationship that entrepreneurship centers and business schools have forged with arts units during the program design process. This partnership typically begins with an arts unit requesting assistance from the business school and customarily, results in many arts entrepreneurship programs employing classes typically found in the undergraduate business curriculum. This is due to a number of factors, though primarily, it is arts decision makers who approach entrepreneurship as a means of fiscal solvency for their students to stem poor professional outcomes. This is a laudable and long overdue sentiment that candidly reflects the realities of arts employment and perhaps, an intrinsic weakness in the way artists – and especially musicians – are trained.[7]

As part of a recent nationwide study that examined representative arts entrepreneurship programs and efforts, arts department chairpersons, deans, provosts, arts students, business educators and directors of entrepreneurship programs shared their thoughts on arts entrepreneurship education (Beckman 2007a, pp. 87–112). These conversations reflected a deep and honest desire on the part of those in the business school to partner with arts units in the development of their entrepreneurship efforts. Without doubt, the collegiality and interest shown by those in the business school was heartening. On the arts side, however, program developers were frequently overwhelmed and confused by the process. Certainly arts decision makers were excited to improve their students' professional outcomes, but this enthusiasm was tempered by a lack of understanding the state of entrepreneurship in disciplinary terms. Specifically, arts administrators seldom engaged the rich discourse of entrepreneurial theory, nor were they aware of alternative definitions and conceptions of entrepreneurship originating from those in the cognitive and behavioral sciences.

The responsibility for this lack of engagement on the part of those in the arts is understandable. Administrators are especially concerned with how their efforts will affect already bloated degree plans. The popular perception of entrepreneurship as a fiscally based concept that is antithetical to fine arts culture is also a concern. Thus, arts decision makers negotiate the educational and professional realties of their students and faculty with the very aesthetic that defines art and arts training. Becoming immersed in entrepreneurial theory to inform these efforts is, for many decision makers, an intellectual luxury seldom undertaken.

A striking finding in the study was a distinct move by arts decision makers to define entrepreneurship idiosyncratically.[8] Sensing dissatisfaction with business-based conceptions of the term, some arts entrepreneurship programs set about crafting a definition that met their needs in the context of the unique micro-cultures of their departments, program goals and disciplines. This is a telling development – an evolution of sorts. Arts units are realizing that entrepreneurship education is not a template that can be applied programmatically. In fact, they have perceived the *spirit* of entrepreneurship as an empowering philosophy rather than solely as a means of fiscal solvency.

This trend by arts units to *envision* an entrepreneurial career for their students instead of adopting a textbook definition has implications for those who assist in the development of these efforts. A formal discussion of the issues arts decision makers face in this context has not been offered to those in the business school and it is our purpose to begin that conversation. Obviously, it cannot address the entirety of the topic, but it does reflect the general concerns of arts administrators and the best practices identified in the study. Note, however, that the following concerns those in the fine arts, not popular arts, or music business programs.[9]

Key issues in arts education

Outlining some of the overarching issues in the arts academy is required to understand the delicate position that arts departments occupy and arts administrators must negotiate when conceiving these efforts. Taken in aggregate, the arts are governed by nineteenth-century aesthetics, which over the past century, has resulted in the objectification of 'Art'.[10] The traditions of that theoretical, historical and educational discourse concerns 'Great Art' to the exclusion of 'Lesser Art' – hence the penchant for dead, white, male and mostly western European composers, artists and playwrights. The consequences of this aesthetic trajectory are significant. It canonizes certain artists and artistic works, certainly, yet it has also marginalized a discussion of the financial outcome and business savvy possessed by arts professionals dating back to the eleventh and twelfth centuries. This has occurred because there remains a strong feeling by many in the arts academy that 'Great Art' should exist autonomously – 'Art for Art's sake' is the refrain. This aesthetic is both implicit and explicit. Music students typically perform the works of 'Great Composers' on stage. Studio artists study 'Great Art' in their history classes; theatre students study and perform 'Great Plays'. The implication of this aesthetic is that art should be created simply because art is art.

Linking any discussion of art and the financial survival of art's creators is viewed as diminishing 'Great Art' for some in the academy that have centered their professional careers on 'Great Works'. Speaking of entrepreneurship in fiscal terms can be professionally threatening for faculty – rendering a life's work aesthetically irrelevant for the expediency of 'better student outcomes' through entrepreneurship education. These perceptions are strong and understandable.

Arts degree plans are bloated. Because of accreditation requirements, many students in state institutions, for example, have only two or three electives available beyond their undergraduate degree mandates. This pressure forces decision makers to focus immediately on curricular delivery when developing arts entrepreneurship initiatives. Additionally, there is a debate among arts educators concerning how entrepreneurship education should be presented – integrated into the degree plan, or adjunct to the degree plan in the form of an academic minor, certificate or as a series of electives.[11]

Given the perception of entrepreneurship as a solely fiscal endeavor, many programs rely on standard undergraduate business classes as central pillars of their efforts. This is an almost default decision for those in the arts as new resources are seldom available to develop and staff such efforts. However, the consequences of this tact are significant in the long term. By arts units relying on business schools for their entrepreneurship curricula, there is no engagement of the unique needs, training or professional culture that arts students have participated in for much of their lives. It is, in essence, a quick fix – we believe that entrepreneurship lives in the business school and arts students need to go there because, that is where it (entrepreneurship) lives.

What the study mentioned above highlighted was that leading arts entrepreneurship efforts *conceive* entrepreneurship first, not define it first. For most, this occurred in two phases: first, defining outcome goals for students and second, defining entrepreneurship uniquely in the context of committee dynamics, perception of the term and departmental culture. Many of the leading programs set goals during the development stage that differed from the status quo 'better outcomes for Arts students'. 'Student empowerment', 'realizing potential' and 'entrepreneurial thinking' are frequently highlighted as goals by more progressive efforts. By envisioning these outcomes, there is an explicit admission that 'fiscal' definitions of entrepreneurship are not suitable for arts students. Simply put, if one conceives entrepreneurship in fiscal terms and develops an entrepreneurship program based upon that definition, students are taught a skill set. Indeed, skill sets are valuable, but some programs perceived the disconnect: entrepreneurship curricula, as it exists in a business school is a contextual curricula designed for the skill sets that business undergraduates receive – not the skill sets that arts students need. Thus, these program designers re-defined the goals of their efforts. Empowering students to envision an entrepreneurial life style through their art became the focus of their development trajectory. This tact not only empowers students, it blunts the nineteenth-century aesthetic outlined above.

Business units should know that their arts colleagues are attempting to revolutionize an educational culture that has largely ignored the professional development and outcomes of its students for many decades. A new generation of faculty and administration have experienced the desire to make the performing arts a career and profit fairly from their creative efforts, yet were stymied when they could not reach their goals. Not wanting to see this occur with students in their charge, some view arts entrepreneurship education as a *moral imperative*. They are passionate about the success of their students, but as importantly, they are concerned about the efficacy of the fine arts in a flatter, more global world. In a strictly business context, the market share for the fine arts (as compared to the popular or entertainment arts) has either declined or stagnated.[12] Thus, some see arts entrepreneurship education as an opportunity to train a vanguard of change agents to spotlight the efficacy of art in cultural and societal contexts.

What arts units need to hear
For those assisting arts entrepreneurship efforts, there are a number of topics that arts units might want to consider from the perspective and authority of the business school. These topics are drawn from the experiences of leading entrepreneurship programs and their moves towards advancing their students to meaningful careers in the arts. For purposes of this chapter, we shall limit this discussion to four issues.

First, arts units exist to train the symphony musicians, arts scholars, painters, actors, playwrights, conductors, moviemakers and dramatists for the next generation. Fine arts higher education is primarily concerned with the performative arts – those who create and perform art. Frequently, these decision makers overlook the arts educators, historians, theorists and other scholarly specialists they train in this process. Certainly the outcome for most of these students is graduate school, then an academic or teaching career. Academic positions for these newly minted PhDs, for example, are scarce (Cherwitz and Beckman 2006, pp. 13–20). Thus, arts units contemplating entrepreneurship efforts should consider a *holistic* approach when designing these programs (Beckman 2004, pp. 13–18). This is a challenging demographic for business and arts units, yet leveraging the training and unique skills these students possess is an extraordinary opportunity that few have recognized as entrepreneurial, and fewer still can realize as profitable for both the students and their institution.

One of the most interesting reactions to defining entrepreneurship in fiscal terms is how business education is integrated into these efforts. Many cutting-edge arts entrepreneurship programs feel that business knowledge is necessary for their students. As a result of the idiosyncratic definitions of entrepreneurship mentioned above, opting for a broader *economic literacy* approach may better suit these efforts instead of putting arts students in standard, core business courses. The justification is simple, yet persuasive: do not make a decent cellist a dangerous accountant. By adopting this trajectory, arts students receive a broader view of the impact that larger economic issues have for the arts economies. Business units may also want to suggest that non-profit business education (and perhaps aspects of the typical arts administration curriculum) become a significant part of this trajectory. Larger arts organizations are non-profit entities and much of the fine arts industry relies on some form (or combination) of philanthropic, university and foundation support. By advancing this larger idea of economic literacy, arts students are better prepared to launch ventures in the economic environment they will inhabit after graduation.

As mentioned above, the typical business entrepreneurship curriculum is a *contextual* endeavor. It places in context the core business knowledge that business students learn as undergraduates. When this curriculum appears in fine arts units, it is so outside of their training, it emerges as a new skill set with no contextual component. Those in business units who are assisting those administrators in the arts should strongly argue for balancing any new skill sets with a cogent and meaningful contextual component within the curriculum.

Lastly, business units must assist in *conceptions* of entrepreneurship that are better suited and closer to the authentic purpose of fine arts training. We must remember that arts students are sequestered in practice rooms, attend two or three three-hour studio classes per day or are at rehearsals late into the night – for four years. With the lack of integrating their liberal arts education into performative training, few opportunities for electives in the degree plan, and years of specialized historical and theoretical studies, students are removed from the very professional culture for which they are trained. The demands of their degree, unfortunately, dictate this intense educational experience. Arts students, then, could be considered professional causalities of the training they purchase through tuition dollars. Espousing a definition of entrepreneurship that is based on fiscal gain does not rehabilitate or leverage the arts training experience for students. In fact, it is counterproductive to what they need and the aesthetics of the fine arts. Put bluntly, students must be empowered by their education to seek an entrepreneurial career through their art, not told that they must become accountants. We would urge those in the business school to present their discipline fully and in a manner that informs arts decision makers of new and progressive definitions of entrepreneurship (already present in the literature) that will empower students and are compatible with the existing aesthetics of fine arts training. For example, Kelly Shaver and Linda Scott in their seminal article 'Person, process, choice: the psychology of new venture creation' argue that the individual is the locus of an entrepreneurial venture: 'a person, in whose mind all of the possibilities come together, who believes that innovation is possible, and who has the motivation to persist until the job is done' (1991, p. 39). William Gartner's advocacy of a behavioral approach to the study of entrepreneurs in '"Who is an entrepreneur" is the wrong question' helps to pull 'entrepreneurship' away from the term's fiscal trappings and can be applied directly to the history of 'Great Artists' and their entrepreneurial behavior as creative iconoclasts (Gartner 1989, pp. 47–68). Hao Ma and Justin Tan's 'Key components and implications of entrepreneurship: a 4-P framework' is especially useful for those in the fine arts as it schematicizes the entrepreneurial process instead of painting the entrepreneur as an exploiter of art (2006, pp. 704–25).

Implications for business and entrepreneurship units
Business and entrepreneurship units can benefit significantly by collaborating with arts programs in the design of these efforts. Although building a cross-campus partnership with a discipline that aesthetically abhors any discussion of fiscal viability is praise-worthy and reflects the realities of arts production, collaborating with arts units in this context provides an opportunity for entrepreneurship programs to demonstrate a new efficacy to fine arts units. Certainly the new generation of arts administrators mentioned above negotiate art's aesthetics in more enlightened terms, but the power of a business and arts relationship lies in the idea that enlightenment breeds practicality.

With the recent financial challenges faced by higher education – especially in public institutions – entrepreneurship programs in fine arts units have a significant advantage in recruitment and retention over those who lack such efforts. Research has shown that arts departments with an arts entrepreneurship degree plan have increased out-of-state enrollment, for example (Beckman 2007a). Although this potential new funding stream is neither realized nor exploited by these departments now, those collaborators from the business school can expose this immediate new source of tuition dollars to arts administrators. By simply advocating for the financial worth of arts entrepreneurship programs in this manner, business units can not only assist their arts colleagues but also demonstrate that interdisciplinarity is not limited to the humanities. This can emerge as a new mission for business schools: generating knowledge that promotes the best aspects of art in society is not antithetical to arts training, but a method of civic responsibility, empowerment, fiscal solvency and aesthetic sustainability. Perhaps most importantly, entrepreneurship departments can create a new efficacy across campus by demonstrating that successful and empowered students can spread the humanities beyond the campus walls, thus developing an increasing relevancy for these disciplines in society.

Yet even with these more tangible potentialities, entrepreneurship units have an opportunity to intellectually align themselves with arts units. Given the perception of business schools as only concerned with fiscal matters, collaborating with arts units on their entrepreneurship efforts is an opportunity to reveal the rich theoretical discourse taking place in entrepreneurial theory mentioned above. By establishing that entrepreneurial theory can possess cognitive, behavioral and interdisciplinary aspects, the business school can align itself with arts units in the context of humanist aesthetics. Since nineteenth-century arts aesthetics are based in the human experience, the cognitive and behavioral discourse occurring in entrepreneurship journals are directly compatible. This alignment eschews any perceptions of the arts being co-opted for financial gain and instead, brings the arts and entrepreneurship to a similar theoretical position of transcending the status quo. This intellectual union of two disparate disciplines, collaborating on empowerment strategies for fine arts students through a common humanist perspective and intellectual tradition through entrepreneurship, can breed new partnerships and model both the IE philosophy and interdisciplinary ideal.

Seeking the authentic in arts entrepreneurship programs: IE in context
For those creating arts entrepreneurship curricula, confronting the authenticity of their work is inevitable. That is, do these programs, classes and activities reflect the aesthetic traditions of fine arts training, and the economic and cultural environment that students will inhabit as arts professionals? Such questions are not simply an academic exercise, but reflect both the context and purpose of arts entrepreneurship education.

In an effort to conceptualize the 'authentic', we must realize that the aesthetic tradition of fine arts training – the 'objectification of art' – is not simply an aesthetic, or simply a tradition. For many in the arts academy, 'Great Art' is not merely a study object but a way of life that is intrinsically worthy of study regardless of financial return. This is because the foundation upon which this ideal is based has everything to do with the desire that humanity has to spiritually transcend the status quo – to seek the sublime. German aestheticians and philosophers developed this idea in the 1800s and its effect is still with us today.

One of the most important aestheticians of the nineteenth century and nineteenth-century music was Eduard Hanslick (1825–1904). A Viennese music critic, Hanslick argued in *Vom Musikalisch-Schönen* (1854) that music itself could not represent 'feelings' (despite having the 'dynamic' trappings of 'feelings') but rather that music was a subjective, autonomous experience and that the trappings of the outside world could taint this experience (Grey 2007). In fact, Hanslick argued that the 'net result' of any musical idea 'determines the aesthetic quality and value of the work' (ibid.). He called this *'das geistiger Gehalt'* – the 'spiritual substance'. Thus, for Hanslick, music was a spiritual experience: it allowed one to transcend human corporality and reach a higher state – the sublime. This is no different from Martin Luther's conceptualization of music's role in the spiritual life of his followers. For Luther, 'music was a means of moving the heart to devotion' and served as a mechanism to reach a higher spiritual state – to transcend the status quo of human existence (Irwin 1983).

Hanslick's ideas about music pervade arts training. When students are taught that Beethoven's music is the premier exemplar of 'Great Art', what is really being said is this: 'Beethoven's music, intrinsically, is so well composed that listening to his compositions can aid in humanity's transcendence – the inherent struggle to seek "place" in the universe. Thus, you [the student] have a responsibility to play his music well. Now, back to the practice room, for a less than perfect performance cheats humanity of his (Beethoven's) gifts'. Beethoven and the music he produced are then objectified by the metaphor of 'Great'. The music he wrote, then, becomes an object – the *substance* of spirituality.

It is easy to see why some arts faculties regard entrepreneurship (perceiving the term as a method of fiscal gain) as antithetical to art, if not 'Art'.

With a conception of entrepreneurship that can fold within the arts academy's aesthetic tradition, entrepreneurship education in the fine arts can take hold extraordinarily quickly. (Hence the discussion above outlining the humanist commonalities between entrepreneurial theories based in the cognitive and behavioral sciences and the arts.) For many arts units, however, entrepreneurship will simply never take root. This is because the standard entrepreneurship curriculum and its perceived nature as the 'co-opter' of art are not authentic to the aesthetic traditions of art – and by proxy, arts training. Thus, entrepreneurship educators armed with new theories of entrepreneurship who stand at the ready to assist in designing curricula specifically for arts students, can aid in bridging the aesthetic tangle that arts administrators confront: how can we empower our students to become successful arts entrepreneurs without abandoning our authentic traditions – the intrinsic nature of how we conceive Art?

The business school has a tremendous opportunity to outline the authentic purpose of arts entrepreneurship programming for the arts academy. That is, developing classes that expose the economic environment of the arts industries and presenting how larger economic forces affect the arts marketplace will arm students to know the economic landscape of the arts. This facilitates sound business decisions because students have the perspective to recognize opportunity in their profession's economic environment. A broad-based business literacy education for arts students in the context of arts entrepreneurship efforts is not only crucial to the mission of these efforts but also an authentic realization of what these programs are designed to produce. If opportunity recognition is an accepted skill that the entrepreneurial artist must possess, then these programs should help to provide not just the recognition skills, but the vital information required to envision the opportunity. At some level, this should be the purview of the arts units themselves as they know and understand the culture of the arts industries. However, basic economic measures such as employment statistics, federal interest rates, stock market psychology, exchange rates, consumer confidence, inflation rates and many other basic issues impact the arts marketplace and arts funding; the business school is uniquely suited to present these issues in a way that is relevant to arts students. Certainly, a New Venture Creation curriculum is valid for those arts students who are predisposed to an entrepreneurial life style, but at what cost to other students who never leave rehearsal spaces except to attend liberal arts classes? We can teach students to start businesses but can we teach arts students to make good financial decisions without an authentic economic context for the desired outcome of these programs?

When considering the design process for arts entrepreneurship programs, every aspect of the training experience that an arts student encounters must be taken into account – including what occurs after the endeavor is complete. This seems obvious, yet many programs, efforts and classes omit such consideration. Far too many courses and programs are designed without a theoretical orientation of entrepreneurship or a serious consideration of the curricular impact, or lack of impact. In order for arts entrepreneurship education efforts to become a ubiquitous part of arts training, the authenticity of the effort must be considered in a myriad of contexts.

Arts students need more than a typical business education – they need a smart and contextualized understanding of the arts economy. They can experience business education in a manner that suits their training in order to become aware of the economic environment in which they will soon operate with the assistance and authority of those who contribute to the design of these efforts. This is the power of the business school; courses can be contextualized to match the unique needs of different disciplinary cultures and target marketplaces. Yet this plea for a contextualized business education does not occur in isolation. Other arts educators have suggested the same. Larry Wacholtz from Belmont University's (Nashville, TN) Music Business Department delivered a paper at a recent US Association for Small Business and Entrepreneurship conference saying 'additional industry related concepts, information, constructs, and methods of operations should be added to the curriculum for performance arts students in entrepreneurship classes' (Wacholtz 2005, p. 1). John O'del from Rhode Island College echoed a similar sentiment: 'some options/topics routinely addressed in an entrepreneurship course may not be appropriate [for Arts Students]' (O'del 2003, p. 3).

The expertise that those in the business school can offer arts units in the early stages of these efforts is crucial for both parties. Arts administrators are seeking guidance at these times and the authority of those experts in entrepreneurship education is valued – literally, in some cases. By understanding the training environment of fine arts students, entrepreneurship departments are in a better position to make critical disciplinary and curricular recommendations that fit the unique needs and culture of arts units and their students. Further, by presenting a conception of entrepreneurship that does not interfere with the nineteenth-century aesthetics in arts education, those in the business school can help to shape an *authentic* arts entrepreneurship program.

Conclusion

The case study presented above demonstrates not only the IE ethos in the context of program development, but also the authentic realization of higher education's purpose. For example, discovery can occur with seemingly disparate disciplines: business units can discover the aesthetic traditions of the fine arts and arts units can discover new conceptions of entrepreneurship suited to these aesthetics. Likewise, both can become accountable to their disciplines and stakeholders: arts administrators can better prepare their students to operate in the economic and cultural environment they are trained to inhabit and business units can leverage their rich theoretical discourse to assist arts units in meeting the goals of arts entrepreneurship education. Collaboration and action permeated the study not only by the transfer of knowledge, but as a means to a shared end. Certainly the case study demonstrated that arts units can achieve their goals with arts entrepreneurship programs, but the 'value added' was the development of a new efficacy for business units.

Adopting IE as a philosophy of higher education can bring new value to the intellectual endeavor. By envisioning IE as a platform to catalyze innovation, leveraging the university's intellectual assets can create significant and meaningful change for society and the university itself. Yet, the power of IE lies not in simply serving the university, but in empowering its citizens to embrace the intellectual endeavor with the goal of becoming authentic citizen-scholars – the change agents of a new age.

Notes

* Portions of this chapter appear in Beckman, Gary and Cherwitz, Richard (2008), 'Intellectual entrepreneurship as a platform for transforming higher education', *Metropolitan Universities Journal*, **19** (3), 88–101.
1. For a recent study on cross-campus entrepreneurship initiatives, see Hulsey et al. (2006).
2. See https://webspace.utexas.edu/cherwitz/www/ie/what.html.
3. Ibid.
4. Aristotle understood the need to put knowledge to work and thus the necessity of integrating rather than segregating theory, practice and production. See Roberts (1954). For a recent study that amplifies his argument as it related to community engagement, see Steffensmeier (2005).
5. This view of the authentic has already been negotiated other disciplines. For example, Gedicks and Hendrix (2005, p. 140) have written (in the context of copyright law) that 'The authentic is also embedded in a tradition which frames its potential meanings and defines its significance'.
6. Note that a longitudinal study determining the effectiveness of arts entrepreneurship education has not been conducted.
7. For a sampling of the recent literature concerning artist employment, see Wassall and Alper (1985); Alper et al. (1996); Galligan and Alper (2000); Alper and Wassall (2000).
8. A short list of these definitions include: 'Entrepreneurship is the notion of thinking metaphorically . . . not thinking literally about the skill-set that one has grown [up with], but the ways these things [skill-sets] can be potentially transferred to other kinds of activities'; 'Searching for, finding, and filling gaps. [As a developing arts entrepreneur, one should] stop "finding" yourself – "create" yourself. Create an individual voice'; 'entrepreneurship is concerned with empowering individuals to see new possibilities and to effect change' (Beckman 2007a).
9. This is a critical distinction. Popular arts disciplines and music business education are not imbued with the aesthetic imperatives (commonly marked as 'tradition') of the fine arts. Additionally, music business education is highly contextualized. For example, as a typical business-based entrepreneurship curriculum is injected into a music business degree plan, it provides a powerful skill set that results in a highly effective and balanced curricular structure.
10. For a single source that eloquently discusses this issue as it relates to music performance, see Hunter (2005). Further discussion of the phenomenon appears below.
11. Note that the University of Iowa (Iowa City, IA) has a major in Performing Arts Entrepreneurship and the University of Southern Maine (Portland, ME) has a major in Art with a concentration in entrepreneurship.
12. See National Endowment for the Arts, *2002 Survey of Public Participation in the Arts*, Research Division Report 45, www.nea.gov/research/ResearchReports_chrono.html, July 2007.

References

Alper, N. and Wassall, G. (2000), *More than Once in a Blue Moon: Multiple Jobholdings by American Artists*, Research Division Report 40, National Endowment for the Arts, Santa Anna, CA: Seven Locks Press.

Alper, N., Jeffri, J., Chartrand, H. and Wassall, G. (1996), *Artists in the Work Force: Employment and Earnings, 1970–1990*, Research Division Report 37, National Endowment for the Arts, Santa Anna, CA: Seven Locks Press.

Beckman, G.D. (2004), 'Career development for music students: towards an holistic approach', *South Central Music Bulletin*, **3** (1), 13–18.

Beckman, G.D. (2007a), '"Adventuring" arts entrepreneurship curricula in higher education: an examination of present efforts, obstacles and best practices', *Journal of Arts Management, Law and Society*, **37** (2), 87–112.

Beckman, G.D. (2007b), 'Disciplining arts entrepreneurship education: a call to action', paper presented at the Hero's Journey Entrepreneurship Festival, Pepperdine University, Malibu, CA.

Cherwitz, R. and Beckman, G. (2006), 'Re-envisioning the Arts Ph.D.: intellectual entrepreneurship and the intellectual arts leader', *Arts Education and Policy Review*, **107** (4), 13–20.

Cherwitz, R. and Darwin, T. (2005), 'Crisis as opportunity: an entrepreneurial approach to higher education productivity', in J. Miller and J. Groccia (eds), *Enhancing Productivity in Higher Education*, Bolton, MA: Anker, pp. 58–68.

Cherwitz, R. and Hartelius, J. (2007), 'Making a "great 'engaged' university" requires rhetoric', in J. Burke (ed.), *Making a Great 'Engaged' University Requires Rhetoric*, San Francisco, CA: Jossey-Bass, pp. 265–88.

Cherwitz, R. and Sullivan, C. (2002), 'Intellectual entrepreneurship: vision for graduate education', *Change*, November/December, 22–7.

Galligan, A. and Alper, N. (2000), 'The career matrix: the pipeline for artists in the United States', in J. Cherbo and M. Wyszomirski (eds), *The Public Life of the Arts in America*, New Brunswick, NJ: Rutgers University Press, pp. 171–201.

Gartner, W. (1989), '"Who is an entrepreneur?" is the wrong question', *Entrepreneurship: Theory & Practice*, **13** (4), 47–68.

Gasset, O. (1944), *Mission of the University*, Princeton, NJ: Princeton University Press.

Gedicks, F. and Hendrix, R. (2005), 'Religious experience in the age of digital reproduction', St. John's Law Review Association, www.lexisnexis.com, August 13, 2007.

Grey, T. (2007), 'Hanslick, Eduard', in L. Macy (ed.), *Grove Music Online*, www.oxfordmusiconline.com, accessed November 1, 2007.

Hulsey, L., Rosenberg, L. and Kim, B. (2006), 'Seeding Entrepreneurship Across Campus: Early Implementation Experiences of the Kauffman Campuses Initiative', No. 6090–250, Mathematica Policy Research, Inc.

Hunter, M. (2005), '"To play as if from the soul of the composer"; the idea of the performer in early romantic aesthetics', *Journal of the American Musicological Society*, **58** (2), 357–98.

Irwin, J. (1983), 'Music and the doctrine of Adiaphora in Orthodox Lutheran theology', *Sixteenth Century Journal*, **2** (14), 157–72.

Ma, H. and Tan, J. (2006), 'Key components and implications of entrepreneurship: a 4-P framework', *Journal of Business Venturing*, **21**, 704–25.

O'del, J. (2003), 'Entrepreneurship in the Arts: an educational approach', paper presented at the United States Association for Small Business and Entrepreneurship National Conference, Hilton Head, SC.

Roberts, W.R. (ed.) (1954), *Rhetoric*, New York: Modern Library.

Shaver, K. and Scott, L. (1991), 'Person, process, choice: the psychology of new venture creation', *Entrepreneurship Theory and Practice*, **16** (2), 23–45.

Steffensmeier, T. (2005), 'Rhetorical invention and becoming local', unpublished dissertation, University of Texas at Austin, Austin, TX.

Tomlinson, G. (1989), 'Authentic meaning in music', in N. Kenyon (ed.), *Authenticity and Early Music*, Oxford: Oxford University Press, pp. 115–36.

Wacholtz, Larry (2005), 'Teaching entrepreneurship to the creative arts', paper presented at the National Meeting of the United States Association of Small Business and Entrepreneurship, Indian Wells, CA.

Wassall, G. and Alper, N. (1985), 'Occupational characteristics of artists: a statistical analysis', *Journal of Cultural Economics*, **9**, 13–34.

4 The microfoundations of entrepreneurial learning and . . . education: the experiential essence of entrepreneurial cognition

Norris F. Krueger, Jr

> Experience is not what happens to you, experience is what you do with what happens to you.
>
> Epictetus

Introduction

Knowing a lot about entrepreneurship is hardly sufficient to make one a successful entrepreneur, 'knowing a lot' can even be dangerous. Knowledge is not just an accumulation of data; knowledge requires both the information content *and* the structure by which we organize it. All too often in our haste to transfer large amounts of important content to students, we lose sight that the knowledge structures are even more important and our ability to influence how students' mental models evolve is the essence of education.

Perhaps nowhere is this as visible as in entrepreneurship education, where we must go beyond teaching facts and teach students how to think like an entrepreneur, to help them toward a more expert entrepreneurial mindset. One way to do that is to situate entrepreneurship education in settings where mental models are not shared, where there is cognitive diversity, that is, a significant diversity of knowledge structures. The success of cross-campus entrepreneurship programs may derive in large part from the inherent cognitive diversity of its students and teachers.

As entrepreneurship educators, we are not training memories, we are training *minds*. Education changes students; entrepreneurial education is no different. Here, more than anywhere, we can assess that change and we can use that assessment to nurture our students' education. Many of our best teaching and training methods visibly affect how students think about entrepreneurship. Of any business discipline, can one readily envision classes where experiential learning does not dominate in the way it typically does in entrepreneurship teaching?

The rise of cross-campus programs in entrepreneurship now offers a golden opportunity to explore this, given the greater cognitive diversity of students who come from different majors, different academic levels and even different physical locations. However, we first need to step back and look at the microfoundations of entrepreneurial learning. We offer here a primer of how the constructivistic paradigm of education applies to entrepreneurial learning; we also hope that it provokes significant discussion about what are, and how we might test, the drivers of cognitive change in entrepreneurship learners.

Constructivistic, not behavioristic

Genuine experiential education changes what learners know but even more importantly *how* they know it. Teaching content is often behaviorist in nature, but to change how we think requires a more constructivistic mode of education. Constructivistic approaches

35

change more than what students know, they change how they *structure* that knowledge. If entrepreneurial education often includes highly constructivistic methods, we can thus make the case that entrepreneurial education can have significant, positive impacts on learning.

However, this then requires us to consider some new questions as we design, implement and assess entrepreneurship education. What is the change we are attempting to induce? We argue here that it is logical to assume that we want to help learners move from a more novice mindset toward a more expert mindset as entrepreneurs. To be specific, we want to help learners move from being novice to expert thinkers!

Considerable research has explored how experts become expert (Ericsson and Charness, 1994), studying chess grandmasters to musicians to pole vaulters. What do all experts share? They may know different things, but what really differs is how they structure their knowledge. Also, there are consistent cognitive processes that develop those deep knowledge structures, processes that we need to take explicit advantage of in our teaching and training.

Thus, we need a better understanding of what course (and curricular) activities influence what cognitive changes. We must also understand what cognitive changes are most desired (and it would not hurt to have a better understanding of what cognitive mechanisms are involved in moving learners toward being more expert entrepreneurial thinkers).

Entrepreneurship education is inherently constructivistic
Entrepreneurship faculty members all want to believe that there is something 'special' about what they do in the entrepreneurship classroom (Fayolle and Servais, 2000). The expectation is that the applied, hands-on nature of class assignments helps students to think entrepreneurially, to see themselves truly as entrepreneurs. State-of-the-art educational theory suggests that the bias toward experiential, action learning found in entrepreneurship training reflects how humans actually learn complex, ill-structured knowledge (Krueger, 2007; Gustafson, Chapter 5, this volume). In fact, these methods reflect the cutting-edge educational theory of 'constructivism' – which is coming to dominate the more familiar and traditional behavioral methods.

Genuine education changes how we think
Perkins (1994) argues that education needs to be 'thinking-centered' – reflecting the reality that education truly involves changing how students think. Truly changing students' entrepreneurial thinking requires more than mere transfer and acquisition of information and skills – students need to move toward a more expert way of structuring that content. To do that, students must take ownership of these new skills and knowledge. This requires significant change in deeper cognitive structures, not just changes in knowledge content but also changes in how individuals structure knowledge.

Krueger (Krueger and Brazeal, 1994; Krueger, 2000) argues that an organization seeking a more entrepreneurial climate requires more entrepreneurial thinking in its members. Classrooms are no different. As with organizations, educators must seek to develop a fertile seedbed that supports entrepreneurial thinking. This cognitive infrastructure supports entrepreneurial thinking and the changes in cognitive structures such as intentions and attitudes, and even deeper cognitive structures such as students' personal mental models of 'what is an entrepreneur? Am *I* an entrepreneur?'.

We must care about these deeper structures. If we are to truly stimulate entrepreneurial thinking in a fundamental way, then it is likely that there will be important changes in students' thinking, including deeper cognitive structures that reflect how humans represent and process information. Mere transfer of information is insufficient to fundamentally alter behavior. This has important implications for *learning* how to think entrepreneurially.

Despite a very extensive – and largely descriptive – literature of entrepreneurship education, academics have been less successful at researching how entrepreneurs actually learn (for example, Alberti et al., 2004). The descriptive work done in entrepreneurship education has, of course, proven of great benefit. The next step for researchers is – as is now being done with intentions – to be much better grounded in educational theory.

Learning and constructivistic education
There are two dominant paradigms in education. The traditional 'behaviorist' approach focuses on fact-based learning (including rote memorization, repetitive drilling and similar mechanisms that focus on transferring content knowledge). Instructors typically provide the models and the framework for knowledge being transferred to students. In contrast, the constructivist approach argues for situated learning where students must develop their own ways of organizing the knowledge (building and changing their own mental models to represent knowledge) as they acquire it. The labels 'learning the answers' versus 'finding the questions' are one way to think about the difference; the author prefers the words of W.B. Yeats about learning. Entrepreneurship educators, it seems, much prefer 'lighting a fire' to 'filling a vessel'. And this makes perfect sense in terms of cutting-edge educational psychology.

Traditional methods provide greater control to the instructor and can appear as more efficient for large groups of students. Constructivistic methods tend to be much more student centered, but this reflects how humans actually learn in daily life: by trial and error in a social setting. Moreover, if one wishes to change deeper cognitive structures such as scripts, then more student-centered learning is imperative. Albert Bandura's social learning theory (for example, 1994) posits learning as an iterative change process by which deeply held beliefs and attitudes co-evolve as learners actively acquire, process and organize new knowledge. That is, students and teachers alike learn from each other – not just facts, but from each other's mental models. The more cognitive diversity, the more opportunities there are to learn from one another.

The number one objective of constructivistic education is deep understanding, the more surface-level skills will follow naturally. Obviously, the more complex the skills required, the more advantageous it is to be constructivistic. Constructivism thus appears essential to nurturing an expert. Moving toward becoming a more expert entrepreneurial thinker is not easy, nor is teaching this. How do we provide critical development experiences for students that accelerate change toward more expert deep knowledge structures?

How knowledge evolves
Again, knowledge is not just an accumulation of data; knowledge requires both the information content *and* the structure by which we organize it. But, this raises one critical

issue: to advance a learner's knowledge almost always requires confronting significant discrepancies and contradictions. Prior knowledge, assumptions and beliefs may prove problematic, even dysfunctional. Constructivistic education offers mechanisms for helping learners confront and learn from challenges and resolve contradictions in their constructed knowledge base. In fact, progress generally requires an ongoing, iterative process of construction and re-construction of knowledge. Consider Thomas Kuhn's *The Structure of Scientific Revolutions* (1962) where he describes a parallel phenomenon of how a strongly held shared mental model (the 'paradigm') evolves in a scientific field. Another parallel lies in the difference between transactional and transformational leadership; too much of education is transactional, despite recognizing that true learning is significantly transformational. A final useful parallel is the process of participatory action research where research subjects become co-investigators.

A big part of being an expert is knowing what you do not know; a big part of staying an expert is continuing to reassess how one structures knowledge and the deep beliefs that anchor those structures. While teachers may intend to assist students toward more expert thinking, they need to model the same learning and openness to cognitive change that they desire in students. In constructivistic classrooms, the teacher–student distinction is thus blurred mindfully; both are learners, both are teachers.

The net result is that we are providing learners with the opportunity and environment to change not just what they think, but *how* they think (see Figure 4.1). This is important. We need to help students change how they structure what they know about entrepreneurship. This requires giving them opportunities for critical developmental experiences that help them to re-shape their mental models.

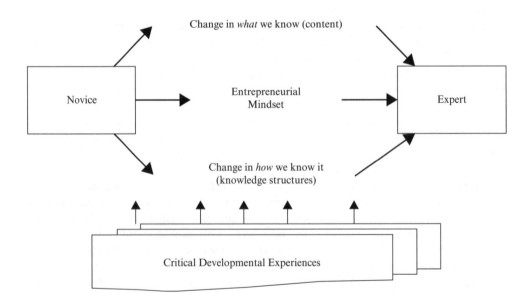

Source: Adapted from Krueger, (2007).

Figure 4.1   What we really do in entrepreneurship education

Thinking-centered learning

Learning is a process by which we construct meaning jointly from our context and from informational cues. Construction of meaning occurs within the learner rather than simply a process of assimilating information from the environment. Learning is situated, though. That is, learning is independent of neither the context nor the learner. The landmark research of Jean Piaget and his successors demonstrates clearly that learning is not a literal transfer of knowledge from teacher to student. Learners of any age construct new knowledge by integrating the new data into relationships with prior knowledge, connecting new information in more than one way. Knowledge is thus constructed as an interrelated whole, not as a set of isolated brute facts. Thus, master educator David Perkins's (1994) felicitous phrase 'thinking-centered learning' proves most appropriate.

Constructivism and the learning cycle

Research has clearly identified a natural learning cycle: first, we discover an issue (and its seeming implications), next we identify critical concepts that may help us explain the phenomenon in question, and finally we seek to apply our newly constructed knowledge and test it against reality (ibid.).

The natural learning cycle assumes that 'big ideas' and 'big questions' are inherently complex. Perhaps oddly, we need complexity to accelerate learning. Oversimplification can actually confuse us when we first confront a 'big idea'. Only after we have immersed ourselves in the problem is it useful to move to a more reductionist approach to isolate key principles. Then, as we struggle to apply the key principles that we have extracted, we return to more complexity. Finally, we must evaluate our resolution to the problem and re-think the process anew, actively seeking contradictions and counter-examples. Note we use the word '*re*solution' instead of 'solution'. The word 'resolution' captures both the iterative nature of the learning process and the recognition that few perfect solutions exist. It also illustrates the dialogic nature of learning a concept. However, as Prawat (1992) notes, students' exploration still requires some sort of 'road map'. Instructors need to provide focus and coherence to prevent the breadth of inquiry from degenerating into unproductive wandering through trivia.

Key principles of constructivistic education

Constructivism's five key principles follow the learning cycle (Brooks and Brooks, 1993):

1. *'Authentic' (and 'important') questions* Learners need to 'own' their knowledge, thus they need to find their 'own' problems in a given subject area. Educators can assist by posing 'authentic' problems of emerging relevance to learners. This has the further advantage of engaging learner emotions productively. For example: planning a desired new business takes on extra meaning when it is potentially 'for real' even though it often complicates our efforts.

2. *'Big ideas'* We should structure learning around primary concepts, not minutiae. If we light a fire with one or more primary concepts with which learners relate directly, they will identify and adopt details as needed. We want students to grasp the essence of a given phenomenon. For example: entrepreneurship is more than identifying an opportunity, it is about understanding how we learn to see the opportunities that we

do (and those we do not). A colleague of the author has introductory entrepreneurship students (many with zero business courses) identify a small business innovation research topic for a feasibility study – and students learn what personally they see as opportunities, often in quite surprising fashion. This is a particularly welcome model for classes including students from science, social science and/or engineering. (Arts and humanities students might also be able to identify grant-based opportunities.) Social entrepreneurship is thus a fast-growing topic in any entrepreneurship course and is often the centerpiece for cross-campus entrepreneurship, as this Handbook demonstrates. Where better to connect learners with big, authentic ideas?

3. *Constructing meaning requires triangulation*   We should focus on and value learners' different points of view; accommodating multiple perspectives often entails team teaching. (This takes advantage of multiple types of intelligence in the class.) For example: team projects that are designed to be truly interdependent force students to bring their differing perspectives to bear in productive fashion. An even better example is the action-learning model that allows students to see how 'book' knowledge squares with practice in hands-on situations (Leitch and Harrison, 1999). Consider how the cognitive diversity in a cross-campus course requires negotiation of often radically different mindsets.

4. *Coaching, not lecturing*   The curriculum should follow students' inquiries (their process of constructing knowledge) not the instructor's own process. (This does not imply an 'anything goes' approach, however.) For example: informal interaction between students and the instructor is critical; but so too is allowing (or requiring) students to coach one another.

5. *Assessment and evaluation techniques should reflect these processes*   They should not reflect the ability to merely 'regurgitate'. Also, different majors are accustomed to often quite different modes of assessment and evaluation (for example, the portfolios used in art). Why not ask students to negotiate the most efficacious metrics? For example: assessment and evaluation processes themselves need to be assessed and evaluated with student involvement.

Re-read the above list and consider how these are reflected in a well-done analysis of a case study or in a hands-on small business institute-type project. (The SBI approach uses real businesses as a 'live-ammo' case.) We begin with a focus on 'big ideas' and authentic questions in an environment that offers a 'safety net' (for example, it is acceptable to try to fail). Learners will accept almost *any* challenge if they frame the learning situation as an opportunity, but to perceive an opportunity requires perceptions of control and competence that are very much in the eye of the beholder. How do we help *them* to frame it as an opportunity? The instructor can foster and reinforce those perceptions, but a student's peers are equally important in promoting a sense of safety and of challenge. Making it safe for students to explore is more difficult than we realize and requires constant vigilance. For example, too much visible knowledge can actually impede knowledge; if students see one possible answer, they can see it as 'the' answer. Similarly, if they see the instructor as having 'the' answer, learners may focus on extracting that answer. The author can attest that instructor ego can be problematic. As such, the constructivists suggest emphasizing questions that clearly have no one single answer. Sound familiar?

The human mind comprises an ever-evolving set of cognitive structures that help us

Table 4.1   A simplified view of how modern pedagogy has evolved

			(more behavioristic)
Key theory	Core assumption	Key activity	Sample tool
Teacher-centered	Expert teacher; passive student	Memorization	Fact-based lectures
Teaching-centered	Expert teacher; active student	Skill development	Pro formas; business plans
Learner-centered	Learners need to control learning process (student as customer)	Teacher–student interaction	Case studies
Learning-centered	Metacognitive understanding of learning (from what we know to how we know it)	Problem-based learning	Self-managed field projects
			(more constructivistic)

Source: Adapted from Krueger (2007).

make sense of our environment and our place in that environment. This includes perceptions of opportunity; we increase the potential for entrepreneurial behaviors if we increase the perceived range of possible opportunities (Krueger and Brazeal, 1994). If we accept this cognitive framework, we must, however, abandon much of the behavioristic tradition that still dominates educational theory and practice (for example, Table 4.1). Learning is not just a stimulus-response phenomenon (Langer, 1994). Memorizing facts or other mimetic activity is not learning; brute facts without context offer little meaning beyond 'We need to know this for the next test!'.

Entrepreneurial learning in practice
The literatures on entrepreneurship, small business, family business and so on all offer considerable evidence that supports the constructivistic paradigm. Bouchhiki argues explicitly that entrepreneurs appear to construct their environments (1993) while Jelinek and Litterer (1995) describe in great detail how a truly entrepreneurial organization encourages its members to construct an opportunity-friendly cognitive infrastructure. Perceptions of self-efficacy, something that constructivistic learning is better at developing, are already closely linked to entrepreneurial intentions (Krueger et al., 2000), opportunity perceptions (Krueger and Dickson, 1994), venture performance (Chandler and Jansen, 1992), and entrepreneurial career choice (Scherer et al., 1989). We also see evidence that entrepreneurial performance is associated strongly with ability in self-directed learning (Guglielmino and Klatt, 1993). Finally, recall that entrepreneurs appear to be motivated far more by intrinsic (for example, autonomy, mastery) than extrinsic (for example, money) considerations (Brockhaus, 1987). These all suggest that if the entrepreneurship-friendly cognitive infrastructure is constructed, then it makes a lot of sense to emphasize learning that is consonant with the constructivist model. If entrepreneurship education works in theory, then it should also work in practice.

Consider the range of best practices that the field of entrepreneurship has developed. While beyond the scope of this chapter, it would be relatively easy to examine, for example, award-winning pedagogies and see the inherently constructivistic principles at work. Many awardees place novice learners in learning situations where they do not answer questions; they must first identify the proper questions. Rather than fulfill a relatively well-structured task such as 'write a business plan for your client', the students must first assess what tasks would solve the client's seeming problem (and may need to assess whether the apparent problem is a root cause or merely a symptom).

True problem-based learning (PBL) is much more than 'learning by doing', as powerful as that may be. Students are forced to structure the problem and the knowledge and skills required (again, as we see prevalent in medical and legal training). Consider, too, the very nature of PBL. We know that genuine PBL enhances students' entrepreneurial thinking to a remarkable degree, even showing evidence of changing knowledge structures in a few months (for example, Krueger, 2001; Hanke et al., 2005; Souitaris, 2005; Cooper and Lucas, 2007; Post et al., 2007; Tegtmeier, 2007; Chapters 11 and 15, this volume). However, the particular value of PBL in entrepreneurship pedagogy is that PBL requires learners to move from answer finding to question creating, to take personal (cognitive) ownership of their projects. Faced with very high uncertainty, extreme time pressures and competing demands on their time and effort, PBL mirrors what an entrepreneur faces on a daily basis. As students proceed, their reflections invariably lead them to that realization: the necessity for further improving their personal role identity as an entrepreneur. (It would be difficult for me to sustain any mental prototype of 'entrepreneur' that does not include 'me'.)

If we are therefore to assist novice entrepreneurial thinkers to become more expert, we need to apply some of the latest research on entrepreneurial cognition to address central questions of how expert entrepreneurs differ, not just in terms of surface knowledge and skills, but in how deep structures affect how they think.

How I think this discussion might apply in the entrepreneurship classroom centers on what we are trying to achieve: we seek to develop more individuals with the entrepreneurial mindset and, more importantly, to develop them better at being entrepreneurial. In the language of cognitive science, we are helping novice entrepreneurs to become expert entrepreneurs. Observers such as former *Inc.* editor George Gendron[1] have argued that entrepreneurship has grown increasingly professionalized and, in turn, that entrepreneurs increasingly require assistance to help them grow as professionals. Whether or not one considers entrepreneurship to be a profession, we now know that there are expert entrepreneurs. As we improve our understanding of what differentiates the expert entrepreneur, we also need to focus our pedagogy in directions that help students and trainees to grow in that direction.

Along those lines, Jack and Anderson (1999) suggest that we should be creating 'reflective practitioners' with higher-level skills, both practical and cognitive. Creating reflective practitioners requires more than the mere acquisition of information and skills. Again, genuine knowledge is both the raw information *and* the structures by which we organize that information. If we are to truly change our students' entrepreneurial thinking, we must also help them develop new cognitive structures at a much deeper level. In turn, this requires creating a cognitive infrastructure in the classroom that mindfully facilitates such changes.

Tom Monroy was perhaps the first to articulate that traditional classroom methods were not only less frequently used in entrepreneurship classes but they are less effective than more experiential approaches (Monroy, 1995). Rather we tend to emphasize 'problem-based learning' where learners focus on real-world issues, a focus that is a staple of most entrepreneurship courses. Indeed, the most popular and successful training techniques used in entrepreneurship tend to strongly reflect the constructivistic model: living cases (for example, small business institute), business plans, shadowing and so on (Krueger and Hamilton, 1996).

Garavan and O'Cinneide (1994; see also Alberti et al., 2004) published an interesting overview of different entrepreneurship training programs as to key approaches used, key constraints and so on and it illuminates the strong bias we have for hands-on, experiential learning. In particular, *action learning* represents a model of education that seems particularly applicable to entrepreneurship training (Leitch and Harrison, 1999). Action learning is perhaps the most prominent incarnation of the constructivist model.

Much of constructivist pedagogy focuses more on cognitive phenomena, while action learning focuses more on a set of techniques to facilitate that change. Creating Jack and Anderson's (1999) 'reflective practitioners' with both practical and cognitive skills requires action learning's iterative combination of both classroom and hands-on learning in synergistic fashion. Action learning is typically most efficacious in a team setting, as befits the situated nature of the learning, especially a team setting that reflects considerable cognitive diversity (for example, Chapter 11, this volume). Think Senge's (1990) cross-functional high-performance work teams.

'Informed' intent

Who would you bet on? An experienced, successful entrepreneur with a moderate intent or a complete novice with an intense, even passionate intent? What can it possibly benefit us if we increase students' attitudes and intentions toward entrepreneurship, if we fail to prepare them (or, worse, encourage them unrealistically). Increasing intent is one thing, nurturing an informed intent is far more important (Krueger et al., 2007).

We have recently seen exciting research expanding the richness of our understanding of entrepreneurial intentions and, in particular, the relevance to pedagogy and the critical importance of expertise. As entrepreneurial expertise is increasingly important to scholars and educators alike, why not ask about 'entrepreneurial intent among novices versus entrepreneurial intent among experts? If entrepreneurship is not fully recognized as a profession, it certainly has become more and more professionalized. What does it mean to be "expert" in the entrepreneurial domain? How can we help people get there?'

As entrepreneurship researchers and educators, we do not want to turn out entrepreneurs *per se*, rather we are attempting to help them become as expert as possible in the skills and processes entrepreneurs need to exhibit. As educators we can assist them in this journey from novice to expert and that is exactly what we need to be doing. But, that begs the question of content – what should they be working to become expert at? The growing body of work in entrepreneurial cognition argues persuasively that what differentiates entrepreneurs is not necessarily knowledge content and even surface-level skills.

What differentiates entrepreneurs is entrepreneurial thinking; our job is to nurture students into thinking like an expert entrepreneurial thinker. That requires changing some very deep beliefs, deep assumptions that anchor our mental prototypes. To do that requires giving students opportunities for critical developmental experiences (again see Figure 4.1).

Current research has focused on how entrepreneurial education changes intentions and attitudes. Formal training/teaching does seem to matter in the emergence and evolution of entrepreneurial thinking. Nicole Peterman's thesis work found that an entrepreneurial training program significantly influenced the various antecedents of entrepreneurial attitudes and intentions (Peterman, 2000). Even formal coursework (Cox, 1996; Krueger, 2001; Lucas and Cooper, 2004; Post et al., 2007; Tegtmeier, 2007) appears to have a small but measurable impact on critical beliefs (for example, self-efficacy) and attitudes (including intent).

Again, however, developing entrepreneurial thinking requires changes in deeper cognitive structures. This offers us many opportunities to research the specific impacts of different training activities and other experiences to further improve our learning (Duckworth, 1986). Prior experience certainly influences perception of future opportunities (for example, Krueger and Brazeal, 1994). For example, we have some evidence that growing up in a family business influences attitudes and intentions toward entrepreneurship (Krueger, 1993; Delmar and Davidsson, 2000). Exposure to competitive sports seems particularly potent in more collective-minded cultures (Neergaard and Krueger, 2005); one might even make the case that children's fairy tales might affect deep beliefs (Neergard and Smith, 2007). While it may be unrealistic to place students in their own family business, what are the 'lessons learned' that we might replicate? (And that we are likely doing already.)

Skills and self-efficacy
What *are* some critical developmental experiences that we can fruitfully offer? What specific kinds of skills, what specific kinds of training and what specific kinds of experiences are truly transformative in terms of enhancing entrepreneurial thinking? For example, Robert Baum and colleagues (Baum et al., 2001) found that a venture's growth depended on both specific motivations and specific skills of the founder. However, education researchers argue that skills acquisition is necessary but not sufficient, whether acquired via hands-on mastery or vicarious learning through behavioral modeling.

Learning a skill changes knowledge content, learning that one can use that skill successfully can change how you structure knowledge. Learners must internalize knowledge and skills to the point where they feel comfortable enough to apply them to new, even highly risky situations. Self-efficacy theory (Eden, 1992; Bandura, 1993) suggests that just acquiring skills is not enough to fundamentally change how we think, it also requires believing in those skills (perceived efficacy versus actual efficacy). No self-efficacy, no long-term skills acquisition – or skill usage.

However, self-efficacy without the actual skills hardly reflects an informed intent. Bandura himself would also argue that acquiring the correct skills is also imperative for long-term, sustained change in our thought processes as we move from a more novice mindset toward a more expert mindset. In the entrepreneurship domain, we are beginning to focus on identifying those skills that appear to make the most impact on subsequent entrepreneurial behavior. These tend to also reflect changes in entrepreneurial thinking. For example, opportunity identification often reflects relatively sophisticated skills of counterfactual thinking. Based on this, Gaglio trains her students in advanced counterfactual thinking techniques to increase their abilities to identify opportunities (Gaglio, 2004). How better to expand students' 'what-if' thinking than to have a broader range of life, work and school experiences in the classroom, as you would find in a cross-campus course.

The entrepreneurship program at the University of Victoria (Victoria, BC) focuses most of their activities explicitly on moving students from a novice entrepreneurial script toward an expert script; the expert script serves as a guide to accelerate student progress (for example, Morse and Mitchell, 2005). Baron's (2006) argument that expert entrepreneurs are better at 'connecting the dots' suggests that we find ways to train students in related skills; and deliberate practice seems to be one such method (for example, see Mitchell, 2005; Baron and Henry, 2006). However, this is a process that requires fairly intense reflection, something that other majors are far more comfortable with – and can assist business students.

For yet another example, Fiet and Barney (2002) show that certain key skills related to identifying highly credible opportunities can be identified and taught, thereby raising students' self-efficacy at opportunity identification in a broader, more diverse range of possibilities. This permits instructors to tailor experiential exercises to develop and assess those skills. However, the more diverse the existing base of knowledge and beliefs that the student have, the easier that task will be.

Deep beliefs

Finally, what is the essence of being successfully 'entrepreneurial'? Expert entrepreneurial thinking seems a critical perspective. Successful entrepreneurs should be characterized by an expert mindset. Evidence indicates that the content of an expert's knowledge base need not differ from that of a novice, but experts typically organize or structure the content differently. This begs the question concerning how expert entrepreneurs structure their knowledge. Ericsson (for example, Ericsson and Charness, 1994) has shown that while some individuals move from novice to expert, yet others do not. And, that change manifests itself in significant changes in deep cognitive structures. One key implication of Ericsson's work is that experts, including entrepreneurs, are definitely made, not born. There may be some innate 'hard wiring' but expertise appears to be learned. Some deep beliefs may coalesce at a very early age (for example, Neergaard and Smith, 2007) but they evolve over time (for example, Erikson, 1980).

The research also indicates that experts consistently and reliably follow recognizable cognitive behaviors and processes (for example, Mitchell, 2005; Baron and Henry, 2006). Consequently, if we want to understand entrepreneurship, then it is vital for the field of entrepreneurship to learn as much as we can about what differs in the deep cognitive structures of expert entrepreneurs (maps, scripts, schemas and so on and the deep beliefs and assumptions driving them). When we gain a better understanding of how such deep structures evolve, our ability to help entrepreneurs grows in parallel.

Cognitive diversity

In recent years, we have found remarkable new insights into how we learn to think entrepreneurially. We have found constructs that fully moderate the intentions model. For a striking example, differences in cognitive style can yield dramatically different pathways in the formation of intent. That is, the intentions model for learners who score as preferring intuitive thinking differs significantly from the model for those scoring as preferring an analytic cognitive style (Krueger and Kickul, 2006). That implies explicit consideration of differing cognitive styles among our students and, given the constructivist paradigm, to encourage a broad range of cognitive style and other learning styles in our students. If the differences in something as simple as cognitive style matters that much, then how about all the other ways that students may differ cognitively?

What better way to do that than to have students from every imaginable major. Barring that, we need to surface the unique mental models that all of us possess. However, consider how business students can influence how non-business students think; consider even further how non-business students can influence business students. But first we must surface as much cognitive diversity as we can, then use that to everyone's advantage.

Building a constructivistic classroom

What teaching tools are constructivistic?
How do we actually implement a constructivistic curriculum? Again, let us turn to Brooks and Brooks (1993):

> A constructivist framework challenges teachers to create environments in which they and their students are encouraged to think and explore. To do otherwise is to perpetuate the ever-present behavioralist approach to teaching and learning. (p. 30)

> [C]onstructivistic teachers seek to ask one big question, to give students time to think about it, and to lead them to the resources to answer it. (p. 39)

In short, we need to focus much more on the learning process going on inside the heads of the learners and less on filling those heads with details. If we improve the students' abilities to learn, the details will follow. Straight lecturing is far from optimal. A charismatic instructor may 'light a fire' in students even in straight lecture mode, but be assured the learning comes from the motivation not the details. Even testing should be a significant learning experience. What do students learn from parroting the text or lecture notes? From multiple-choice, true–false, or matching types of tests? They may even learn that they do not do these kinds of test very well, reducing both their interest level and their self-efficacy perceptions.

Operationalizing constructivism
Brooks and Brooks also offer 12 concrete steps to operationalize these principles. Let us look at them in the context of the entrepreneurship classroom, where students engage in hands-on projects that offer the potential for critical developmental experiences:

1. *Explicitly encourage, accept, and honor students' autonomy and initiative* Self-managed, self-organized work teams require that students take considerable initiative.
2. *Try to use raw data and primary sources as fodder for student inquiry* Requiring student initiative and responsibility also requires that the instructor give them the authority to guide the direction of their own projects after launching.
3. *Students' tasks are to classify, analyze, predict, and create (not simply memorize)* Real-world projects inevitably involve both primary and secondary data collection as grist for the students' mill.

4. *Student responses on a topic should direct strategy and content of teaching* The projects (and essay exams) force the students to think critically, to integrate and apply what they are learning with projects (and with past life, work and school experiences).

5. *Ask for students' understanding before we give them our perspective* They also require that class discussions be centered around the students' authentic questions, often about how to apply a concept to their project.

6. *Encourage dialogues between students and teacher, each other, family, even outsiders* The projects require students to discuss their efforts with each other, clients and others in the community with the knowledge and expertise needed for the project.

7. *Ask open-ended questions; encourage students to also do so* The exam takes this approach, while experiential projects themselves naturally induce open-ended questions (often to a harrowing degree). Moreover, students feel free to ask tough questions of each other.

8. *Ask for elaborations of initial responses* Similarly, students in self-managed team projects rarely let their peers give evasive answers (but are coached to be supportive as well.)

9. *Don't accept quick answers; encourage reflection* Similarly, giving the students two months for the essay exam affords them an opportunity to elaborate and reflect, even argue with one another.

10. *Actively seek contradictions* Interestingly, hands-on projects under high cognitive diversity appear to naturally encourage the students increasingly toward initiating dialogues that are more Socratic in nature, as they struggle to make sense of ill-structured projects in ill-structured domains.

11. *Actively seek metaphors* Metaphorical reasoning is not inherent in these projects (nor in the exam) although students have a propensity toward analogical reasoning, even where spurious, affording teaching moments for the instructor. Here again, cognitive diversity becomes a true ally.

12. *Take advantage of the natural learning cycle (from discovery to concept introduction to application), balancing both challenge and safety* For example, the extended time afforded by take-home exams with deep, 'stretch' questions allows students to work through this cycle. Extremely challenging team projects work best when students realize that there is a safety net in the form of both the instructor *and* their fellow students.

Impediments to constructivistic curricula

Another aspect of that is how educators' prior expectations can cloud their perceptions of what is happening in the classroom. A trap we are all familiar with: it is very easy in case-study discussions to assume that the discussion will eventually end up taking the same general directions and end up with the same general conclusions. Prawat (1992) notes the existence of four critical cognitive impediments to implementing a more constructivistic curriculum:

1. dichotomous view of teaching and learning;
2. student interest and involvement is necessary and sufficient for deep learning;

3.   dichotomous view of comprehension and application; and
4.   the curriculum is a fixed agenda (dichotomous view of content and process).

These erroneous assumptions reflect instructors' own role identity as a teacher. We can test ourselves – are we guilty of these assumptions? Assumptions may be hard to change, but we can raise our awareness of them. Prawat suggests that these assumptions reflect dichotomous, 'either/or' thinking about learning, though experienced educators are fully aware of the sizable 'grey areas'. Let us consider this in terms of cross-campus entrepreneurship education.

Teaching and learning as distinct implies the folk wisdom that education is a transfer of knowledge from teacher to student. An entrepreneurial setting often requires the student to bring considerable information to the class and, in many cases, a distinctly different mental model of the problem at hand. The latter is particularly powerful in helping students (and teachers) to construct newer, more apt mental models.

A classroom where many different majors are present (and not just different business majors) forces these differing mental models to the surface immediately. It is this iterative, reflective process of constructing and re-constructing deep knowledge structures that makes for deep learning. All the student and teacher passion in the world will not help if we ignore the constructivistic nature of deep human learning.

Prawat's third impediment is that we often think of learning as a sequential process: we learn, then we apply our learning. Action learning models (for example, Leitch and Harrison, 1999) have long argued that deep learning is accelerated when we act, then seek to understand. Entrepreneurs need to act and learn essentially in tandem, making it difficult to arbitrarily separate even classroom learning from action. Our classroom exercises must reflect that, rarely being mere transfers of knowledge without the context of action. It is easier to get students to routinely ask 'Why?' and 'How?' when their mental models differ as much as they do in a cross-disciplinary setting.

Prawat's final impediment is really the culmination of the first three. How do we overcome the first three impediments, while following a rigid syllabus? Even with students with a shared mental model (for example, accountants) one never quite knows when important teaching (and learning) moments can occur. The more cognitive diversity in the classroom, the more likely it is that any key learning moment can occur at almost any time and the instructor (and the students) need to be prepared. If entrepreneurs thrive on serendipity, then so too should entrepreneurship education.

Let us look briefly at how one might grow a constructivistic learning partnership.

Exemplars of constructivistic classrooms
Providing learners with authentic questions (or helping surface them) that engage them at a deep level and letting them take ownership of how they address those questions (and how that changes how they think) is key. Doing so requires that the instructor truly understand the entrepreneurial mindset, but the payoff is significant. Not only does the engagement benefit the community, but the constructivistic process enables learners to change how they think about entrepreneurial thinking. You simply cannot change the entrepreneurial mindset through 'memorize and regurgitate' training

Appendix 4A offers two examples that the author is closely familiar with and most readers will find them well within their comfort zones. Again, much of what entrepreneurship educators do routinely leans heavily toward the constructivistic; these examples lean even further, including an intensive engagement with the community. Both examples also lend themselves quite readily to university-wide programs.

What other kinds of exercise are congruent with the constructivistic learning approach? Case studies seem an obvious approach. Case-study analysis compels students to construct working models and to re-construct them as they work through the ramifications. The iterative process is immensely valuable as it enhances students' ability to 'learn how to learn' in new directions. (When we learn to do mathematics, we engage in the same 'patterning' process.) Cases can surface students' most stubbornly held assumptions, but only if we encourage reflective thinking and we encourage 'out-of-the-box' thinking. For example, some case instructors insist that students not invoke outside knowledge, but we are rarely dealing with legal cases where precedent is paramount. If you are teaching case studies and students 'go the extra mile' to find additional data, why punish them?

One useful approach in this domain is the semi-structured 'living cases' such as those used by many schools. The reality of a living case compels action learning and a constructivistic approach. The good news is that most entrepreneurship educators have embraced the reality aspect and many focus heavily on experiential learning. However, a deeper understanding of the key principles of constructivism and of methods that embrace them (for example, action learning) will enhance learners' experience even further.

Once again, a caution: experiential exercises need to be *truly* experiential exercises. Not all such named exercises are really so. 'Hands-on' does not necessarily equal 'experiential'. Truly experiential exercises give careful consideration to process and content – and give students room to make mistakes. An example of this would be a business simulation game that in the long run rewards early mistakes, rather than a game that overly rewards early success, even if it results purely from chance. In short, truly experiential exercises change how students think – not just changing the content of knowledge but also changing deeper cognitive structures.

Consider examples from this Handbook. Entrepreneurship in the sciences requires an entrepreneurial approach. Biologist Daniel Johnson asked his students to write a chapter for an authentic biology text, while biophysicist Jed Macosko engaged students in computer graphics, both with a truly entrepreneurial spin and genuine problem-based learning (Chapter 9, this volume)

A remarkable example from this Handbook is Lynnette Claire's entrepreneurship film project (Chapter 12, this volume) where students with little or no exposure to entrepreneurship or to film-making were tasked with studying a local entrepreneur and creating a compelling short film on their subject. This required bringing in resources from across the University of Puget Sound (Tacoma, WA) and engaging the community at a deep level, all the while helping students reflect on their experiences and the impact on their own entrepreneurial self-efficacy.

Community engagement in general is a potent way to get learners to identify truly authentic questions. We have already noted that social and sustainable entrepreneurship is often at the heart of cross-campus entrepreneurship programs. What better than projects that allow learners to learn at a very deep level and channel their passion in ways that enhance their cognitive development toward more expert entrepreneurial thinking?

Getting started

Business students are often well-schooled in the traditional learning approaches. True collaboration is likely to seem threatening to students who assume that education is a competitive process. Perkins and others argue that we can begin the process with deceptively simple exercises such as 'Fermi' problems. (A Fermi problem asks a simple question with no simple answer, such as 'How many pencils are there in Chicago?'.) The pursuit of a Fermi problem forces students to be creative and to use multiple perspectives and approaches. In turn, this leads them toward collaboration and toward the realization of the world's inherent messiness and noisiness. We observe other simple approaches such as using metaphors ('firm as a machine' or 'firm as a tree' and so on as suggested by Morgan, 1986) or debates or even a mock 'town meeting'.

'Students as true co-investigators' is another powerful model (Yager, 1991). Consider John Bunch at Benedictine (Atchison, KS) who lets students do 'How-To' papers that show the reader how to handle some useful task such as how to arrange a letter of credit for exporting to France. The student identifies the topic area (thus an 'authentic' problem), negotiates its scope with instructor as essentially co-learner, then delivers a report that is available to classmates, present and future. We are developing a program where students will co-write white papers with local technology clients; this may even become a profit center to help support student activities.

Not all group projects offer such benefits; poorly structured group projects can impede learning. True group projects involve pervasive collaboration and exhibit many characteristics of cooperative learning (true interdependence in goals, in the means to those goals, and in rewards). Some instructors have found success in journal writing and other tangible supports to students' ability to think reflectively on the learning process in that class – how their thoughts have changed and how their ways of thinking have changed. One tangible output might be writing a case study, especially now with formal case-writing competitions that are welcoming student efforts.

Any such approach lends itself to a cooperative learning environment where students are wholly interdependent on each other for their goals, their strategies, and their rewards. Many business school programs use such teams exclusively with great success. A low-risk approach is the group outside presentation where the team must present to some real-world group on a topic of value and interest. This pushes students to select an 'authentic' problem and grants them the freedom to pursue it autonomously. As might be expected, team teaching is often useful, offering multiple perspectives to the students. A prominent example is the Experiential Classroom Program at Syracuse (NY) that teams entrepreneurs with academics.

We need to provide a safe environment where failure is clearly and emphatically a learning experience. Some entrepreneurship classes even insist that students must 'push the envelope' until they actually fail, learning that adversity really is a learning experience. One popular model is to assign students a project to induce some actual, visible change in some organization that involves more than one person (who must be persuaded, not ordered). Setbacks on an 'impossible' task are often much less ego-threatening.

Daryl Mitton (1994) offered a series of experiential exercises to build what he calls entrepreneurial 'clout' (essentially tacit knowledge and self-efficacy). Exercises many use include the 'dollar' exercise (create a profitable, legal business for $1) and the 'five strangers' (go ask five strangers about your business idea). Learning experiences such as these are generally done outside of class at the student's choice of time and place. The exercises encourage breadth of thinking and, more important, increase student perceptions of self-efficacy at the task or skill in question. They allow students to change their mental models with a minimum of risk to ego or self-image.

How do we evaluate progress?
One key advantage of the behaviorist, content-oriented model is that it is relatively easy to assess whether the content knowledge has been transferred. It is considerably more challenging to assess whether knowledge structures have changed (and in positive directions). What we can do is focus on the constructivistic process and to keep firmly in mind that our goal is to help students move toward more expert entrepreneurial thinking.

Let us return to the issue of how learning processes can change deep mental models in the direction of better entrepreneurial thinking, whether in terms of learning to see more/better opportunities or to see oneself as an entrepreneur (or, as we have noted, both). Both Baron (2006) and Gaglio (2004) demonstrate how the cognitive mechanism of counterfactual reasoning is a potent lever for stimulating students to question their existing mental models. And, again, at the University of Victoria, Ron Mitchell, Brock Smith and Kristie Seawright and Eric Morse have developed a pedagogy that heavily emphasizes helping students acquire expert scripts (2000). This clearly suggests that measures of deep structures, whether scripts or maps or other possibilities, can be usefully deployed to research how entrepreneurial thinking changes across a training program (Mitchell et al., 2000; Krueger, 2001).

How do we best evaluate student performance formally? We have suggested above that in constructivistic learning, it can be powerful indeed to engage the students in designing assessment and evaluation metrics. An excellent starting-point is something that students, especially non-business majors, often suggest: the 'portfolio' concept that collects a wide variety of student outputs. Perkins (1994) argues for 'process-olios' which also include throughputs to vividly demonstrate student progress. (That is, the process-olio includes interim and draft reports.) Requiring multiple projects in the portfolio/process-olio taps into more than one kind of intelligence and more than one type of skill, showing how students take advantage of their strengths and how they remediate their weaknesses. In short, they show how the students learn how to think more entrepreneurially. SBI reports are ideal candidates. However, we would be remiss if we neglected the growing use of portfolios in entrepreneurship education with at least three Academy of Management pedagogy awards going to portfolio-based programs, two of which are explicitly script focused (San Francisco State and Victoria.) Never lose sight that the metrics and the evaluation process itself should have visible connection to the change in deep beliefs and knowledge structures that we are seeking.

Where next?
More important questions remain. As models and methods continue to evolve, especially those suggested by recent breakthroughs in neuroscience, we will be able to take closer and closer looks at how specific educational experiences affect specific changes in how we structure knowledge. However, we still have relatively limited evidence even at the surface level. Unlike the education field (for example, Hamilton and Hitz, 1994) we have not studied how students' reflections change over time (for example, through

even simple mechanisms such as reflective journals). Would it not be amazing to track the changes of business majors versus non-business majors? Even if they converge at the same points, the paths will likely differ. (Even if they start at similar spots, the paths may differ!) We already know in social entrepreneurship (a frequent theme in cross-campus programs) that someone with the role identity of an 'entrepreneur' starts with very different knowledge structures from someone with the role identity of 'social activist', even if they too end at the same point (Simms and Robinson, 2006). Cross-campus courses represent a powerful venue for cutting-edge research in entrepreneurial cognition.

It is also imperative that entrepreneurship educators do more assessment of the impact of their teaching. As noted, we consistently see that our classrooms do change students' thinking. From the constructivistic perspective, it is almost unthinkable that we would not. However, that begs two questions. First, why are we not doing more of this research? Why are we not doing research that addresses directly the legitimacy of what we do? With accrediting bodies nudging schools to use practitioners less in the classroom and administrators trying to shoehorn entrepreneurship into the mainstream, why then are we not providing the very evidence that demonstrates that what we do matters? That how we do it matters?

Second is a more troubling question: are we always changing minds in the right directions? Are we actually moving them in the general direction of expert thinking? If the constructivist model has a large drawback, it is that the instructor needs to fully understand (and likely share) the expert entrepreneurial mindset. What if the people teaching entrepreneurship have serious misconceptions about the entrepreneurial mindset? Even a talented, passionate amateur may be painfully hostage to the novice mindset to the detriment of students.

Entrepreneurship is not linear; entrepreneurial thinking must not be linear
Considering that entrepreneurial processes are rarely linear, becoming an entrepreneur comprises a set of ill-structured, even wicked tasks. We know that planning a venture requires effectual, not causal logic (Sarasvathy, 2004). However, what about instructors who teach entrepreneurship as essentially a linear process? There is growing evidence that simply teaching someone to write a business plan is dysfunctional at best, educational malpractice at worst. Meanwhile, leading educators have grown increasingly contemptuous of 'cookbook' business plan classes – and contests (for example, Meyer, 2001).

On the other hand, we are seeing the rise of cross-campus competitions such as the University of Texas's 'Idea To Product' (www.ideatoproduct.org) global contest where multidisciplinary student teams turn raw intellectual property into plausible products. Helping students learn to turn ideas into reality is powerfully constructivistic in itself; adding the cognitive diversity of multiple disciplines makes it work.

The political context? ('Anyone can teach entrepreneurship!')
Yet, little of this has seen print. Why? Business plans are essentially the 'killer app' that brought entrepreneurship into wider acceptance in business schools. Business plan contests are great theater and potentially great fund-raisers for schools, even if we cannot identify measurable impacts on entrepreneurial thinking. What administrator wants to hear that business plans are too often mediocre pedagogy? We have seen how

problem-based learning is far more powerful and more productive, yet if it requires an expert thinker to do it properly, then that constrains administrators who would prefer to believe that 'anyone can teach entrepreneurship' (Fernandes, 2006). However, do we really know what the impacts are, positives as well as negatives, of using the business plan 'cookbook' as the centerpiece of entrepreneurship education? Would we not be better off if we took a constructivist approach to teaching business plans (Honig, 2004)? That is one nettle we need to grasp; we now have the tools to do so. How does this linear approach actually change deep knowledge structures?

Instructor effects?
Case studies are a middle ground that can also be fruitfully explored. An inexperienced case teacher may be too prone to follow the 'recipe' suggested by the teaching notes, both the intended conclusions and the paths to get there. Meanwhile, an experienced (expert?) case teacher can operate in a much more nonlinear fashion, yet providing linearity where needed. As such, we could hypothesize that instructor differences might play a significant role. In much of the foregoing, we have argued that the key instructor difference lies in him/her having or knowing the expert entrepreneurial mindset. Here we may find that the key difference is being an expert in case teaching. Hanke et al. (2005) seem to argue that having expertise in true problem-based learning is the critical leverage point, not necessarily having the expert entrepreneurial mindset. Finally, we would also be remiss in not arguing that we need to study student effects. (Might not cross-campus courses provide fertile ground for studying that?) Our research needs to tease out the differential impacts of instruction, instructor and student.

In sum, it should be obvious that not only does the constructivist model offer us a powerful, productive way to understand and improve entrepreneurship education, but there is also a rich, deep array of theoretically interesting – and practically useful – topics for future research.

Constructivism: major conclusions

1. The number one objective of constructivistic education is: deep understanding, not just superficial skills. Even complex skills necessary for success are acquired more quickly and thoroughly through this kind of approach. Being a successful entrepreneur requires this. And, as we have seen, the cognitive diversity offered by a cross-campus program can accelerate this process measurably.
2. Gaining a deep understanding requires 'learning how to learn' from multiple perspectives. How better to do this than in settings where the multiple perspectives define the setting (as in cross-campus classes)?
3. The constructivistic model of education confirms conceptually much of what we already know to be efficacious educational practice.
4. The constructivistic model affirms the criticality of context: the situation and co-learners are vital to students gaining a deep understanding of the subject area.
5. Constructivistic teaching works (but it is not easy!).

'Education is not the filling of a vessel but the lighting of a fire' (William Butler Yeats). To borrow an old adage, our goal as entrepreneurship educators is not human resource development, rather the goal is developing resourceful humans. Where better than in entrepreneurship to light – and fan – the fire?

Appendix 4A   Two examples of constructivistic classrooms

Example 1   The virtual accelerator course for nascent gazelles
The University of California at Los Angeles (UCLA) pioneered a model program (GAP) where MBA capstone (all majors) students were matched as teams with nascent gazelle entrepreneurs with high potential for explosive growth and figured out ways to help them toward meeting their promise. (UCLA was not the only pioneer, in fact, many schools now follow this general model such as Georgia Tech's TiGER program, the multi-school program developed by N2TEC (www.n2tec.org, led by USC and Fresno State, CA). However, UCLA's Alan Carsrud was first to market with this model.)

Basic GAP model   Student teams are matched with nascent tech entrepreneurs (firm already started but not yet launched). Team goal is to help accelerate the business's development, ideally resulting in major external funding, acquisition and/or major customer acquired.

- *Step 1: Recruitment*   Obviously, the client businesses are carefully vetted, but so too are the instructors required to support this process (comfort with and skills with regard to problem-based learning is imperative).
- *Step 2: Launching*   Students (and faculty) and entrepreneurs come together for a 'kickoff' weekend where the teams and their entrepreneurs can bond and develop the initial action plan for the semester. This includes a 2+ day entrepreneurship boot camp that gets students and others up to speed on the task ahead. This crash course can also be shared with a broader audience. The event closes with brief student presentations on their proposed 'battle plan' (including benchmarks and milestones), pitched to a 'murder board' of experts in new ventures and the firm's industry.
- *Step 3: The work*   Student teams go home to begin work on their plan, revising as need be. They identify an advisory board for their project using members of their community (wherever possible), even national experts. It really is up to the team; however, at regular intervals, additional course material is presented to students and other material is provided to faculty and team advisors to use.
- *Step 4: The celebration/competition*   Student teams return at the term's end for a celebration of what all the teams have been able to do and a final formal presentation to an extremely high-powered, experienced 'murder board' selected specifically for each team. (This can obviously be structured as a competition, of course.) The celebration combines this with a second boot camp that can be shared with the public, this time focusing on later-stage issues such as presentation skills.

From a constructivist perspective, note how the GAP program lives up to the key criteria for constructivistic learning, using the criteria provided by Brooks and Brooks (1993).

1. 'Authentic' (and 'important') questions.
2. 'Big ideas'.
3. Constructing meaning requires triangulation.
4. Coaching, not lecturing.
5. Assessment and evaluation techniques should reflect these processes.

- *Authentic questions and big ideas:* GAP offers projects with genuine, significant real-world consequences, where both success and failure will be highly visible. Students realize immediately that they will play a significant role in what happens.
- *Triangulation:* Nascent entrepreneurs operate in an environment where information is problematic, requiring students to work with all manner of information sources, including human sources whose intel requires triangulation, but also teach them about the mental models of industry insiders and outside experts.
- *Coaching:* The instructors provide key information in the initial boot camp and are available for consultation (and intervention, if need be) throughout the term. However, it is common that student teams must teach themselves key skills.
- *Evaluation:* Students are evaluated by the 'murder board' expert panels and by their peers.

Example 2:   Technology commercialization and economic development

A 'TEAMS' approach?   TEAMS was at the heart of a complex partnership between Boise State University (Boise, ID) (later other schools), the Idaho National Lab (www.inl.gov) and the Inland Northwest Research Alliance (Idaho Falls, ID) (www.inra.org) and the universities in the INRA region, supported by these partners and the Ewing Marion Kauffman Foundation (Kansas, City, MO). Student project teams work on a diverse set of entrepreneurial projects that provide a rich, ill-structured learning environment while helping their communities via commercializing novel cutting-edge technologies and economic development (including social ventures).

The TEAMS process   Each team works with external clients to negotiate project scope. Teams working with a community negotiate their project with local contacts and the instructor. During the semester teams share their progress (and their hurdles) with other teams, including a midterm formal progress report and presentation. At the end of the semester the team presents formally to their clients, usually on-site, with a final formal presentation with guests from the local business and technology communities.

Technology commercialization projects   Most of a wide range of technology projects were recruited from the large federal research lab here in Idaho, the Idaho National Lab (INL). Commercialization assessments begin with a thorough industry analysis followed by a market analysis (*à la* QuickLook). Student teams develop a strategic plan for implementing commercialization, presented to the inventors and tech transfer professionals.

Students primarily worked with new technologies developed that INL wants to license, such as software (data warehousing, computer security monitoring), biotech, and environmental remediation, plus the local high-tech community (for example, www.kickstand.org).

Economic development   Similarly, INL's economic development group and others offered projects where student teams can help local communities. With the technology projects the successful student work attracted interest from other development entities in the region.

- *Community assessments*, such as developing opportunity-capacity matrices to guide future projects. (For these, students present to development professionals and local leaders.)
- *Feasibility studies for new industries*   One project proved the high potential for a new industry cluster based on hydroponics, while another team prepared a feasibility study for the Sacajawea Interpretive Center in Salmon, Idaho.
- *Designing new development efforts*   Past projects include designing a next-generation producers' co-op for rural Idaho and designing a distance learning center in northeast Idaho.
- *Specialized projects*   Teams from three different Idaho universities inventoried telecommunications resources in several Idaho cities, presenting their findings to the Governor and other top officials from government and industry at a major conference to ramp up rural connectivity.

Key student lessons learned   TEAMS projects gave an opportunity for hands-on experience at creating true entrepreneurial value in constructivistic problem-based learning where they applied process skills such as:

- ill-structured problem solving (and project management under such conditions);
- building and maintaining a self-managed high-performance cross-functional work team;
- integrating and applying a wide range of business skills in an entrepreneurial setting; and
- an inside look at how large real-world projects get designed and implemented.

Tangible outcomes

1.   Student excitement: Students now maneuver to be in these capstone sections.
2.   Tangible impact on high-stakes technology commercialization decisions.
3.   Tangible impact on local communities, often rural (but could easily be urban).
4.   Improved student skills at team building, problem-solving and written/oral presentation skills.
5.   Projects provide real-world context to illustrate key concepts such as business models, competitive intelligence, industry analysis, benchmarking and, of course, business plans.

TEAMS as constructivistic learning   How does the TEAMS program live up to the key criteria for constructivistic learning? Let us return to the useful criteria provided by Brooks and Brooks (1993):

- *Authentic questions & big ideas:* Projects have genuine, significant real-world consequences, something that catches the students' attention – and keeps it. Student projects have provided INL with information used directly in patenting and licensing decisions. Economic developers have used student projects to advance their communities (for example, the producers co-op for eastern Idaho relies heavily on the students' research and analysis).

- *Triangulation:* Projects also require using multiple sources of information, often conflicting, and sometimes working with key contacts who themselves have very different agendas. Students get multiple perspectives on their projects directly and en route gain multiple perspectives on critical course concepts. Working in a true self-managed work team adds additional triangulation (for example, Senge 1990). With the addition of other universities to the TEAMS effort, students also triangulate with the experiences of others.

- *Coaching:* The bulk of the instructor's time is spent working with the teams and clients. To further move away from lecturing, each student team is charged with teaching a text chapter, explicitly linking that chapter's key concepts to their own project. Students also coach each other on peer teaching presentations.

- *Evaluation:* Students are evaluated on their projects by their peers, clients and outside experts.

Note

1. See www.pioneerentrepreneurs.net/bigidea_gendron.php.

References

Alberti, F., S. Sciascio and A. Poli (2004), 'Entrepreneurial education: an ongoing debate', paper presented at the Int-ENT Conference, Naples, July.

Bandura, A. (1993), 'Perceived self-efficacy in cognitive development and functioning', *Educational Psychologist*, **28**(1), 117–48.

Baron, R. (2006), 'Opportunity recognition as pattern recognition: how entrepreneurs "connect the dots" to identify new business opportunities', *Academy of Management Perspectives*, **20**(1), 104–19.

Baron, R. and R. Henry (2006), 'The role of expert performance in entrepreneurship: how entrepreneurs acquire the capacity to excel', paper presented at the Babson Entrepreneurship Conference, Bloomington, IN, June.

Baum, J.R., E. Locke and K. Smith (2001), 'A multidimensional model of venture growth', *Academy of Management Journal*, **44**(2), 292–303.

Bouchhiki, H. (1993), 'A constructivist framework for understanding entrepreneurial performance', *Organization Studies*, **14**(4), 549–70.

Brockhaus, R. (1987), 'Entrepreneurial folklore', *Journal of Small Business Management*, **25**(3), 1–6.

Brooks, J. and M. Brooks (1993), 'In search of understanding: the case for constructivist classrooms', Alexandria, VA: Association for Supervision and Curriculum Development (ERIC #ED366428).

Chandler, G. and E. Jansen (1992), 'The founder's self-assessed competence and venture performance', *Journal of Business Venturing*, **7**(3), 223–36.

Cooper, S. and W. Lucas (2007), 'Developing entrepreneurial self-efficacy and intentions: lessons from two programmes', paper presented at the ICSB World Conference, Turku, June.

Cox, L. (1996), 'The goals and impact of educational interventions in the early stages of entrepreneur career development', paper presented at the Int-ENT Conference, Nijmegen, Netherlands, July.

Delmar, F. and P. Davidsson (2000), 'Where do they come from? Prevalence and characteristics of nascent entrepreneurs', *Entrepreneurship and Regional Development*, **12**(1), 1–24.

Duckworth, E. (1986), 'Teaching as research', *Harvard Educational Review*, **56**(4), 481–95.

Eden, D. (1992), 'Leadership and expectations: Pygmalion effects and other self-fulfilling prophecies in organizations', *Leadership Quarterly*, **3**(4), 271–305.

Ericsson, K. and N. Charness (1994), 'Expert performance', *American Psychologist*, **49**(8), 725–74.

Erikson, E. (1980), *Identity and the Life Cycle*, New York: Norton.

Fayolle, A. and I. Servais (2000), 'Exploratory study to assess the impact of entrepreneurship programs on student entrepreneurial behaviors', Babson Entrepreneurship Conference, Babson Park, Wellesley, MA, June.

Fernandes, J. (2006), Keynote address, US Association for Small Business and Entrepreneurship Conference, Tucson, AZ, January.

Fiet, J. and J. Barney (2002), *The Systematic Search for Entrepreneurial Discoveries*, New York: Quorum.

Gaglio, C. (2004), 'The role of counterfactual thinking in the opportunity identification process', *Entrepreneurship Theory and Practice*, **28**(6), 533–52.

Garavan, T. and B. O'Cinneide (1994), 'Entrepreneurship education and training programmes: a review and evaluation – Part 1', *Journal of European Industrial Training*, **18**, 3–12.

Guglielmino, P. and L. Klatt (1993), 'Entrepreneurs as self-directed learners', paper presented at the ICSB World Conference, Las Vegas, NV, June.

Hamilton, D. and R. Hitz (1994), 'Reflections on a constructivist approach to teaching', *Journal of Early Childhood Teacher Education*, **17**(1), 15–25.

Hanke, R., E. Kisenwether and A. Warren (2005), 'A scalable problem-based learning system for entrepreneurship education', *Academy of Management Proceedings*, E1–E6.

Honig, B. (2004), 'Entrepreneurship education: toward a model of contingency-based business planning', *Academy of Management Learning & Education*, **3**(3), 258–73.

Jack, S. and A. Anderson (1999), 'Entrepreneurship education in the enterprise culture: producing reflective practitioners', *International Journal of Entrepreneurial Behaviour and Research*, **5**, 110–21.

Jelinek, M. and J. Litterer (1995), 'Toward entrepreneurial organizations: meeting ambiguity with engagement', *Entrepreneurship Theory and Practice*, **19**(3), 137–68.

Krueger, N. (1993), 'Growing up entrepreneurial?', *Proceedings*, Academy of Management, Atlanta.

Krueger, N. (2000), 'The cognitive infrastructure of opportunity emergence', *Entrepreneurship Theory and Practice*, **24**(3), 5–23.

Krueger, N. (2001), 'Adapt or select?', paper presented at the Babson Entrepreneurship Conference, Jönköping, January.

Krueger, N. (2007), 'What lies beneath? The experiential essence of entrepreneurial thinking', *Entrepreneurship Theory and Practice*, **31**(1), 123–38.

Krueger, N. and D. Brazeal (1994), 'Entrepreneurial potential and potential entrepreneurs', *Entrepreneurship Theory and Practice*, **18**(3), 91–104.

Krueger, N. and P. Dickson (1994), 'How believing in ourselves increases risk taking: perceived self-efficacy and opportunity recognition', *Decision Science*, **25**, 385–400.

Krueger, N. and D. Hamilton (1996), 'Constructivism and entrepreneurship education', in T. Monroy, J. Reichert and F. Hoy (eds), *The Art and Science of Entrepreneurship Education*, vol. 3, Cambridge, MA: Ballinger, pp. 11–21.

Krueger, N. and J. Kickul (2006), 'So you thought the intentions model was simple: cognitive style and the specification of entrepreneurial intentions models', paper presented at the US Association for Small Business and Entrepreneurship Conference, Tucson, AZ, April.

Krueger, N., M. Reilly and A. Carsrud (2000), 'Competing models of entrepreneurial intentions', *Journal of Business Venturing*, **15**(5/6), 411–532.

Krueger, N., M. Brannback, A. Carsrud and J. Kickul (2007), 'Informed intent', paper presented at the ICSB Conference, Turku, June.

Kuhn, T. (1962), *The Structure of Scientific Revolutions*, Chicago, IL: University of Chicago Press.

Langer, E. (1994), 'A mindful education', *Educational Psychology*, **28**(1), 43–50.

Leitch, C. and R. Harrison (1999), 'A process model for entrepreneurship education and development', *International Journal of Entrepreneurial Behaviour and Research*, **5**(3), 83–9.

Lucas, W. and S. Cooper (2004), 'Enhancing self-efficacy to enable entrepreneurship: the case of CMI's connections', MIT Sloan Working Paper 4489-04, Cambridge, MA.

Meyer, G.D. (2001), 'Major unresolved issues and opportunities in entrepreneurship education', Coleman White Paper, US Association for Small Business and Entrepreneurship Conference, Orlando, FL, January.

Mitchell, R.K. (2005), 'Tuning up the global value creation engine: road to excellence in international entrepreneurship education', in J. Katz and D. Shepherd (eds), *Advances in Entrepreneurship, Firm Emergence and Growth*, vol. 8, Greenwich, CT: JAI Press, 185–248.

Mitchell, R.K., B. Smith, K. Seawright and E. Morse (2000), 'Cross-cultural cognitions and the venture creation decision', *Academy of Management Journal*, **43**(5), 974–93.

Mitton, D. (1994), 'Entrepreneurial clout: honing the intuitive behaviors necessary to sustain entrepreneurial success', paper presented at the Babson Entrepreneurship Conference, Babson Park, Wellesley, MA, June.

Monroy, T. (1995), 'Getting closer to a descriptive model of entrepreneurship education', in T. Monroy, J. Reichert and F. Hoy (eds), *The Art and Science of Entrepreneurship Education*, vol. 3, Cambridge, MA: Ballinger, pp. 205–17.

Morgan, G. (1986), *Images of Organization*, Thousand Oaks, CA: Sage.
Morse, E. and R.K. Mitchell (2005), *Cases in Entrepreneurship: The Venture Creation Process*, Thousand Oaks, CA: Sage.
Neergaard, H. and N. Krueger (2005), 'Still playing the game?', paper presented at the RENT XIX Conference, Naples, Italy, July.
Neergaard, H. and R. Smith (2007), '"The Pilgrim Story,": an alternative entrepreneurial fairytale from Denmark', paper presented at the ICSB World Conference, Turku, June.
Perkins, D. (1994), *Smart Schools: From Training Memories to Educating Minds*, New York: Free Press.
Peterman, N. (2000), 'The impact of entrepreneurial training on entrepreneurial beliefs', Honours thesis, University of Queensland, Australia.
Post, C., J. Elfving, T. Pohja, M. Brannback and A. Carsrud (2007), 'On becoming "informed": exploratory study of the impact of education and social norms on entrepreneurial intentions', paper presented at the ICSB World Conference, Turku, June.
Prawat, R. (1992), 'Teachers' beliefs about teaching and learning: a constructivist approach', *American Journal of Education*, **100**(3), 354–95.
Sarasvathy, S. (2004), 'Making it happen: beyond theories of the firm to theories of firm design', *Entrepreneurship Theory and Practice*, **28**(6), 519–31.
Scherer, R., J. Adams, S. Carley and F. Wiebe (1989), 'Role model performance effects on development of entrepreneurial career preference', *Entrepreneurship Theory and Practice*, **29**(4), 32–6.
Senge, P. (1990), *The Fifth Discipline*, Garden City, NJ: Doubleday.
Simms, S. and J. Robinson (2006), 'Activist or entrepreneur? An identity-based model of social entrepreneurship', paper presented at the 2nd International Social Entrepreneurship Research Conference, New York University, April.
Souitaris, V. (2005), 'The value-added of entrepreneurship education', paper presented at the Academy of Management Conference, Honolulu, HI, August.
Tegtmeier, S (2007), 'Empirical implications based on the theory of planned behaviour', ICSB World Conference, Turku, June.
Yager, R. (1991), 'The constructivist learning model', *The Science Teacher*, **58**(6), 52–7.

5 Entrepreneurship as a liberal art

Jerry Gustafson*

Introduction

In spite of an explosion of programs in colleges and universities, entrepreneurship education still lacks wide acceptance across the breadth of academe. Although things have improved, the subject is still regarded with skepticism in many quarters. Perhaps hostility remains particularly in the small, classic liberal arts college. Objections there to entrepreneurship go beyond the complaints frequent in the business schools about the putative lack of disciplinary standing, rigor, or careful research. In the liberal arts context, entrepreneurship is often taken as vocational, materialistic, self-interested, and of questionable ethics. On such grounds, many think it beyond the pale of liberal education.

Yet entrepreneurship education is of essential intrinsic value. It is also a powerful encouragement to the engagement in learning that so heightens the quality of the entire educational experience. As one attempts to craft a thoroughgoing apology for inclusion of entrepreneurship in the liberal arts one is struck further by its promotion of the achievement of self-agency so coveted by the arts for its graduates. The rationale for entrepreneurship as a vital complement to traditional curricular fare is strong enough that an advocate senses, perhaps with surprise, the possession of the high ground. An initial polite tapping on the curricular door gives rise eventually to a more full-throated offense.

Readers might logically expect the case for inclusion to be addressed directly to those skeptical academics in accepted fields who hold the keys to entry. Those persons need to be won with earnest respect and reason. This outline of the offensive is addressed not so much to them, however, as to the community of entrepreneurship educators and scholars. As this group has moved the subject gradually towards the mainstream, many have suffered wounds. Their shared war stories reflect some indignity, impatience and even pride arising from the common cause. I succumb to the temptation to appeal to this group with occasional irony and sarcasm at the expense of our imagined adversaries. For the first twenty years of a career spent at a single classic liberal arts college, I was a purist academic myself. As a convert to entrepreneurship teacher for the last twenty years, I have atoned through a continuing effort to defeat many of the same attitudes I used to hold. So where the tone of the argument may rankle it is because my urge towards commiseration with those in the trenches outweighs sensible forbearance.

My views are informed by my time of marinating in the environment of the small, liberal arts college. That perspective has its limits. What a small liberal arts college teaches proceeds from a sense of mission that differs from that of professional, vocational, or graduate schools. So points below may not generalize. But the route towards full acceptance of entrepreneurship across the curricular spectrum surely must pass eventually through the terrain of the liberal arts.

The aims of any institution of higher learning are, of course, multiple. Any college is engaged to a degree in training persons in essential skills, imparting existing knowledge, creating new knowledge through research, educating for professions and career, improving society through outreach and sharing of expertise, heightening sense of civic responsibility, and so on. Emphasis and truly core purpose change with the context.

What is the truly fundamental purpose of the liberal arts college? This topic is surely one for the ages but, on one level, the answer is clear enough. Look in any college catalog to see what they say and do. Such colleges offer a wide array of the scholarly disciplines and creative arts. They encourage breadth of intellectual reach, and attach high significance to the acquisition of general qualities of curiosity, imagination and creativity. They discourage early specialization, emphasizing distribution of course work. Major requirements are usually pared to the essential. Theory and abstraction are stressed at the expense of practical affairs. They tend to eschew the vocational, often zealously, and even as a marker of superior quality. They evince high regard for social experience, promoting 'well-roundedness' and interpersonal skills by encouraging high participation in extra-curricular activity and residential life.

The goal of this approach must not actually be to turn graduates uniformly into researchers and learned, contemplative library-goers. Alumni of the colleges apparently pursue lives of practical and public affairs at the same rates as those anywhere. The purpose is to liberate and empower the student. The liberal arts program intends to provide students with the imagination, concepts, perspectives, and intellectual tools with which to design their own lives. A rich stew of pure knowledge, distilled through the ages, uncluttered by much specific knowledge of instrumental purpose, avoids fitting students to preordained slots. It aids them to make their own life choices. They do the choosing; college is to make them wise and competent choice makers.

This observation is of essential importance. The liberal arts are taught primarily to enable the learner. In contrast to providing narrow mastery, creating new knowledge, promoting democratic citizenship, inducing graduates to lives of service, or whatever aim might occasionally be claimed, the primary mission of liberal education is to liberate students so they may wisely choose how to pursue fulfilling lives marked by high personal as well as civic achievements. The liberal arts intend to be a vehicle for empowering graduates to lead an effective life in their day.

This assertion is not without controversy. Like other schools the liberal arts claim multiple aims. But what other driving force seems so central in explaining what liberal arts colleges actually do? This inference of purpose is crucial to understanding the role of entrepreneurship in liberal education. For the study of entrepreneurship is powerfully liberating. Its very nature is the freeing of the individual to find effective means to achieve one's chosen aims. Entrepreneurship study supports and clarifies the core outcome of liberal study.

To establish this point is the central cause of the argument that follows. To proceed, it first must be clear that entrepreneurship as an area of serious study has the status of a discipline. The arts, however, exclude many disciplines from their curricula. So it is necessary to consider next the characteristics of a liberal discipline and to show how entrepreneurship meets those. The nature of the rationale suggests, however, that the claim to status as a liberal art is actually a call for educational reform that transcends mere acceptance. We must discuss the points of resistance, principled and other, that the academic may raise in opposition to both the subject and the implied reforms. In particular, we must consider the seemingly powerful clash of values between the academics and the entrepreneurs and their champions, and suggest how it might be resolved. Given the nature of the opposition, the chapter then suggests that the battle is not likely to be won by debate. However valuable a good case may be to entrepreneurship advocates, progress is more likely to be gained by inching ahead, exploiting small opportunities and openings. I end with modest ideas about how to create such openings.

What is a 'discipline'?

Faculty love their disciplines. Teachers through secondary school offer mere 'subjects'. But the professoriate lives, much as it teaches, its disciplines. Faculties refer to their disciplines for standards of content and quality of teaching and research. They base their very self-evaluation as professionals upon them. Disciplines prescribe content, the level of rigor, the pace, the comprehensiveness, and the testing of learning. One's scholarly obsessions derive from one's specialization. Obligation to profession contends in conscience with service to institution and to student need.

The academic disciplines define subjects for study but they are also clubs that significantly define a professor's professional identity. A discipline is a set of habits shared by an easily distinguishable community of scholars. On ceremonial occasions, these habits are literally worn as professors pull on the colored hoods and robes that symbolize the shared practices of the various scholars. These communities constitute, if by small margins, alternative cultures. Practitioners in each share a unity promoted by common ideas and preoccupations. The quest for answers to similar categories of questions makes members of interest to each other. Specialization of argot and discourse serves not only to bind each group, but to set it apart. Faculty enjoy identification with their own fields, want to stick within them, and, in the main, expect others to do likewise.

For membership is not easy to come by. Each discipline comes equipped with features that require many years of study to master. First, there is a canon of foundational works and readings. These provide doctrine. They illuminate a distinctive point of view about what phenomena are important and worth study, together with some variety of permissible viewpoints of what one may think and conclude about them. One is not required to accept doctrine but membership does require that one know its history and current status. Second, there are prescribed methodologies for pursuing advancement in knowledge. These are typically rigorous. The discipline demands their employment for truth-seeking and testing, and assessing current work. Third, there is an accumulating body of work. Members know basic trends in accumulation, at least some in depth.

Scholarly identity is won with effort, so it is no wonder that professors are jealous of disciplinary status and grumble at presumptuous colleagues, who, as entrepreneurship educators, wish too easily and casually to create new ones.

Nevertheless, by these standards, the field of entrepreneurship has become a discipline, like it or not. It is true that many foundational works have emerged from other fields, such as history, economics and social psychology. But that is true of many disciplines. In any event, major works from Jenks to Schumpeter, McClelland to Drucker, Knight to Bhide, and countless others exist in a coherent, common context. Entrepreneurship educators know their roots are there. The body of research has grown large. Journals proliferate. They are competitive, well-edited, demand peer review, and bear all the trappings of professionalism. The literature is well-defined, addressing a range of considerations, rules, and techniques pertaining to venturing and growth of enterprise.

Similarly, there is wide agreement on appropriate methods. Self-critical of excessively casual past work, scholars in the field increasingly demand close observation, theoretical grounding, rigorous empirical techniques and general fastidiousness.

More telling are the cultural manifestations of this nascent discipline. That culture celebrates individual achievement. Its habit is not only to describe but to laud the creativity and wit employed by the successful entrepreneur. It appreciates a rapid, clever, and crisp use of practical knowledge and street wisdom in executing plans. This culture values study, to be sure, but its members are also drawn to aid and promote the success of emerging ventures. Its shared ideas and preoccupations possess a distinctiveness and unity that distinguish it from other fields. It is *sui generis*. Its missionary spirit and clear agenda are those of a movement. Entrepreneurship is a discipline.

What is a liberal discipline?
The emerging recognition of entrepreneurship as a discipline is clear, as universities continue to create new majors and departments in the field. Still, the notion is that entrepreneurship is a business discipline. A corollary assumption is that the goal of 'entrepreneurship across the curriculum' would be achieved simply by bringing liberal arts students (and others) into the business departments for a bracing dose of enterprise. The deeper question for purposes at hand is whether it can be considered a liberal discipline in its own right and a candidate for inclusion in liberal arts curricula. As the ancient mariners' maps used to label unknown territories, 'Here there be dragons.'

The faculty who teach in the liberal arts determine curriculum. These faculty have long recognized a duty to protect existing scholarly traditions. By temperament and role, in contrast to university specialists, they are more sensitive to conservation of knowledge than to its creation. The institutions they serve are mostly small and intimate. Agreement to break new ground may be more easily achieved than at larger, more bureaucratic places. Most of the durable innovations in higher education have likely originated in some liberal arts college. But any decision to innovate happens slowly. It took years, for example, to make the radical step of adding the natural sciences and, later, economics and sociology, to the traditional classical curriculum. In the selection of permissible subjects, there has always been a simple rule based upon the degree to which a subject may have vocational intent. Geriatric nursing or electrical engineering are not liberal; French literature is.

Liberal arts colleges have accommodated, over time, to the social environment and demands of the workplace, as well as to student career concerns. Curricula have changed greatly. But change is cautious, even grudging, and the resistance to strictly vocational programs has applied, especially at leading and prestigious places. Economics was in, business was out, creative writing was in, journalism out, sociology in, social work out, and so on. Even the crafting of pre-professional programs from logical combinations of liberal subjects raised suspicion. The successful exclusion of the vocational and practical has left faculty in the better colleges to worry only about what to do with their teacher-training education departments.

Anti-vocationalism has been compounded by the antipathy of liberal arts faculty for the ordinary and material. The making of money is often judged a base motive in the ethics of the wider society, too, but the unyielding aversion in the colleges must surely be a survival from their clerical roots. At any rate, the faculty evidently does not wish either to teach vocational courses or to have their students worry overmuch about how to make a living. They prefer to leave that to a career services office.

Instead, their lasting impulse, as suggested above, has been to open students' minds through the sampling of a rich environment of coursework, all of which is subject to wide and general application. Exposure to science, philosophy, languages, literature, and the arts helps students to find their deeper interests. It fires their imagination. It provides a fabric for students to examine their roots, their possibilities, and purposely to build their newly found identities. They become lifelong learners.

In the view of the liberal arts colleges, this is the sort of education that liberates students. Freed from ignorance, parochialism, and prejudice, they are empowered to think critically about major issues and more to enjoy the fullness of human experience. They are on the road to wisdom. How tragic it would be to deflect such learning by obsession with the ordinary and material stuff – like earning a living.

If entrepreneurship is to be defended as a liberal discipline, it has two strikes against it. It seems fairly to wallow in the material aspect of life. Tangible reward seems both its driving force and its satisfactory end. And it seems to possess vocational intent to excess. It appears inevitably a business subject. To qualify as a liberal discipline, entrepreneurship must supersede its roots in business study to proclaim its source in liberal study.

Entrepreneurship is rightly a fascinating business subject, of course. But it is not inescapably tied to business. Entrepreneurship is a process and a set of concerns and behaviors, to wit: One makes choices about what one wishes to accomplish. One considers one's objectives and commits to pursuing them. Since success may be difficult, the commitment is necessarily firm. One seeks resources. A variety of combinations of resources might lead to the goal. Which are easiest to obtain? Most efficacious? One must plan and examine what techniques one must learn, what logistics are involved, what contingencies are likely. One must assess the relative values of the objectives and means. Will the flame be worth the candle? If so, the scheme must be implemented. With great patience and creativity, the doer begins to assemble and manipulate the resources, including those persons who must be signed on to help. An organization arises. Objectives are achieved. Rewards are harvested and distributed. The doer expresses and reveals ethics and values every step.

This process obviously is not confined to commercial objectives. It describes how one approaches an effort to achieve any self-selected objectives when success is not assured. Thrilling entrepreneurs include film characters such as the English teacher in *Dead Poets Society*, the rabble-rousing McMurphy in *One Flew Over the Cuckoo's Nest*, and the boy Homer Hickham, in *October Sky*. Each goes heroically through a process like that above. In each case, we recognize pure entrepreneurship, all the more inspiring for its being lifted from a business context.

Not just about business, entrepreneurship is rather a kind of science of *doing*. The emphasis on action is a requisite complement to the arts' stress upon theory, criticism and personal responsibility. Critical intelligence and awareness, together with responsibility, call for action. Not a subject of business separated from the arts; entrepreneurship is rather the other side of the coin of the arts.

A common definition is that entrepreneurship is 'the creation of value without regard to resources currently controlled'. Akin to the artist, the entrepreneur, not yet in possession of means, commits to a process creating a vision and bringing it to fruition. In the business context, the realization of the vision as a new product or service is familiar. But that definition applies to a wide range of behavior. Much of the literature, developed with the first context in mind, nevertheless applies broadly, at least by extension, analogy and metaphor. For any would-be creator-of-value, knowledge of appropriate strategies, such methods as may fit particular tasks, what plans should be drawn, what needs to be measured and monitored, how to assess changing circumstances, how to spread and limit risk, and other familiar issues all come into play. As research further informs them, entrepreneurship as a general science of doing grows more elaborate and compelling.

Perhaps in contrast to other subjects, in entrepreneurship study, application, more than theory, provides the true complexity and challenge. Every deal is unique. Similar themes, behaviors, and principles are at play in countless different settings. Each one is a story of creation that leads to enhancement of welfare for the many, of adroitness in setting goals, resourcefulness in gathering means, and of effective accomplishment. The content of the details and materials of achievement differ vastly from case to case. The careful consideration of a wide variety of such cases can cause the quest to create value to be habitually ingrained. Entrepreneurship becomes a way of thinking and a way of life. The broad educational role of entrepreneurial study is to examine the process and to describe that way of life.

Entrepreneurship so viewed is the study of principles of effective self-agency and action. Its focus on value creation underscores its contribution to public good. Such study is valuable, useful and necessary for anyone. It is clearly pursuant to the primary liberal arts aim of enabling the learner to achieve the goals that lead to a fulfilling life. That is a liberal discipline. To describe entrepreneurship as the study of getting things done, to extricate it from its traditional context of business start-up and growth, and to place its focus on value creation that turns private motives to public service as well as to individual gain, unloads much baggage in its trip to the liberal arts.

Moreover, although this 'science of doing' may seem elementary, many students tend to be unaware of it. They often do lack skills of goal-setting, planning, achievement of plans, or other requirements of competent action. Liberal arts students, by background and academic orientation, may be especially limited owing to a lack of savvy and street smarts that is sometimes startling. Students have too little experience in setting and working out their own plans. It is as if no one has given them permission. Students need instruction in how to get things done.

Students sense their weakness on this score. They commonly complain about excessive abstraction and irrelevance of curricula but seldom get to the heart of the felt lack of capacity and competence that unnerves them. Faculty, too, sense there is a problem but one seemingly beyond their responsibility or ability to help. This unsettling sense of unmet need provides a key opening for entrepreneurship education. It is a vehicle – perhaps the best available vehicle – for enriching the liberal curriculum with the motivation and skills relevant to competent action. The liberal discipline of entrepreneurship informs and motivates successful action on choices made. Doing so brings the other liberating arts to fruition.

Entrepreneurship education as educational reform
Entrepreneurship education both teaches and urges useful means of action. That is appropriate and necessary in the context of an education heavily oriented otherwise to

contemplation, reflection, the abstract, and the theoretical. The call for increased attention to both learning by doing and learning about doing is a call for reform. The entrepreneurship educator is an educational reformer. In turn, those reforms that specifically place education in greater service to students have long been the province of the liberal arts college. This opportunity is what the entrepreneurship movement uniquely offers to these schools.

In their zeal to get entrepreneurship into the curriculum, educators may not yet have realized the relevance of their movement to broader issues of reform of higher education. Entrepreneurship, with its focus on individual agency and doing, can be seen as important to improvement in all educational outcomes. It encourages the student to consider all of his or her education as a resource and confers responsibility upon the student to think of ways to capitalize all of it. It sets the student to making useful meaning of the whole realm of educational experience. College itself becomes an entrepreneurial venture. Awareness of entrepreneurship grants permission to transcend the educational box, to shape one's experience to one's own ends, and to take charge. This impulse is all for the best; a more aggressive student is a better student.

A proactive orientation contributes to richness in all venues of living. To achieve fulfilling lives, graduates must be able to act on their choices. We need to think critically because we must think how to act. Academics typically assume that study will, without further instruction, lead to action. That is wrong. An active response to insight, as entrepreneurship teachers know, is not always natural. Many are slow to recognize the occasion to act and proceed with difficulty. For some, the spontaneous combustion never occurs at all. Effective means to proceed from thought to action must be taught and urged. Most important of all, students need to appreciate the limitless fascinations of achievement and the deep personal rewards of getting something done.

Passivity and boredom are the twin enemies of education. Together, they are the source of educational failure. Opposition to passivity and boredom is rallied by what educators can pull out of a student rather than by what they can put in. Educational reform calls for means to energize and involve the student. That is what entrepreneurship does. The possibilities implicit here should be more fully exploited.

The reformer then sees entrepreneurship as a discipline that is essential to any student's liberal education. Its value derives specifically from its differences from other disciplines. It is a complement to routine emphasis on contemplative values, abstraction and theory that mark the other arts. It serves both as counterbalance and antidote to excesses of scholarly cerebration. Its encouragement of action comes as a relief to those students weary of what seems to them often pointless and artificial academic study.

As a liberal art, entrepreneurship is special in its unremitting stress upon animating the learner. The very purpose of its study is to set the learner in motion. Students sense that the point of learning is not mere familiarity with the arts and facility in imitation of teachers. The point is to employ the arts effectively to intervene in affairs in ways of one's choosing. Entrepreneurship provides a process and outlet for vigorous self-expression and assertion not just in business, but in the fullness of life. That is precisely what the arts are supposed to do. No matter what the student's major, the study of entrepreneurship encourages one to ask 'What is it that I wish to be doing? What is it that I truly wish to accomplish? What resources have I available or could I gain that I could employ for my self-selected purposes? How might I benefit from creating something for others?'. Such questions should be asked by all students. The strength of entrepreneurship is to provoke the questions and to provide outlets for acting upon them.

These entrepreneurist reforms have outside support. For many years, studies and critiques of higher education have noted that education is best and most durable when it engages the learner. That student learns most who is not passively absorbing but who is deeply and actively involved. To be deeply involved in some things, such studies suggest, leads persons to perform better in all things. Setting one's own educational objectives, and pursuing and managing them appropriately, obviously heightens the degree of engagement. These critics and reformers have proposed ways to energize students. They call for better advising, more collaboration with faculty in research, more internships and experiential education. They have not yet noticed that entrepreneurship is a powerful agent of engagement. They are important potential allies.

Other obstacles to entrepreneurship education
It is good to have a case statement for entrepreneurship as a liberal discipline. The argument for its inclusion in liberal study must be won eventually on broad principle. But we should hardly expect the foregoing argument soon to carry the day. The clash of values between entrepreneurs and academics is too deep. The temperamental and value differences may be more important than points of principle. The real disputes are potentially more visceral than notions of academic philosophy.

The entrepreneurship community has met its obligation to stick to principle. It has responded constructively to standard complaints of traditionalists that the field lacks rigorous theory, research of good quality, adequate scholarly journals, that it draws too eclectically from existing disciplines, and perhaps also that it just does not seem hard or complex enough to merit status as a stand-alone subject. The straightforward answer has been to admit to weakness and to improve on all counts. But this response has tended to be entirely defensive. Acceptance has grown but remains far from complete. That may be because an appeal based solely upon quality and rigor of scholarship overlooks that entrepreneurship is not scholarly, in central intent, in the way other subjects are.

Of course, we learn about entrepreneurship through research. The research is essential to exploring and understanding the myriad facets of the field. Research, however, cannot communicate the thrill of accomplishment or the devil in the details of trying. Undergraduates, especially, must learn the immediate and personal rewards of effective doing, by doing. Entrepreneurs themselves are not scholarly. But scholars run universities. It is ironic if the promotion of entrepreneurship primarily as a scholarly subject were to place it in service to the values of those who oppose its basic nature.

Of course, the more good entrepreneurship scholarship produced the better. But one wonders whether this matter, or supposed vocationalism, or emphasis on material or pecuniary phenomena, really cut to the heart of the matter. There is reason to suppose that entrepreneurs (and their promoters) and academics have a natural suspicion of and distaste for each other. The potential for negative stereotyping is distressingly great.

Think of the conflicting values. The academics relish contemplation and painstaking thought above all else. They are slow to conclude. Long suspension of judgment is a virtue. They are obsessive about methods of knowing and argument. A favorite metaphor is college as a 'community of scholars', all working towards greater understanding of things in the universe in a spirit of diligent, tolerant, cooperation. They are affiliative, even clannish. Learning is for its own sake, not instrumental. Attempts to deepen ideas and make them complex are good. Profundity is admired. The material world is banal; the world of ideas is preferred. Security is an essential working condition.

In opposition, the entrepreneur values action over thought, decisiveness over accuracy, haste over temporizing, individualism over community, achievement over affiliation, the useful over the impractical, the heuristic over the proven, the simple over the complex. Further, some risk is acceptable and any materialism involved is just fine.

This is caricature. But the truth in it can and does lead to belittling stereotypes each of the other. These go beyond mere anti-business cliché. They are more personal. The academic may casually dismiss the entrepreneur as superficial, opportunistic, brash, unsubtle and materialistic. The entrepreneur, in turn, scoffs at the academic, that muddle-headed, indecisive, long-winded, victim of paralysis by analysis – the so-called 'academic slows'.

This is bias, and is neither thoughtful nor principled. The bias, truly, is unfounded. Consider from the foregoing how much in common the academic and entrepreneur actually share. Each believes fervently that knowledge must be discovered, produced, and used. Each refers to the same set of scales in assessing the other. Each takes it to be an essential human obligation to engage thought and action. Whether intrinsic or instrumental, each believes that knowledge is of supreme importance. Each recognizes that there is a time-value of knowledge to be spent in either extended searching or urgent application of findings. Both agree that insight and intuition are of central importance whether the outcome be profundity or worthy use. Both take it that, whatever one's lifework, personal exposure is at stake and one must choose whether to seek certainty or accept risk. Both agree that, whether ideas are simple or complex, they must ultimately be subject, whether in the short run or long, to a test of the actionability of truth. A good case can be made that the entrepreneur and academic hold fast to the same virtues even as they manifest them in different form.

Insofar as the bias persists, however, and remains unexamined, it does great harm. One can judge from one's academic experience the relative power of principles versus knee-jerk inclination. Quality of research and rigor may be a problem. But so might be ill-considered, prejudicial views of entrepreneurs and what they do. In that case, even a ringing defense of rigor and research may fall on deaf ears. If our colleagues simply assume that entrepreneurs and their promoters are not worthy of admiration or attention, it would surely do no good either to lecture them to respect risk-taking, embrace action, convert to Friedrich von Hayek (more plausibly and just as good, Jean-Paul Sartre), and hail entrepreneurship. Instead we must insinuate our subject in as gentle ways as are available.

Making liberal arts values serve the cause: do not confront – co-opt

Let us hasten to observe that whatever the degree of ideological closing of the mind to which liberal arts faculty may be subject on this issue, it is also true that most, especially in the small residential colleges, hold other values and predispositions that are both remarkable and admirable. We cannot elide their love for truth, beauty, and the highest of standards, of course. But the less lofty focus here is on more immediate attitudes that relate to the way they practice their craft. Some of these offer opportunity for reaching them on behalf of entrepreneurship and lifting their suspicions about teaching it.

A typical small college liberal arts teacher has unusual affinity and even love for students. That is not to say that other faculty do not. But the liberal arts undergraduate teacher is free of some of the professional pressures, at least in scale, and free of the world of politics inside large departments, that preoccupy and demand time of university colleagues. Teaching tends to be the coin of the realm and there are reasons why the faculty who are in that environment are there.

Small colleges do tend to be student-centered and their faculty like it that way. They take high interest in student success, engage in close advising, and can keep up with their charges' full range of courses and activities. They are concerned for their effectiveness as teachers not only of subjects but of students. They are more prone to experimentation and innovation than many faculty elsewhere, even if they tend to prefer the general idea of innovation to any specific proposal for change. There are ways to promote entrepreneurship within this group without hitting the controversial issues head-on, thus raising up whatever biases and complaints may rest in hearts and minds. A few tips follow, meager but perhaps useful, to redeem the lengthy foregoing arguments.

First, much as we recognize entrepreneurship as a liberal discipline, it is not necessary to proclaim it. Small colleges tend to love the interdisciplinary. So bill entrepreneurship as an interesting intersection of psychology, economics, history, sociology, education, and whatever, and design your course or courses accordingly. This design will be an advantage; the interdisciplinary billing will attract a wider audience than otherwise, and you will be a step closer to a desirable and ultimate goal of getting entrepreneurship into your general education curriculum. Problems will not arise until and unless you need a separate department. Cross that bridge when you come to it.

Still better, bill your entrepreneurship program as 'experiential education'. Let 'learning by doing' become your mantra, for entrepreneurship is all about doing. Limit your coursework and supplement it by supervising lots of opportunities for students to develop projects (and businesses). Find opportunities for internships, shadowing, and consulting with small businesses. Your liberal arts colleagues may tend not to know what 'experiential education' is, because nobody does. But they think they approve it, know it is currently all the rage, and that if you are doing it, maybe they will not have to. This has a big advantage. Let your public relations emphasize how different entrepreneurship is from other subjects, and should be judged by the amount of student learning through accomplishment. Claim your special mission within the institution: effective doing to go with the critical thinking. They will eventually get how this effort serves student needs.

Make a special appeal to a wide spectrum of students across the curriculum. Focus especially in the arts. These students can be coached to see that their art requires them to learn to promote themselves and to be small business entrepreneurs. Stress your pure (and lonely) intentions to serve them on this score. For you, they are the route to their faculty, many of whom, though they would hate to admit it, wish that they had taken some business themselves. They will quietly appreciate that their students have the opportunity. Do not, by the way, expect to teach the artists entrepreneurship in the same way you teach business students. Rather than to stress analysis, rational planning and profit, appeal to their nature with emphasis upon the creativity and ingenuity involved in business start-up.

Share with colleagues, especially in the arts and literature, that entrepreneurship is not only a social science but is also an action learned by practice. Point out how much it has in common with musical performance, studio art, or creative writing. In each case, learning comes not through books. Rather, it comes from continuing practice under a master teacher who gives expert feedback. Learning is in the doing and criticism. These are the methods of the conservatory. The methods are good for entrepreneurship students, too. That is why we have internships and practitioner guest teachers. Arts faculty can identify with that. A hazard is that the performing arts, also at the wrong end of the thought-versus-action scale, are at the low end of the semi-official pecking order among the disciplines, and might not be the most influential of friends.

Stress to your colleagues that students who have outlets to pursue their own goals tend to do better in their academic courses, too. Claim that you are actually doing therapy. All faculty recognize the itchiness and impatience displayed by those students who always are doing their own thing rather than their assignments. Entrepreneurial urges are sometimes (not always) the cause. Colleagues will thank you for your willingness to 'reach' these students, and will hope that providing outlets for these troublemakers might actually calm them down. It often does.

Mix your invited practitioner/teachers with colleagues as well as students. We know entrepreneurs tend to be lively, determined, engaged, committed, and habitually and delightfully curious. It will not be lost on your colleagues that your guest is living an interesting life as an epitome of what colleges seek in their graduates. It will not be long before your most ardent anti-business colleague tells you he (or she) would like to discuss with you an idea he has for a deal of his own.

Let your colleagues help you. Give them some tips and put them in charge of advising the students they share with you regarding jobs and careers. Include them in advising students' entrepreneurial projects. Take them to seminars and professional meetings. Show them how general an aid entrepreneurship education is to a person of any background who wants assertively not only to set goals but to accomplish them.

Finally, raise lots of money for your program. When it comes to ingratiation, nothing else comes close.

Note

*   I would like to thank two anonymous reviewers who made numerous suggestions that vastly clarified and improved the argument.

PART II

PLANNING AND IMPLEMENTATION

6 Academic entrepreneurship: possibilities and pitfalls

Anthony Mendes and Cynthia Kehoe

Background

In 2003, the Ewing Marion Kauffman Foundation issued a request for proposals for a funding opportunity to support the development of cross-campus entrepreneurship education in American colleges and universities. This was a new direction for entrepreneurship education in four-year colleges and universities.[1] Other than such noted exceptions as Cornell and Iowa State Universities, entrepreneurship education, though growing, was still primarily available to engineering and business students.[2] Some business schools had recently begun to create undergraduate entrepreneurship minors for non-business students, and individual faculty in other departments taught single courses related to entrepreneurship. Still, in the early part of this decade, while the majority of college graduates who started businesses did not have business degrees, the majority of students who had ready access to an entrepreneurship program were majoring in business or engineering. The challenge from the Kauffman Foundation to grant applicants was to create new models for cross-campus entrepreneurship education. The eight recipients represented a diverse group of campuses with different types of proposed programs.

The University of Illinois at Urbana Champaign (UIUC) was one of the Kauffman Foundation award winners, with a proposal to work with faculty and graduate students as well as undergraduates. The proposal was created based in part on knowledge obtained from a 2002 inventory of the status of entrepreneurship education in over 3,100 two- and four-year US colleges and universities. The study confirmed a weakness in the academic legitimacy of entrepreneurship.[3] Problems included the lack of tenure track faculty to teach entrepreneurship courses; exacerbation of this by the expansion of entrepreneurship across multiple disciplines; lack of doctoral programs to educate and train the future professoriate; and failure to support faculty research to develop the scholarly bibliography that would legitimize the field. These problems can be significant barriers to the promotion of cross-campus entrepreneurship.

Illinois wished, therefore, not only to provide entrepreneurship skills to undergraduate and graduate students, but also to strengthen entrepreneurship research and teaching. Entrepreneurship education at Illinois appeared to be largely confined at that time to the College of Engineering, a few undergraduate business courses and an occasional MBA course. Although the College of Engineering had an academic entrepreneurship center, the College of Business did not, though it did provide some small business consulting that involved students. This cross-campus initiative represented a new direction for the University of Illinois.

The University of Illinois is a large, complex organization – a public, land grant institution founded in 1867, which currently has an enrollment of nearly 43,000 students, of which about 11,000 are graduate and professional students. In addition there are nearly 3,000 faculty and 8,000 administrative and professional/support staff. Research is a major focus, with over $500 million in research and development (R&D) expenditures yearly, ranking Illinois among the top 20 US research universities.

In such an environment campus-wide entrepreneurship education cannot be imposed by the Academy for Entrepreneurial Leadership. The campus culture, resource model and decision-making processes of the university do not allow any one academic unit such authority. Organizational theorist Karl Weick has characterized universities as loosely coupled systems – organizational elements are responsive, but retain some separateness and identity (Orton and Weick 1990, pp. 203–23). Loose coupling results in modularity, variety and some decision-making autonomy and behavioral discretion. Such systems can be particularly adaptable and effective, especially when accompanied by shared values and a good leader. However, the internal fragmentation means that one strategy alone is unlikely to be effective in reaching the majority of people. An entrepreneurship program is not likely to have a highly authoritative position within the university, and must work through persuasion, cultivating champions in various units and understanding the interests and concerns of various constituents.

Diagnosis to identify the heterogeneous needs, characteristics and expectations of the targeted 'customers' was considered an important first step. Alignment of the Academy's efforts with its environment would be the base from which the Academy could achieve long-term goals. This formal diagnostic effort was undertaken beginning in spring 2004, though a more informal information-gathering process was part of the proposal preparation. The diagnostic effort became the basis of the initial strategic plan of the Academy and continues to inform Academy activities. Undertaking this effort also had additional benefits: raising awareness of the grant and the initiative and creating a discussion about entrepreneurship on campus. Diagnosis was an integral part of a '4-D' approach adopted to identify, prioritize and implement initiatives of the Academy: (i) diagnose; (ii) design; (iii) deliver; and (iv) determine.

The diagnostic components included:

- administrator stakeholder interviews;
- needs assessment survey of faculty;
- faculty career development study;
- graduate student survey;
- freshman survey; and
- inventory of entrepreneurial interests, activities among faculty.

This chapter highlights some of the findings and overarching implications of the diagnostic efforts. The goal is to illustrate strategies for the diagnosis of entrepreneurship interests, activities and concerns on university campuses, and to summarize some of our diagnostic results which may resonate with the environment on other campuses.

The next section gives an integrated summary of the findings of three studies of faculty and administrators is presented. The following section provides the results of two surveys, one of graduate students and a second of freshmen. The final section discusses how the diagnostic activities influenced Academy strategies and programming.

Faculty and administrators

Is the concept of 'academic entrepreneurship' a contradiction in terms? Do university administrators and faculty hold different views on the role of entrepreneurial activities in a university? What are the characteristics that differentiate faculty who engage in entrepreneurial activities and more traditional faculty? How can faculty who are interested in entrepreneurial activities be supported by the university, and to what degree should they be? These are intriguing questions, which are stirring debate on campuses across the country and the Academy set out to explore faculty and administrator opinion on the University of Illinois campus through three studies.

An external research team was brought in,[4] to provide objectivity, greater anonymity, external validity and an environment that might encourage the participants to be more candid.

Key administrators

For the administrator interviews, 51 people were asked a set of open-ended questions. Interviews took about 45–60 minutes each. Participants included academic and administrative leaders – college deans, representatives from research, economic development, technology transfer, public engagement, alumni affairs and development, the provost and chancellor. The Academy management team identified the stakeholders to be interviewed, and reviewed the interview guide. The external research team conducted the interviews, and analyzed the results, with input from the Academy leadership that might aid in interpretation based on knowledge of the university environment.

Most participants had some level of awareness of the new initiative because of interactions during the proposal process. Among the objectives for the stakeholder interviews were:

- determine how the concept of entrepreneurship is defined and operationalized campus wide;
- identify campus wide entrepreneurial needs and opportunities and desired Academy objectives;
- obtain candid opinions about the challenges the Academy faces; and
- surface the success criteria by which key stakeholders will evaluate the Academy.

As additional benefits the interviews aided in identifying Academy supporters, generating program ideas and surfacing perceptions of the new initiative.

Among the questions asked in the semi-structured interviews were:

- What is your definition of entrepreneurial thinking as it relates to the teaching, research, and professional development opportunities provided to faculty and graduate students by your unit?
- What are your goals for bringing entrepreneurial thinking to the university, or your area? What have you accomplished to date? What support (internal/external) have you had?
- What are the current entrepreneurial needs of the university, or your unit? What have been some of the obstacles? What do you need to meet your goals? What if any resources have been committed to reach these goals?

- What entrepreneurial activities and professional development offerings could be provided by the Academy in your department or area?
- What if any are some of the possible synergies you see between your department or area and the Academy?
- What in your view are some of the primary challenges you think will be faced by the Academy, and how can these be overcome?
- What would success for the Academy look like to you? What tangible outcomes would you like to see from the Academy: (a) within 18 months; (b) within 5 years; (c) within 10 years?
- What ideas do you have to encourage entrepreneurial thinking by faculty as they approach their teaching, research or professional development?

Administrator opinion
The level of support for the Academy and the cross-campus entrepreneurship initiative was very high. Stakeholders saw a potentially powerful, critical role for the Academy. Most stakeholders expressed an interest in being involved with the Academy and all wished to be kept informed of its progress.

The Academy was perceived as an entity that could assist the university in:

- institutionalizing entrepreneurship;
- capitalizing on and changing the university's culture;
- crossing disciplinary boundaries;
- augmenting existing resources;
- responding to changing student interests; and
- attracting and retaining faculty.

There was a general consensus that the activities of the Academy could be of benefit to all key constituent groups of a major university, students, faculty, alumni, administrators, members of the community and governing bodies, as well as serve as a model for other colleges and universities. The advantage of this positive, broad view is that there will be no shortage of opportunities. The disadvantage is that it will be extremely important for the Academy to determine (and communicate) its primary objectives – what it plans to accomplish and how its efforts can be assessed.

Entrepreneurship defined
The most common definition of entrepreneurship in an academic context that emerged was 'encouraging faculty, students, and administrators to work, act and think differently about opportunity recognition and identification of resources to pursue new ideas'. Sample definitions offered were:

- being innovative in the classroom;
- applying problem solving and creativity to all academic disciplines;
- being innovative in research; transferring intellectual capital into ideas and products either that are marketable or that can be applied in new settings;
- managing careers entrepreneurially;

- encouraging students, faculty, and administrators to work, act and think differently; and
- creating value (for example, new ideas or products).

Stakeholders viewed entrepreneurship in its broadest terms (that is, encouraging innovative thinking and action). However, many said that a challenge for the Academy would be faculty who narrowly define entrepreneurship as for profit activities and starting a new business. In effect, stakeholders considered that others on campus have an inappropriately narrow view of entrepreneurship, as contrasted with their own broader view of its value in a multiple context – that it can, for example, encompass working and thinking more creatively as well as managing one's career more entrepreneurially. This suggests the importance of Academy communications (and that perceptions about others' understanding may not be accurate given the widespread positive views found).

Challenges
Stakeholders noted a number of challenges the Academy will face:

- changing the university culture;
- redefining entrepreneurialism and educating the audiences;
- measuring progress over time;
- incorporating entrepreneurial activities into the faculty recruiting and reward systems;
- mobilizing resources and gaining campus-wide support;
- capturing the attention of faculty and gaining faculty buy-in;
- finding new funding sources; sustainability;
- working within a highly decentralized environment in which much communication and decision making is handled at the departmental level; and
- making a real impact will take time and the Academy should devote the time necessary to building an appropriate infrastructure that can support the broad mission of the Academy to lead the university's initiatives to become more entrepreneurial.

The stakeholders also provided ideas about programming and other entrepreneurship activities for a range of audiences, and suggested courses and collaboration opportunities.

The Academy was seen as having the opportunity to function as a true cross-campus initiative and to serve as a catalyst to encourage innovative, entrepreneurial activities. The perception of the Academy as a potential catalyst continues – the Academy staff has been invited to participate in a range of activities, many sponsored by the chancellor and provost, including:

- presentation of entrepreneurship awards for faculty (for which we successfully sought the addition of an award for social entrepreneurship);
- service on a committee to strengthen institutional entrepreneurship at the university;
- programming on entrepreneurial behavior in the university to several audiences including Extension professionals and College of Business academic professionals;

- partnerships with career services units for programming; and
- partnerships for grant proposals, cosponsorship of events and service on advisory groups.

Impact assessment

Stakeholders noted that the Academy has an opportunity to think broadly about and redefine how success can be measured. Meaningful success can be evidenced by faculty who feel more supported in their efforts to think innovatively and collaboratively; students in non-professional colleges who wish to incorporate entrepreneurial concepts in their coursework; and department heads who are willing to entertain non-traditional mechanisms for evaluating faculty for tenure and promotion. Additional success measures include:

- more class offerings with an entrepreneurial focus; more students who take entrepreneurship courses;
- more collaboration among faculty on campus;
- inclusion of entrepreneurial job strategies and development of self-management skills for all students;
- gaining additional funding for Academy programs and activities;
- attracting alumni to participate in cross-curricular activities; and
- an increase in the depth and breadth of entrepreneurial activities that exist across the campus.

Additional strategies

Stakeholders provided a number of other strategic recommendations for the Academy:

- Academy messaging is critical;
- partner with colleges and departments with no prior entrepreneurial history;
- create and communicate a unique niche;
- start small and do it well;
- offer faculty incentives and rewards;
- avoid duplication of resources; and
- customize content for the audience.

Faculty needs assessment

An online needs assessment survey was sent to all full-time tenured and tenure-track UIUC faculty in the late spring of 2004, with a follow-up printed version. A total of 542 responses were received, for a 27 percent response rate.[5]

As well as those objectives mentioned for the stakeholder interviews, the faculty survey had additional purposes:

- determine faculty attitudes toward entrepreneurship;
- obtain examples of entrepreneurial activities, traditional and non-traditional, in which faculty are currently engaged;
- identify obstacles that faculty who wish to be more entrepreneurial currently face; and

- identify ways in which the Academy can address the needs of faculty who wish to be more entrepreneurial, including programming.

Faculty were given a list of activities and asked to identify which were most important, in their view, in describing entrepreneurial faculty. Among the activities considered most entrepreneurial were:

- seek funding;
- collaborate on research with colleagues outside UIUC;
- manage one's career in a multifaceted way;
- collaborate on research with colleagues at UIUC;
- incorporate creativity themes into teaching; and
- conduct applied research.

The activities viewed as least important in describing entrepreneurial faculty were consulting for a fee, starting a business and publishing a textbook – that is, those seen as being of primary benefit to the individual rather than the organization. Definitions of entrepreneurship by faculty place a greater emphasis on process issues such as collaborating with others, rather than tangible economic forms of entrepreneurship such as consulting. Faculty were open to a broad interpretation of entrepreneurship. This echoes the broad definition held by the stakeholders.

Faculty were also asked about their own activities. A strong relationship was found between what people considered to be entrepreneurial and activities in which they engaged.

When asked about their perceptions of university culture, more than 70 percent responded that entrepreneurial activity should be rewarded. Over half of the faculty reported encountering barriers to being entrepreneurial. Conversely, almost half stated that UIUC promotes creativity. The words 'traditional' and 'bureaucratic' were the two most popular descriptors of UIUC's culture. Approximately one-third of respondents described the university as both, one-third described it as one but not the other, and one-third described Illinois as neither. The 'traditional' description was not necessarily a negative one nor necessarily a barrier to entrepreneurship. Rather, faculty showed appreciation for the university's traditions and this should be taken into account in promoting an entrepreneurial outlook. For example, an emphasis on Illinois as an innovative environment can celebrate the university's scientific and academic achievements of the past.

More than half of all respondents reported encountering barriers to being more innovative, and often more than one barrier. Many of the reported problems are typical of large research universities. The most commonly reported barriers include:

- university bureaucracy;
- lack of resources:
  a. predominantly economic;
  b. peer support;
  c. lack of opportunities to explore possibilities and/or to meet collaborators;
- reward/tenure system does not foster entrepreneurial behavior;
- counter to academic/discipline culture/norms;

- politics; department chair or dean disapproves; and
- not enough time/too many other activities/responsibilities.

Some findings represented immediate opportunities for the Academy. Some suggested longer-term opportunities and other findings were primarily information to be shared with the university's faculty and administrators since action must primarily be taken by others.

Interest in various types of programming and other potential Academy activities was sought. Faculty did express an interest in career development programming. As well they welcomed programming for their graduate students. Aiding students in their career is one route to reaching faculty.

Implications of faculty perceptions
For some activities that the Academy might perceive as entrepreneurial behavior – for example, managing one's career in a self-directed fashion and incorporating themes of creativity, problem solving and so on in teaching – faculty indicate that they are engaged in these activities but do not view them as particularly entrepreneurial. Faculty may be more 'entrepreneurial' than they realize. The Academy must consider this together with faculty definitions of entrepreneurship in its communications, and use language focusing on improving the university (for example, focus on collaborative research, idea generation and creativity in the classroom).

Entrepreneurship inventory
Beginning in fall 2003, an inventory was undertaken of entrepreneurial interests and activities among faculty. Its purpose was, in part, to identify potential champions. This inventory has several components and is periodically updated. The course catalog and departmental course pages were examined to identify courses that focus primarily on some form of entrepreneurship or small business management or include this as one component in the course.[6] Faculty inventors who work with the Office of Technology Management and/or faculty who have their own businesses were identified when possible. Also noted were faculty who have written about entrepreneurship-related topics, through searches of scholarly journal databases that include faculty affiliations.

Among the outcomes of this inventory are the following: entrepreneurial activities were found to be higher than expected; the publications list serves as a way to celebrate entrepreneurship on the Academy web site; and the faculty identified became the initial membership of the Faculty Affiliates program.

Faculty career management
The third diagnostic tool was a career management study conducted in spring 2004. This research was exploratory only. Given its small sample size and research design, it is useful primarily in interpreting other results and providing a starting-point for further research.

The research method was to interview 32 successful/effective faculty, half entrepreneurial and half traditional, as identified primarily by deans. Entrepreneurial faculty were defined as those who bring innovative approaches to their teaching, research and service and/or go beyond research and teaching to incorporate other activities into their faculty role.

Half of the faculty were tenured and half tenure track assistant professors. The group was also segmented equally into four disciplinary categories: arts and humanities; life sciences and veterinary medicine; physical sciences and engineering; and social and behavioral sciences.

Using content analysis on the recorded and transcribed interviews, a career management model was developed. The model includes two profiles: one of successful faculty based on traits possessed by *both* entrepreneurial and traditional faculty, and one of *entrepreneurial faculty only*.

Faculty perceptions

Both traditional and entrepreneurial faculty were pleased with their professional experience at UIUC. Faculty in areas other than arts and humanities generally felt that the university does a good job in providing resources for faculty development. Traditional faculty expressed interest in grant writing assistance and release time to seek funding. Entrepreneurial faculty requested research support, teaching workshops and both release time and assistance with start-up companies.

While the majority of entrepreneurial faculty viewed describing a faculty member as entrepreneurial positively, only a minority of traditional faculty did so. This often appeared to be a problem with the term rather than the behavior – traditional faculty suggested that the term 'innovative' would probably be viewed more favorably by themselves and their department.

When asked about the characteristics of successful UIUC faculty, the traditional faculty pointed to the need for faculty to be student centered and enthusiastic about teaching. Entrepreneurial faculty, while not disagreeing with this belief, described a successful faculty member more broadly, citing the need to be engaged in numerous areas of academic life, teaching, research, service and outside activities.

Participants were asked about the degree to which their involvement in non-traditional activities was supported by the university and/or their colleagues. Examples of these activities, which were mainly engaged in by entrepreneurial faculty, include starting or being involved in a start-up company, commercialization of research, teaching innovations, establishing an externally funded research center and consulting and executive education. The majority believed that their involvement in these activities was supported by their colleagues. A minority believed that some colleagues supported it, while others did not. Sometimes the department heads were viewed as supportive while departmental colleagues were not supportive.

Career management model

The content analysis of the interviews identified six key characteristics emulated by the majority of both traditional and entrepreneurial faculty, and a separate list of nine traits that distinguished entrepreneurial faculty (Table 6.1). Although there is much overlap in the traits of successful entrepreneurial and traditional faculty, those more entrepreneurial are particularly strong in initiating new activities, building connections and actively managing their career in imaginative ways. The results are preliminary but suggest further exploration and a framework to use in talking with faculty.

Selected characteristics of successful entrepreneurial faculty

Certain characteristics were more strongly applicable to those faculty identified as entrepreneurial.

Table 6.1   Approach to faculty career

All faculty	Entrepreneurial faculty
● Collaborative	● Enthusiastic optimists
● Motivated by curiosity	● Initiators
● Organizational citizens	● Applied in orientation
● Dedicated to learning	● Multi-experiencers
● Engaged in their work	● Creators/innovators
● Logical	● Non-traditional
	● Imaginative career managers
	● Connectors/builders
	● Strategic/visionary

Enthusiastic optimists   While most faculty, both traditional and entrepreneurial, were engaged in their work, entrepreneurial faculty exhibit an exuberance when discussing their career. Similarly, entrepreneurial faculty express great resilience when encountering career barriers and setbacks.

Initiators   Entrepreneurial faculty are proactive in creating new research streams, forming professional collaborations with others and inaugurating new programs and services.

Applied in orientation   Entrepreneurial faculty are interested in making an impact and seeing a direct or immediate application of their work. Entrepreneurial faculty seek out real-world applications for their research.

Multi-experiencers   Entrepreneurial faculty have diverse work histories and link their previous experiences to current projects. They use this diversity of experience as a springboard for new classroom applications and research areas of focus.

Creators/innovators   For entrepreneurial faculty, creativity is more than just being curious. These faculty are highly creative, innovative and seek non-routine approaches to their work. In particular they are very creative in their approach to their research.

Non-traditional   Entrepreneurial faculty engage in activities that cannot be easily classified as teaching, research or service (such as an externally funded innovative research center, consulting or a start-up company).

Connectors/builders   Entrepreneurial faculty do not define their interests in a narrow, discipline-based manner. They are open to building on existing ideas as well as working with new people in disciplines other than their own.

Strategic/visionary   Entrepreneurial faculty see situations and problems holistically, as part of a coherent whole rather than disparate parts. They are also willing to focus on the larger objective and to cut their losses for the greater good or ultimate goal.

Implications of initial diagnostics
The three studies suggested strategies and activities for the Academy and issues of which to be mindful. Among these are the following.

Structure/organization
- develop a strategic plan specifying the Academy's overall mission and short-, mid- and long-term objectives; and
- determine desired outcomes and ways to measure/evaluate progress.

Communication/decision making
- develop protocols and procedures that are viewed as inclusive of groups across campus;
- stay in close contact with career management study participants and other faculty and staff who have indicated their interest in the Academy;
- plan carefully the Academy's brand, messaging, communication materials and program offerings. Distinguish the Academy from other entrepreneurial efforts both on campus and nationally; and
- coordinate with existing efforts, centers, programs and courses.

Academy activities
- incorporate the findings from assessment efforts into an activities plan. The plan can be matrixed to include a mix of activities by major function (teaching, research) and by constituent group;
- when possible engage faculty from diverse departments in the activities of the Academy as Fellows, proposal reviewers, program advisory group members and so on;
- offer faculty fellowships for the explicit purpose of generating papers on academic entrepreneurship for acceptance by peer-reviewed academic journals;
- develop a database of the interests and skills of faculty looking to engage in cross-disciplinary research;
- offer the opportunity for faculty to work in a 'thought incubator' setting;
- an important function of the Academy could be to simply bring together people and give them the opportunity to interact; and
- monitor perceived barriers to entrepreneurship at the university and advocate for appropriate changes.

Program design
- expand the understanding and definition of academic entrepreneurship across campus by sponsoring programs with a strategically determined, eclectic array of departments and centers. Initially involve colleges that have not developed entrepreneurial offerings;
- announce campus-wide entrepreneurial faculty initiatives and work with those most interested and engaged;
- develop a portfolio-based approach to program design offering an initial menu of programs and services that are tangible and that can yield short-term, measurable results, as well as activities whose impact will be evident over time;

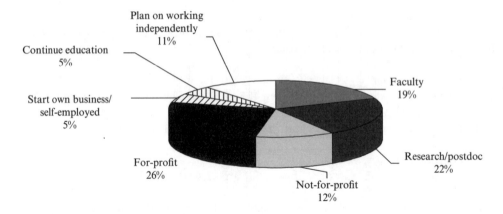

Figure 6.1   What do you plan on doing immediately after receiving your degree from UIUC?

- work with the university's 27 career services offices on programs that can aid students in their professional career development; and
- offer faculty incentives including stipends and/or small grants to revise or design new courses.

Entrepreneurial thinking, no matter how broadly interpreted, will not be accepted by all faculty. The Academy, however, is seen as having the potential to be a major source of support for those faculty who are creative and innovative. These research findings affirm the Academy's need to define entrepreneurship in the context of higher education. By focusing on faculty and departments across campus; broadening the definition of entrepreneurship to include educational and non-commercial applications; and offering programs that foster entrepreneurial values in both academic and administrative areas, the Academy can help to shape the entrepreneurial university.

Student-focused diagnostics[7]

Graduate students
A web-based survey was distributed to all (10,237) graduate and professional students, with a response rate of 24.5 percent. The survey objectives were to ascertain graduate students' career paths, interest in entrepreneurship and preferred modes of learning about entrepreneurial skills.

Interest in entrepreneurship was found to be high, and was not limited to such expected fields as business or engineering, but encompasses graduate students in all areas.

Students were asked 'What do you plan on doing immediately after receiving your degree from UIUC?' (Figure 6.1). Together the options of starting a business/being self-employed and of working independently were chosen by 16 percent of all graduate students.

Asked whether they ever planned on working independently as an artist/writer/inventor or starting their own business, 68 percent of the respondents planned to do so at some point in their career. When examined by college, over 50 percent in each college

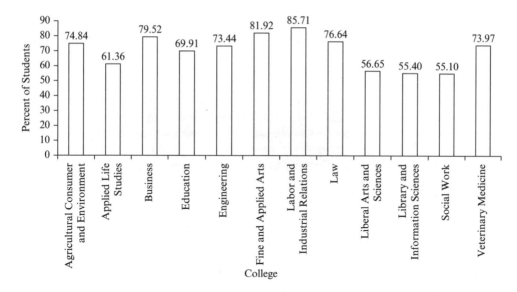

Figure 6.2   Do you ever plan on working independently on starting your own business, at some point in your career?

said they had this goal. This matches the reality that most entrepreneurs do not have a business degree. (Figure 6.2.)

Students were asked about their interest in entrepreneurship education and the means by which they would like to learn more about entrepreneurship. This latter issue arose because of the concern that graduate students might find it difficult to add additional coursework or substitute an entrepreneurship course for another elective.

Analysis does reveal significant differences in preferred learning modes in relation to the colleges in which students are enrolled and interest in particular forms of entrepreneurship. However, across the campus there is a strong interest in learning more about entrepreneurship. Among the findings are the following:

- strongest preference overall, with 67 percent selecting, is for internships and mentoring;
- little interest in formal coursework;
- lack of knowledge about basics expressed: finance, finding markets and selling ideas/inventions; and
- uncertain about own abilities and willingness to take risks.

Entrepreneurial topics that graduate students were most interested in included how to communicate ideas, how to organize resources and how to recognize opportunities.

Graduate students prefer to learn through the type of instruction the Academy is most suited to provide directly; real-world experience and workshops that are not constrained by the limits of formal instruction.

The interest in career development programming by graduate students dovetails with the need perceived by their faculty. As well, it meshes with campus and national concerns about graduate education, especially in the humanities and social sciences, which is often devoid of any discussion of careers other than as faculty.[8]

Freshman survey

In fall 2005, a survey was administered to all first semester freshmen. The respondents (29.47 percent of the population of 4,747 students) were a good representation of the freshman class as a whole. The purpose of the survey was to assess entrepreneurial inclinations and attitudes. Students were asked about their past, current and prospective plans for owning their own business or working for social change. The latter option was used to indicate potential interest in social entrepreneurship, a term with which students were less likely to be familiar. The freshmen were also asked about taking entrepreneurship-related courses while they were undergraduates.

Among the overall findings are the following. Almost one in ten (9.5 percent) UIUC freshmen have owned their own business or worked as a creative artist or inventor. More than one in ten (11.1 percent) plan to own their own business or work independently while they are undergraduates. The college in which a student is enrolled is highly correlated with such post-graduate plans. Students in fine arts, engineering and business are most likely to indicate interest in owning their own business or working independently as a creative artist or inventor after graduation. Students in education are least likely to express interest in such careers.

Social change/social entrepreneurship   Students were asked about their interest and involvement in working for social change. Somewhat less than half (43.0 percent) of freshmen have already been involved with an organization whose purpose is to bring about social change. Almost two in three (61.2 percent) freshmen expect to be involved while they are earning their undergraduate degree. When they graduate, 64.4 percent expect to work to bring about social change within an organization.

Undergraduate entrepreneurship education   Freshmen were asked whether they would take courses to help start a business, succeed as an independent inventor/creative artist and/or work for social change. Overall, 71.2 percent of respondents indicated that they would take such courses if available (Figure 6.3). Such interest is spread across the disciplines. In addition:

- more than half (52.3 percent) of UIUC freshmen are interested in learning how to start their own business;
- almost one in three (31.8 percent) is interested in learning how to succeed as an independent inventor or creative artist;
- almost half (47.5 percent) are interested in learning about how to work effectively for social change;
- men are more interested than women in start-up businesses (53.7 percent of male freshmen are interested in starting their own business after graduation, compared to 32 percent of women); and
- women are more interested than men in social entrepreneurship: 55.9 percent of women versus 37.2 percent of men are interested in taking courses on working effectively toward social change.

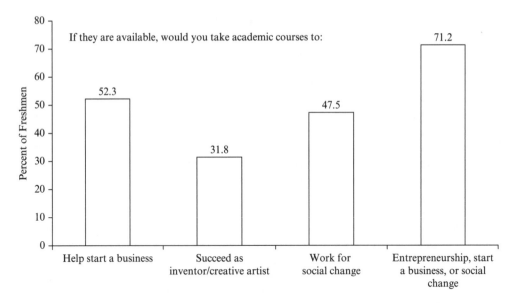

Figure 6.3   Freshman interest in entrepreneurship courses

Implications of faculty, administrator and student diagnostics
What did the Academy for Entrepreneurial Leadership learn from undertaking these diagnostic efforts?

The diagnostic process itself is valuable. It surfaced perceptions and opinions, and served to gather significant information, but also served as a messaging tool about the entrepreneurship initiative. Results were more positive than perhaps expected, and the level of entrepreneurial activity and interest among all groups was significant. Sharing the results with stakeholders through meetings and documents led to further discussion and input.

We began with a broad definition of entrepreneurship. This allowed faculty who would not ordinarily identify as entrepreneurs to see a place for themselves. One example: a dance professor interviewed for the faculty career management study later became a panelist for a presentation on entrepreneurial faculty. She noted that she had not previously used the term 'entrepreneurial' to describe herself, but rather had thought of herself as 'scrappy', as aggressively managing her career and looking for opportunities. This attitude and career strategy was one she was trying to impart to her students, and she could now see the role that education related to entrepreneurship might strengthen those efforts.

We learned that terminology matters. 'Entrepreneurial', for example, is less problematic than entrepreneurship. It allows people to see it as behavior, a process, which may be useful in multiple contexts. Innovation and creativity are also often useful as terms to accompany entrepreneurship as part of the explanation of its broad perspective.

Social entrepreneurship was included as one form of entrepreneurship in the diagnostic studies. It was found to be of interest to both faculty and students – in fact, to a greater extent than the Academy staff might have predicted – and interest continues to grow. Its inclusion in the Academy's mission allows us to work with faculty and administrators interested in civic engagement, service learning and outreach. It will be a track in the undergraduate minor under development. Social entrepreneurship has, in fact, become a signature component of the Academy.

The diagnostic process began our networking. Discussions with stakeholders identified champions. The inventory of entrepreneurial activities led to the establishment of a Faculty Affiliates initiative. The wide interest in entrepreneurship, broadly defined, also led to a cross-campus advisory board of deans; establishment of an Opportunity Fund to support ideas that do not fit within our funding frameworks; co-sponsorship of events and seeking partnership opportunities based initially on suggestions that arose through the diagnostic process; and opting not to control the curriculum. Faculty Fellows are encouraged to develop their own courses tailored to their areas.

Academy strategy
Campus-wide entrepreneurship education and a change in organizational culture to create a stronger appreciation for entrepreneurial behavior cannot be imposed by the Academy. The campus is large and complex – as Weick describes, a loosely coupled system. Diagnosis to identify the heterogeneous needs, characteristics and expectations of the targeted 'customers' is a necessary first step. To effectively accomplish the succeeding steps, the Academy adopted a '4-D' framework for transforming the entrepreneurship orientation of the UIUC campus: diagnose, design, deliver and determine. These components are closely linked in a dynamic process and used to achieve both strategic consistency and appropriate changes in responses to the environment.

Before the Academy was established, entrepreneurship endeavors at UIUC were rather traditional, in that the business and engineering schools were the primary homes of entrepreneurship curriculum and organizations. These efforts, though influential within their individual schools, were limited in their influence on campus-wide entrepreneurship education and awareness. Long-term success of a university-wide program to promote academic entrepreneurship requires cultural support from the entire campus, rather than one or two individual schools.

However, the diagnostic process did identify pockets of entrepreneurship that had long gone unnoticed. The Human Resource Education (HRE) program had produced many graduate students with a focus on entrepreneurship training. In fact, within the national Small Business Institute (SBI) program, Illinois was the first campus to host an SBI program outside of a school of business – within the HRE department. The diagnostic effort aided the Academy to identify champions, partners and activities to celebrate and use in advocating that the culture change being sought was not a completely new perspective.

Figure 6.4 exhibits an outline of the Academy's approach to establishing a campus-wide program. The right-hand side shows a flow from strategy formulation to strategy implementation, and the left-hand side shows the corresponding stage in the 4-D model. The four Ds constitute a dynamic process through which entrepreneurial needs are identified, entrepreneurship education is provided, entrepreneurship-related activities are sponsored and entrepreneurship awareness is continuously enhanced. These two parts are not independent. The specification of strategic plans is drawn from the diagnosis stage, and the modification of strategic plans is made according to the determine, or evaluation, stage.

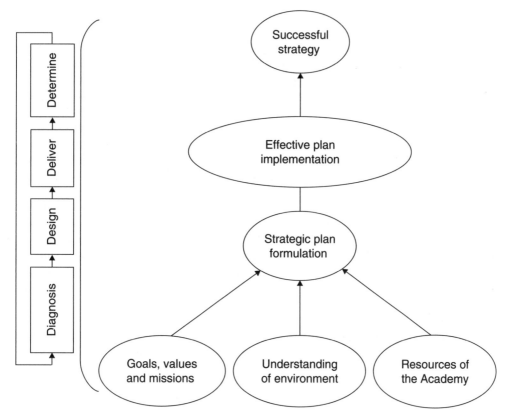

Figure 6.4   A 4-D strategic management framework

Although entrepreneurship education can be dated back more than 60 years (Katz 2003, pp. 283–300) the field is far from mature. In 2002, a comprehensive inventory of the status of entrepreneurship education in over 3,100 two- and four-year colleges and universities confirmed a weakness in the academic presence of entrepreneurship.[9] Problems include the lack of tenure track faculty to teach entrepreneurship courses; exacerbation of this by the expansion of entrepreneurship across multiple disciplines; lack of doctoral programs to educate and train the future professoriate; and failure to support faculty research to develop the scholarly bibliography that will legitimize the field. These problems can be significant barriers to the promotion of cross-campus entrepreneurship.

For the efforts of the Academy in transforming entrepreneurship culture of the entire campus to be successful, a strategic process is indispensable. The 4-D model depicted in Figure 6.4 is one manifestation of the Academy's efforts in integrating formulation and implementation of its strategic plans. The right-hand side of this figure gives a general presentation of common elements in successful strategies. Consistent and long-term goals and mission are the guiding post for the activities of the organization. The mission of the Academy (2008) is to advance the understanding of entrepreneurship as 'a vehicle for the creation of social, economic, and intellectual value through (1) advancing opportunity for human creativity and (2) identifying and leveraging resources for inter-disciplinary collaboration'.

During the preparation of the initial Illinois proposal, an informal diagnostic process was undertaken. The strategy and program components expressed in the proposal were derived from this and from knowledge of the campus culture and the level of entrepre-neurship activity; and knowledge of the higher education environment more broadly, and the state of entrepreneurship education and of entrepreneurship as a discipline nationally. With the awarding of the grant from the Kauffman Foundation, a more formal diagnostic effort was undertaken. The left-hand side of Figure 6.4 exhibits the Academy's efforts in initiating the 4-D model in accordance with the general model on the right-hand side. The Academy investigated the different constituents of the campus in terms of their perceptions of, participation in and expectations for entrepreneurship education and activities across the campus. The diagnostic efforts served to confirm program components developed in the construction of the initial proposal to the Kauffman Foundation, and surfaced opportunities which had not been apparent. It aided in reprioritizing, fleshing out more specific objectives and approaches and creating a strategic plan. The 4-D framework provides a process to draw up and implement the plan and then to evaluate and modify it as needed.

Strategic plan formulation
The faculty and administrator studies collected viewpoints from different constituents of the campus, providing valuable information for the Academy in terms of its structure and organization, the appropriate decision-making procedure, the proposed activities and the design and contents of the programs that the Academy will provide.

The design stage: objectives
The results of the diagnostic efforts were translated into objectives for the Academy. Table 6.2 shows a list of the entrepreneurship needs identified in the diagnosis stage, and the programs and projects that the Academy designed in response to these needs.

The plan outline includes: (i) strengthen entrepreneurship as a respected field of study; (ii) establish a local, national and international identity for the Academy; (iii) develop entrepreneurial skills; (iv) identify entrepreneurship champions; and (v) create sustain-ability for the Academy. The more detailed objectives integrate the original strategic plan of the proposal for establishing the Academy and the diagnosis results.

Strategic plan implementation
The design stage helps the Academy to identify not only the strategic objectives, but also the ways to execute those objectives, through programs and projects. For example, how can we support faculty and graduate student research in entrepreneurship? The Academy developed a research fund to support faculty; partnered with the Center for International Business Education and Research (CIBER) and the Center for Global Studies to promote international/global entrepreneurship, including research; estab-lished a Graduate Scholars program and a Faculty Fellow program; and hosted lectures by entrepreneurship scholars. Participation in the broader community of entrepreneur-ship scholars was encouraged through the publicizing of research and conference oppor-tunities, and support for conference participation by faculty and graduate students. As

Table 6.2   From strategic plans to strategic objectives

Strategic plans	Objectives
Strengthen entrepreneurship as a respected field of study	Create mentoring networks for faculty and students
	Identify and nurture faculty champions
	Nurture opportunities for cross-disciplinary and trans-domain networking
	Support faculty in developing curricular and co-curricular activities
	Support faculty and graduate students in participation in national community of entrepreneurship scholars and educators
	Establish programs to support faculty and graduate student research in entrepreneurship
Establish a local, national and international identity for the Academy	Broaden the understanding and appreciation of entrepreneurship on the UIUC campus
	Communicate and disseminate best practices/models
	Collaborate with universities and other national organizations to expand awareness and best practices
	Promote the development of entrepreneurship ventures, whether social, economic, intellectual or cultural, in the UIUC community
	Develop various publications to highlight entrepreneurial activity and opportunity on the UIUC campus
Develop entrepreneurial skills	Raise awareness of how to manage careers more entrepreneurially
	Expand entrepreneurial understanding among administrators
Identify entrepreneurship champions	Identify and nurture faculty champions
	Identify and nurture champions among administrators and other academic professionals
Create sustainability for the Academy	Raise minimum $10 million endowment
	Identify and secure funding for the Academy from public sources
	Secure grants from various local, state and national organizations

well, the Academy created a research resource page on its web site and collaborated with the Kauffman Foundation on scholarly database projects.

The Faculty Fellows program is an example of the effort to integrate the needs and expectations identified from the initial stage with the Academy's resources and values. In response to the request for rewarded entrepreneurial activities from the faculty, this program supports the development of entrepreneurship course and course modules across the Illinois curriculum. A faculty member can apply for funding to design a new course or revise a current offering. The Academy will also provide successful applicants with experiences to enhance understanding of entrepreneurial principles and sponsor educational and mentoring activities. As the course is taught, students acquire entrepreneurship skills or principles, within the context of a particular discipline.

Delivery
Implementation of the designed programs constitutes the delivery stage for which the Academy has designed a set of functional strategies, including marketing and operations. Because it is rather new and non-traditional in its approach, the Academy must actively promote both itself and an entrepreneurship orientation in the campus. Approaches are

tailored to the various audiences. For general promotion, for example, multimedia materials have been designed specifically for faculty, for alumni and for students. Among the efforts to market the Graduate Scholars initiative are e-mail announcements sent to prior scholars for distribution to colleagues, to Faculty Fellows and Affiliates who may know students they can encourage and to the directors of graduate programs in each department. An electronic newsletter distributed by the Graduate College reaches students of whom the Academy would never otherwise be aware. Advertising workshops to undergraduates takes a quite different approach.

At the deliver stage, the Academy collects feedback for evaluations at the determine stage. Broad evaluation criteria were suggested by the stakeholders during the diagnosis process, and more specific criteria are also determined for individual events or types of events. For example, at a workshop a feedback form would ask whether the event met their expectations and whether they would recommend it to a colleague. Together with these specific evaluation criteria, strategic consistency is important for evaluating the efficiency and effectiveness of the organizational efforts. The Academy's strategic activities should be consistent with the goals of the university, the individual academic units on campus, and the values or long-term goals of the Academy itself. In the university strategic plan, economic development and global reach are important components of the vision of the university and fostering innovation and creativity is one of the most important values.

Initiatives must also meet Academy goals and objectives. For example: an analysis of the events organized in the 2005–06 academic year shows that workshops are very popular, that graduate students and undergraduate students comprise the majority of attendees (62 percent), and that 99 percent of the workshop attendees rate the workshop content as satisfactory, valuable or surpassed expectations. More workshops targeted to students are therefore a viable choice. However, a significant minority of participants were members of other Academy constituencies and should also be considered in deciding on programming. Workshop offerings and workshop partners were therefore expanded for 2006–07.

The Academy formally examines its strategies and objectives twice each year at an annual all-day planning meeting and a briefer review halfway through the year. As well, major events are followed by debriefings, in addition to the typical capture of notes about execution for the next similar event.

Model Dynamics
Figure 6.5 presents the dynamics of the 4-D model. The 4 Ds constitute a strategic management process – establishing strategic plans at the beginning, going through the diagnosis, design, deliver and determine procedures and modifying the specifics of the original strategic plans if necessary. The four stages of this process are not independent of one another. The process is dynamic, involves observing the environment in which the Academy operates and often leads to refining of strategies and objectives, or deemphasizing one activity in favor of another that was more effective in reaching an objective. Given the high interest in working with us that has arisen on campus, it also helps the Academy to prioritize the many opportunities that are presented.

The Academy is the initiator of each 'D' of this framework. For each stage, the Academy brings in a variety of participants whose inputs help to identify the entrepreneurship

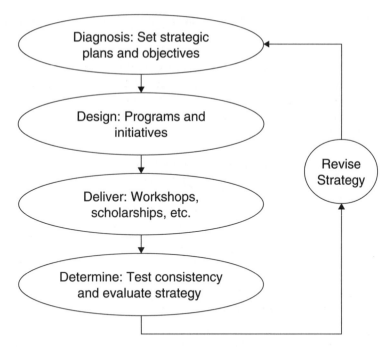

Figure 6.5   Dynamics of the 4-D model

needs, to provide resources deployable by the Academy or to redefine the direction of the Academy's efforts. The sequential process of this 4-D framework can be rephrased as following: for the first step, the Academy studies the cross-section campus in terms of entrepreneurship awareness, needs and resources; then designs and delivers programs identified through the initial diagnosis process; finally, feedback is then obtained from the audience, as well as staff (and where applicable, Advisory Board) input.

One distinctive attribute of the 4-D framework is that its inputs are from the campus, and its outputs are for the campus. Input from the faculty, administrators and students helped to define the initial plans, roles and activities of the Academy. Many activities can only be carried out with the cooperation and shared resources of other units. The programming output is evaluated based upon the effect on campus-wide entrepreneurship education, and only the initiatives regarded by faculty, students and other stakeholders as valuable are retained for further development. In this sense, the 4-D framework is rooted in the campus rather than being imposed by the Academy.

This approach enables the Academy to identify those important components that may affect its efforts (for example, existing entrepreneurship activities; the university strategic plan; stakeholder views), and therefore successfully catch opportunities and avoid some risks. The Academy is better able to allocate its resources effectively because every component of the Academy is organized and guided by the same strategic objectives. The strategic consistency that the Academy continuously tries to maintain is the key to its success because it enhances the legitimacy and sets consistent guidance for the revision of strategy.

The divergence between traditional entrepreneurship education and a university-wide approach needs to be considered. Entrepreneurship education cannot be imposed by the Academy; a diagnostic effort to identify the heterogeneous needs, characteristics and expectations of the targeted 'customers' is the necessary first step. Alignment of the Academy's efforts with its community, the university and the environment is critical to the achievement of long-term goals. No strategy can guarantee success; appropriate modification and revision is indispensable. The framework described herein provides an approach for making these modifications and revisions.

Notes

1. Kauffman Campuses Initiative, www.kauffman.org/items.cfm?itemID=475.
2. Inventory of Entrepreneurship Education in U.S. Two Year and Four Year Colleges and Universities', University of Illinois, 2002, Study conducted by Cynthia Kehoe and Paul Magelli, in collaboration with Illinois Business Consulting.
3. Ibid.
4. Karen Dowd, from the Empower Group, a change management consultancy, worked with Courtney Price from VentureQuest Ltd, an innovation and entrepreneurship consulting firm.
5. The respondents represented a diverse group: 63 percent of respondents were male; 22 percent were minorities; 69 percent of all respondents were tenured. The disciplinary distribution was 31 percent in the social sciences; 23 percent in other sciences; 18 percent in the humanities; 17 percent in engineering and 8 percent in health sciences.
6. This is not solely a matter of searching for key words, but requires some browsing of more likely types of courses – for example, a practice management course in veterinary medicine.
7. The surveys of graduate students and of freshmen were conducted by the Library Research Center, in the Graduate School of Library and Information Science at the University of Illinois.
8. The Responsive PhD Woodrow Wilson Foundation, www.woodrow.org/responsivephd/index.php.
9. See note 2.

References

Academy for Entrepreneurial Leadership (2008), 'Strategic Plan 2008–2009', University of Illinois at Urbana–Champaign, IL.
Katz, Jeremy A. (2003), 'The chronology and intellectual trajectory of American entrepreneurship education: 1876–1999', *Journal of Business Venturing*, **18**(2), 283–300.
Orton, J. Douglas and Karl E. Weick (1990), 'Loosely coupled systems: a reconceptualization', *Academy of Management Review*, **15**(2), 203–23.

7 Entrepreneurship education: meeting the skills needs of graduates in Ireland

Briga Hynes, Michele O'Dwyer and Naomi Birdthistle

Introduction

Educators, including universities, 'have an obligation to meet students' expectations with regard to preparation for the economy in which they will operate' (Galloway et al., 2005: 1–14). Educational institutions need to ensure that they respond to this obligation by preparing graduates to engage in a more enterprising and innovative manner, thereby adding value to the business in which they work. The needs and structure of the work environment are constantly changing. Of particular note is the change in the composition and profile of the size of firms (Hynes and Richardson, 2007). On a European-wide scale there is an increasing emergence of the small firm as a key component of the industrial profile of countries. This is very evident in Ireland where it was estimated, in 2003, that the number of small firms was approximately 186,114, an increase of 16,114 over a three-year period since 2000 (Revenue Commissioners Statistical Unit, 2003). Given this, embedding enterprise across the population through education programmes is a central element of policy across the world (Martin, 2006). Such policy initiatives promote the need to ensure that graduates are familiar with, and equipped to work effectively in such an environment. In addition, there is a need to provide enterprise education for graduates who are interested in acquiring the knowledge and skills to become entrepreneurs.

This chapter addresses the manner in which a University of Limerick postgraduate entrepreneurship education course, the Master of Business Studies in International Entrepreneurship Management (MBS in IEM), is an effective mechanism for accommodating the changing needs of the work environment, while instilling in graduates of all disciplines, an interest and knowledge in international entrepreneurship and self-employment as a career option. The programme is described based on the components of a proposed framework for entrepreneurship education. This framework has been identified as a useful template to guide entrepreneurship programme design and development. It also provides for a means of analysis of the strengths of the programme and the identification of issues which could be enhanced in its future development. Finally, the research promotes the adoption of this proposed framework for entrepreneurship education for other institutions in programme development.

The changing work environment: a need for a flexible employee

During the last decade in Ireland, both large and small firms have seen changes in terms of downsizing, restructuring, outsourcing and an increase in the use of technology in determining where, when and how tasks are accomplished. These factors coupled with changes in the economy, increased globalisation and liberalisation of markets, increased competition and a changing profile and composition of the workforce have posed significant challenges for the owner/manager in managing firm growth. The owner/ manager assumes a myriad of roles in managing a new business (Muir and Langford, 1994; O'Gorman et al., 2005). The ability to perform a number of roles requires skills and competencies in a number of technical, functional and process areas which are rarely all found in nascent entrepreneurs. Nascent entrepreneurs generally have a skill set biased towards a technical or product/service knowledge area; thus, it is a requirement for employees in the firm to possess a range of complementary and compensating skills to those of the owner/manager in order to effectively grow the business.

In addressing these needs, the University of Limerick has been successful in providing a suite of entrepreneurship education programmes designed to develop and transfer knowledge about the enterprise process, and to encourage students to examine entrepreneurship as a viable career option. Programmes operate at both undergraduate and graduate levels. They range from structured courses consisting of lectures, assignments, case studies and readings to innovative, integrated programmes where students actively participate in the small business sector, develop business plans and are exposed to prominent entrepreneurs who operate their businesses both nationally and internationally.

At a graduate level, the MBS in IEM has been specifically designed to meet the needs of recent graduates from all disciplines, graduates with work experience or owners/ managers of small businesses who wish to understand how to manage and grow a small business internationally. This one-year (full-time) programme or two-year (part-time) programme focuses on assisting participants in understanding the development of an international strategy for a small business. Specifically the objectives of the programme are:

- To provide participants with an insight into the role, functions and characteristics of the entrepreneur and owner/manager that are needed to grow a small business internationally.
- To provide students with an understanding of the functional disciplines of a business and how they change as the small business grows and internationalises.
- To provide participants with the knowledge and competencies to develop an international business strategy for a business.
- To develop useful skills and perspectives such as creative problem solving, diagnostic skills, communication and project management skills that are needed to grow a business internationally.

These objectives were set in accordance with industry research such as that provided by the Expert Group on Future Skills Needs (EGFSN, 2007), which identified that small and medium-sized enterprise (SME) employees require a range of generic and transferable skills and attitudes, with a requirement for flexibility, continuous learning, and individual initiative and judgement. In summary, the EGFSN indicated the need for employees in the workplace to have a number of skills and competencies in addition to subject knowledge expertise acquired from the completion of a formal educational qualification. These skills influenced the design of the MBS in IEM at the University of Limerick and can be grouped into four areas as follows:

- practical experience, project-based and flexibility/innovation skills;
- management skills for the twenty-first century;

- information and communications technology skills; and
- generic skills.

Practical experience, project-based and flexibility/innovation skills
Given that industry is increasingly looking to recruit graduates with practical work experience and commercial understanding, students with strong technical or pure theoretical knowledge but little practical experience are losing out on potential jobs. Education courses such as the MBS in IEM need to foster adaptability, flexibility and innovation skills which must become integral to the education system at all levels if the needs of a changing workforce are to be met. The introduction and expansion of project-based learning, team work, assignments on the programme addresses the provision of these skills. By moving in this direction, there is significant scope for programme developers to improve both the quality of learning and the development of soft skills relevant to the workplace without compromising the intellectual content of courses.

Management skills for the twenty-first century
Management skills such as creativity, opportunity sensing, decision-making competencies, risk-taking propensity and people management skills have become increasingly important for businesses of all sizes. Such graduates from the MBS in IEM need to be well equipped in both people-related and conceptual skills. Such people-related skills are based on effective communication, interpersonal, team-working and customer-service skills. In addition, conceptual skills required by graduates include those such as collecting and organising information, problem solving, planning and organising, learning-to-learn skills and systematic thinking skills. The design of the MBS in IEM is such that learning outcomes have been created so that the modules engender these management skills within the participants through the pedagogical approaches adopted.

Information and communications technology skills
The rapid diffusion of information and communications technology (ICT) in all aspects of the business has resulted in the need for graduates of all disciplines to be ICT proficient. This is particularly pertinent for the small firm, where there is a need for both owner/managers and employees to understand how ICT can be adopted to create greater efficiencies in areas such as sales, customer service, market research, product development, research and development (R&D) and so on. Students on the MBS in IEM programme are provided with an opportunity to use ICT in an integrated manner in project work and in presentations relevant to the small firm scenario.

Generic skills
Generic skills, which include basic skills such as literacy, numeracy, personal and professional development-related skills, are integral to the MBS in IEM. Graduates need to possess effective skills in self-understanding and self-confidence which will provide them with freedom to think in a creative manner, contributing to their workplace.

Therefore, it is evident from the above that industry requires a graduate who is not just trained as a subject-specific expert, but increasingly there is a need for graduates to have skills beyond their core discipline. There is a definite requirement for graduates to have skills which are based on the ability to adopt a flexible, creative and innovative approach to work, to perform as a member of a team using their people management skills. The educational experience should provide individuals with the attitude, abilities and competencies to excel and participate in the highly dynamic business and technological environment of the future (EGFSN, 2007).

In addressing these needs, and in creating the graduate for the future, it is argued that there is a need for third-level institutions to adopt a much greater and more strategic enterprise focus, both in terms of satisfying the knowledge and skills requirements of graduates, and thus satisfying business and industry needs, as well as fostering new business start-ups. Galloway et al. (2005) suggested that in order to adopt this strategic focus, universities should develop as entrepreneurial institutions and become more proactive in addressing the needs of employers and the business community when devising courses, thus exploiting the creative potential and encouraging enterprising behaviour.

Entrepreneurship education: a means for creating the future graduate
From a policy perspective, the importance of enterprise education has been acknowledged by the European Commission, which advocates that entrepreneurship education is important to create the 'correct mindset' to foster greater enterprising behaviour. The focus and objectives of entrepreneurship education programmes should involve the acquisition of a broader set of lifelong skills and not simply training for business start-ups (Audretsch, 2002; DfES, 2002; Martin, 2004), and in developing enterprise capacity (NCIHE, 1997; DfES, 2003). Entrepreneurship education should contribute to the development of a range of skills, including the ability to innovate and to provide leadership, which pays dividends for the individual and the economy in any employment context. It should instil an interest and the potential to start a new business (Galloway and Brown, 2002). Research conducted by Birdthistle (2006) reveals that entrepreneurship is a potential career option for Irish students either directly after completing their studies or within five or more years after graduation.

According to Gibb (1993), the real challenge for educational institutions is to acquire staff with an orientation towards an enterprising mode of learning, and a capability to teach it. The lecturer plays a crucial role in the overall effectiveness of any enterprise programme, encouraging an 'enterprising' style of learning as opposed to the more traditional 'didactic' teaching approach (ibid.). Teaching enterprise via the formal didactic processes will ultimately result in the simulation of the 'knowing how' not occurring. Gibb suggested that the lecturer needs to act as more of a guide and a partner in the learning process as opposed to a dictator who delivers knowledge to a largely passive audience. Moreover, lecturers need to recognise and understand the different ways that people learn, and lecturers should aim to facilitate this process.

As is illustrated in Table 7.1, if lecturers are to effectively teach enterprise then they need to make the transition from 'didactic to enterprising teaching modes', (ibid.:14). This may involve a perceived loss of power and control, as the lecturer becomes a facilitator and is no longer the centre of attention in the classroom.

In addition, it is necessary to extend enterprise education outwards from business schools, which has been endorsed by Brush et al. (2003) and Galloway and Brown (2002). Galloway further suggested that a 'cross disciplinary approach' to enterprise education can influence a range of industry sectors including the arts, science and technology disciplines (Galloway and Brown, 2002). In an assessment and evaluation of a number

Table 7.1   Didactic and enterprising learning modes

Didactic	Enterprising
Learning from teacher alone	Learning from each other
Passive role as listener	Learning by doing
Learning from written texts	Learning from debate and exchange
Learning from 'expert'	Learning by discovery (under guidance)
Learning from feedback from one key person (the teacher)	Learning from the reactions of many people
	Learning in a flexible informal environment
Learning in a well-organised timetabled environment	Learning under pressure to achieve goals
	Learning by borrowing from others
Learning without the pressure of immediate goals	Mistakes learned from
	Learning by problem solving
Copying from others discouraged	
Mistakes feared	
Learning by notes	

Source: Gibb (1993:14).

of entrepreneurship programmes, Hytti and O'Gorman (2004) found that more success-ful programmes were those which had the ability to integrate learning across the general educational experience of students, and provided them with exposure to subjects which extended beyond their core disciplines.

In essence, entrepreneurship education for graduates (business and non-business disciplines) involves education for the acquisition of entrepreneurial attitudes and skills, not simply training for business start-ups, and should be provided to all students. However, a challenge facing educationalists is how best to design programmes which contain the most appropriate content and delivery mechanisms to accommodate differ-ent student groups in acquiring the necessary entrepreneurial knowledge and skills. In exploring this concept, this study adopted a process approach to the design of entre-preneurship education programmes which provides for the design of more-relevant programmes to address the needs of diverse student groups and the demands of the business environment.

A process approach to entrepreneurship education
A process framework of entrepreneurship education devised by Hynes (1996) following an evaluation of third-level entrepreneurship courses suggested that entrepreneurship education is process driven. Stakeholders in the process have a range of needs, which may differ in nature and scope. This results in the need for a flexible approach to course design and delivery. Essentially, the process consists of three key elements: inputs, process and outputs. The inputs refer to the profile and characteristics of the student prior to partici-pation in the programme. The process consists of two elements that reflect the content and teaching methods adopted to suit the characteristics, objectives and requirements of the inputs. The outputs reflect the 'take-away' element of the course – the resulting increase in knowledge and skills the participants obtains from the course and the added value accrued to the host institution delivering the course. (Table 7.2.)

Table 7.2   Process framework for entrepreneurship education

Inputs	Process		Outputs
Student's profile and characteristics	Content focus	Teaching focus	Professional/Personnel
Prior knowledge base	*Entrepreneurship* Entrepreneurship, innovation, new product development, innovation, idea generation, R&D	*Didactic* (reading/ lectures) *Skill building* (case studies, group discussions, presentations, problem solving, simulations, teamwork, projects)	*Personal* (confidence communication) *Knowledge* enterprise, initiative, self-employment, business, management and market skills, analytical, problem solving, decision making, communication, presentation, risk taking
Motivation/ attitudes			
Personality			
Needs/interests			
Level of independence	*Business content* Marketing, accounting & finance, human resources		
Attitudes			
Parent influence			
Self-esteem		*Discovery* brainstorming, personal goal setting, career planning, consultancy	
Values (work and personal)			
Work experience	*Legal aspects* Intellectual property rights, employment legislation, insurance		*Confidence* Greater self-awareness
Gender			
			Career Improved knowledge, broader career options
	Competency/soft skills development Interpersonal skills (communication, presentation, writing)		

Source: Hynes (1996: 13).

The process framework focuses on the transfer of two primary constituents, namely knowledge and learning, to the student. Hall and Andriani (2003) describe knowledge to include all factors that have the potential to influence human thought and behaviour, which sometimes allow the explanation, prediction and control of physical phenomena. This definition includes factors such as skills, intuition, organisational culture, reputation and codified theory, all of which can be placed on a spectrum of knowledge. This spectrum of knowledge runs from tacit (uncodified) knowledge at one extreme, to explicit (codified) knowledge at the other; understanding the nature of knowledge exchanges within the context of this spectrum is essential to the successful development of an effective teaching and learning programme (O'Dwyer and O'Flynn, 2005).

Grant (1996) regards tacit knowledge as the know-how, skills and practical knowledge which is acquired by experience; it is knowledge of what works, whereas explicit knowledge is knowledge that has been captured in a code, or a language that facilitates communication (Hall and Andriani, 2003). There are two distinct categories of knowledge acquisition: experiential learning (comprising scanning, organisational experiments, organisational self-appraisal, experimenting organisations, unintentional or unsystematic learning) and external learning (comprising vicarious learning, scanning, focused search and performance monitoring). The process framework provides for multiple alternative structures and learning mechanisms to ensure that learning is targeted to accommodate students' requirements and serves as a basis for the design of targeted and focused entrepreneurship programmes.

Adopting the process framework of entrepreneurship education: the MBS in IEM
The MBS in IEM has been designed to educate students from diverse disciplines in the theoretical and practical aspects of managing and growing a small business internationally. Participants therefore explore their own entrepreneurial potential and learn in a practical manner how to develop and grow a small business internationally. In the development of this programme and in ensuring as far as possible, that the correct balance of both the different types of knowledge and a mix of formal and informal learning were incorporated, the process framework for entrepreneurship education was adopted to guide the design of the programme. This programme was introduced in September 2007 and is discussed in the context of the proposed framework for entrepreneurship education.

Inputs
Before the content or teaching focus is finally decided upon, it is important to define the personal profile and personality characteristics of the students ('inputs'). It is at the input stage of the MBS in IEM programme that many of the needs of the workplace can be accounted for and accommodated in the content, teaching and delivery process. As most student groups are heterogeneous in nature, characterised by different levels of subject-specific knowledge and career aspirations, the completion of an 'entry questionnaire' or 'entrepreneurial self-assessment questionnaire' by students is a useful mechanism to assess the requirements of the group and the commonalities between the various groups.

The detail obtained from these questionnaires provides baseline data on which to design more relevant content and delivery methods. This is significant in the MBS in IEM programme where the students varied in terms of age, prior educational awards, work experience and experience in a small firm context, resulting in a heterogeneous student group. These characteristics influence the pace of the delivery of certain introductory subjects and also require faculty to have experience as a facilitator and have a practical understanding of the operations of a small business.

Process
Given the heterogeneous nature of the student group, emphasis was placed on how both the content and delivery addressed the skills needs of the student, and how they aligned with the needs of the external workplace that the student will enter, either as an employer or as an employee. While the process comprises two elements, content and teaching, it is important that they are integrated in order to ensure that programme objectives are achieved. Decisions on one of the stages will impact on and influence the other.

Content/subject focus
The MBS in IEM programme consists of 10 modules completed over two academic semesters (for full-time candidates) or four academic semesters (for part-time candidates)

Table 7.3   MBS in IEM description

Semester 1	Semester 2
• Establishing New Ventures • Managing Innovation and Intrapreneurship • Human Resource Management for Small Business • Internationalising Entrepreneurial Ventures • Small Business Economics	• Entrepreneurial Marketing and Research Methods • Financing International Small Businesses • International Small Business Planning/Consulting • Managing International Business Growth • Family Businesses: Generational Challenges and Growth

International Entrepreneurship Management thesis (individual piece of research completed by the student)

and a thesis which is submitted in September, see Table 7.3. The thesis is completed under the supervision of an appropriate faculty advisor.

Key topics include introducing students to the theory and practice of entrepreneurial creativity and innovation, providing an understanding of the nature of entrepreneurship and the characteristics of the entrepreneur, and the transfer of both tacit and explicit knowledge. As there is an applied emphasis throughout the programme, students are encouraged to generate a number of business ideas and develop practical options to grow existing businesses. Furthermore, topics such as international marketing, accounting and finance, and human resource management add value to the knowledge of necessary business subject areas. In addition, more-specific modules such as Family Businesses, Small Business Economics and Innovation and Intrapreneurship provide the students with an insight into a broader perspective of the small business sector. The completion of the International Entrepreneurship Management thesis provides students an opportunity to complete an individual piece of research which they have an interest in. This challenges the students' ability to blend and integrate both tacit and explicit knowledge in a defined research topic. They will also develop the skills base to encourage more enterprising behaviour and will have gained a more integrated and holistic business management perspective.

Graduates need to have soft skills such as communication, presentation and writing skills. As owner/managers, they need to be able to present themselves effectively to the business community around them, while also being capable of marketing their product potential/service to customers. Thus, students are required to make presentations, engage in problem-solving and negotiation scenarios, and participate in simulation games. The challenge for educators is to provide graduates with the relevant mix of the content focus, while ensuring that students acquire and develop the skills and competencies required to establish and manage an international business. This is achieved through the adoption of multiple flexible delivery methods in teaching.

Teaching focus
A variety of pedagogical approaches, appropriate to both the discipline and the level of the award, are employed in the delivery of the programme including taught lectures,

case studies; role playing, videos, field visits and guest speakers. Students attend formal classes and workshops which facilitate the integration of theory and practice in an applied and practical manner. The inclusion of guest lecturers, role-playing exercises, case analysis and discussion, and team assignments are fundamental aspects of the delivery methods adopted. Although Kirby (2004) found that traditional lecture-driven teaching methodologies were less relevant to entrepreneurship courses, as they may inhibit the development of entrepreneurial skills and characteristics, it is argued that there is a role for the lecturer in providing a medium for the transfer of tacit knowledge to students. Essentially the educationalist moves from the traditional 'sage on the stage' to becoming a 'guide on the side' (Hannon, 2005: 108), adopting the role of coach, mentor and challenger, while providing constructive and relevant feedback in order to facilitate the transfer of explicit knowledge.

Hannon (ibid.: 108) suggested that the need to encourage 'experiential, practice-based, action learning' and to create different learning environments and opportunities for participants is important. Furthermore, Binks (2005) suggested that the inclusion of different activities encourage 'integrative learning', that is, rich intentional learning characterised by the individual student's ability to make deep-level connections between the processes of academic learning, reflective self-awareness/personal development and experiential learning in a range of practical contexts. One such context is the owner/manager and the small firm. Through working with small firms as business consultants, students on the MBS in IEM programme are able to integrate the benefits, knowledge, realisations and understanding gained on the programme to a 'live' SME client.

The teaching process focuses on active learning, problem-based learning and discovery teaching. The active learning technique places greater emphasis on students exploring their own skills, competencies and general self-awareness levels. In the problem-based learning environment, either on their own or in teams, students assume responsibility for solving problems and making decisions which will have consequences in real-life scenarios. Discovery teaching provides students with a learning environment which will equip them with the ability to continue educating themselves throughout their career. Furthermore, role models, guest speakers and case studies are incorporated to complement the multiple teaching methods, encourage skills development such as self-efficacy confidence, initiative and problem-solving skills. Essentially, the combination of these approaches provides students with personal and career development and aids the transfer of both tacit and explicit knowledge to the students.

The combination of content and teaching focus, with an emphasis on enterprising learning modes as promoted by Gibb (1993), provides students with an understanding of the stages of the entrepreneurial process and equips them with a range of skills considered necessary by the Expert Group on Future Skills Need (EGFSN, 2007) for the workplace. The process focus combined both formal and informal teaching methods, encouraging topics such as problem solving and career planning in an interactive action-based learning environment. In essence, the pedagogical approach adopted in teaching modules on the MBS in IEM adopts these teaching methods.

As with the delivery of entrepreneurship programmes, issues arise with regard to the most appropriate means of assessing such programmes. Robertson et al. (2003) stated that assessment and examination form the basis of how well the students have utilised the time and resources available to them, to accomplish the objectives of the course studied.

Conventionally at the third level, a final examination – which is generally theory based – forms the primary component of assessment. Gibb (1996) and Henry et al. (2003) suggested that entrepreneurship education did not fit neatly into these models of assessment of the traditional examination. Assessment methods need to mirror the objectives of the entrepreneurship courses and also accommodate the different non-traditional teaching and delivery methods discussed above. The assessment method adopted for the MBS in IEM programme includes a variety of methods such as 100 per cent project-based assessment, and continuous assessments combined with an exam. Continuous assessment is by assignments, such as the completion of business growth plans, consultancy projects for small firms in the region, report writing, interviews, project work and end-of-term examinations.

Outputs
The outputs from participation in the MBS in IEM programme combine both tangible and intangible aspects. The tangible outputs are associated with the theoretical knowledge acquired, the establishment of networks or membership of professional organisations. Moreover, students have completed a growth plan for a business or a feasibility study for a proposed business idea. These documents are used for funding from government organisations, for securing venture capital funding or in the development of strategic alliances. In addition, the student acquires a number of intangible outcomes which may not be readily apparent or easily assessed but will enhance both personal and professional development. The more immediate outcomes which are more easily assessed are those relating to the improved levels of self-confidence, communication skills, report writing skills and team-working skills.

The environment for entrepreneurship education: an entrepreneurial educational institution
In developing the MBS in IEM programme, consideration was given to the physical and learning conditions that exist internally in the environment of the relevant educational establishment, and also the external general environment which will impact on the career choices available. It is important that educators and facilitators ensure that the immediate environment (learning environment) is conducive to learning. This will involve ensuring that facilities and resources are available and accessible to students. The larger external environment which includes the broader work, economic, social and technological environment needs to be understood to provide students with the necessary skills to be successful in this environment. The provision and access to resources such as the Student Enterprise Centre, a commercialisation fund, and mentors are made available to students to ensure that the MBS in IEM programme operates to the level of the expectation of the student and facilitates and supports the completion of the practical work required by students.

Summary
It is critical that entrepreneurship education is adopted in an integrated manner where interdisciplinary teams and project work are encouraged. This allows educational institutions to benefit from the expertise and synergies that can be obtained from cross-functional learning.

This integrated learning which is provided in the MBS in IEM programme will provide students with an improved awareness of the reality of working in progressive organisations, but perhaps more importantly it will provide students with the awareness, interest and preparation for self-employment as a career alternative. For education institutions to adopt this integrated approach, it is critical that faculty endorse it and are prepared to allocate resources and time to ensure that this enterprise culture is evident in their institution. It is considered that the MBS in IEM programme, when examined against the process framework of entrepreneurship education, highlights how this framework can be a useful template not only to guide programme design, but also to be an effective mechanism for evaluating programmes. The feedback provided from students highlights the positive experience of students on the MBS in IEM:

Very enlightening and appropriate module, great learning experience.

Meeting entrepreneurs and hearing from people who are actually out there doing it, is a great learning experience.

The teaching approach is completely different to what I am used to. It is much more engaging and quite thought provoking.

Each day when I go back to my own business, I think 'how can things be done differently around here'. I have a new lens for looking at my own business.

I never gave a presentation before in my life, now I am giving them on a weekly basis. My confidence has soared.

Conclusion

Entrepreneurship education in its broad sense has key strengths such as equipping graduates to contribute in different capacities to the strategic economic needs of a country. The process framework for entrepreneurship education can be modified to target graduates who will enter industry sectors where small firms are becoming increasingly important. This approach has the added advantage of the promotion of self-employment as an alternative career option for the graduate. Additionally, the framework can be applied in a transferable manner to meet industry-specific sector needs. Ultimately, entrepreneurship education should be viewed as a flexible mechanism through which important knowledge, skills and competencies can be imparted to accommodate specific industry needs.

References

Audretsch, D.B. (2002), 'Entrepreneurship: A Survey of the Literature', Prepared for the European Commission, Enterprise Directorate General, Research (CEPR), London, July.

Binks, M. (2005), 'Entrepreneurship education and integrative learning', National Council for Graduate Entrepreneurship Education (NCGE) Policy Paper, 1, July.

Birdthistle, N. (2006), *Irish Survey on Collegiate Entrepreneurship 2006* (online), www.isce.ch/PDF/ISCE06_Irish_finalised_report.pdf, 9 February 2008.

Brush, C.G., Duhaime, I.M., Gartner, W.B., Stewart, A., Katz, J.A., Hitt, M.A., Alvarez, S.A., Meyer, G.D. and Venkataraman, S. (2003), 'Doctoral education in the field of entrepreneurship', *Journal of Management*, **29** (3), 309–31.

Department for Education and Skills (DfES) (2002), *Howard Review of Enterprise and the Economy in Education*, London: DfES.

Department for Education and Skills (DfES) (2003), 'The Future of Higher Education', www.dfes.gov.uk/hegateway/uploads/white%20Pape.pdf, accessed 9 August 2006.

Expert Group on Future Skills Needs (EGFSN) (2007), 'Tomorrow's Skills: Towards a National Skills Strategy', The 5th Expert Group on Future Skills Needs Report, www.skillsireland.ie, February.

Galloway, L., Anderson, M., Brown, W. and Whittam, G. (2005), *The Impact of Entrepreneurship Education in Higher Education*, Edinburgh: Heriot-Watt University.

Galloway, L. and Brown, W. (2002), 'Entrepreneurship education at university: a driver in the creation of high growth firms', *Education and Training*, **44** (8/9), 398–408.

Gibb, A. (1993), 'The enterprise culture and education', *International Small Business Journal*, **11** (3), 11–34.

Gibb, A. (1996), 'Entrepreneurship and small business management: can we afford to neglect them in the twenty-first century business school?', *British Journal of Management*, **7**, 309–21.

Grant, R.M. (1996), 'Prospering in dynamically-competitive environments: organizational capability as knowledge integration', *Organizational Science*, **7**, (4), 375–87.

Hall, R. and Andriani, P. (2003), 'Managing knowledge associated with innovation', *Journal of Business Research*, **56**, 145–52.

Hannon, P. (2005), Philosophies of enterprise and entrepreneurship education and challenges for higher education in the UK', *International Journal*, **6** (2), 105–14.

Henry, C., Hill, F. and Leitch, C. (2003), *Entrepreneurship Education and Training*, Aldershot: Ashgate.

Hynes, B. (1996), 'Entrepreneurship education and training: introducing entrepreneurship into non-business disciplines', *Journal of European Industrial Training*, **20** (8), 10–17.

Hynes, B. and Richardson, I. (2007), 'Entrepreneurship education: a mechanism for engaging and exchanging with the small business sector', *Education and Training*, **49** (8/9), 732–44.

Hytti, U. and O'Gorman, C. (2004), 'What is enterprise education? An analysis of the objectives and methods of enterprise education programmes in four European countries', *Education and Training*, **46** (1), 11–23.

Kirby, D. (2004), 'Entrepreneurship education: can business schools meet the challenge?', paper presented at the RENT XVIII Research in Entrepreneurship and Small Business Conference, Barcelona, November.

Martin, L.M. (2004), 'Developing an international entrepreneurship programme; a work in progress', paper presented at the IEEE Conference, University of Wolverhampton, 11 June.

Martin, L.M. (2006), 'Regional innovative capacity; global trends; local needs', Keynote speech to DG Regional Policy, Committee of the Regions, Brussels, 31 March.

Muir, I. and Langford, D. (1994), 'Managerial behaviour in two small construction organizations', *International Journal of Project Management*, **12** (4), 244–53.

NCIHE (1997), 'Higher Education in the Learning Society' (The Dearing Report), National Committee of Inquiry into Higher Education, www.leeds.ac.uk/educol/ncihe, accessed 10 July 2006.

O'Dwyer, M. and O'Flynn, E. (2005), 'MNC–SME strategic alliances: a model framing knowledge as the primary predictor of governance modal choice', *Journal of International Management*, **11**, 397–416.

O'Gorman, C., Bourke, S. and Murray, J.A. (2005), 'The nature of managerial work in small growth-oriented small businesses', *Small Business Economics*, **25** (1), 1–16.

Revenue Commissioners Statistical Unit (2003), *Annual Report 2003*, Dublin.

Robertson, M., Collins, A., Wilson, K. and Lyewllyn, D. (2003), 'Embedding entrepreneurial studies across the curriculum paper', paper presented at the 26th National Institute for Small Business and Entrepreneurship Conference: SMEs in the Knowledge Economy, Surrey, UK, November.

8 Building an entrepreneurial university: a case study using a new venture development approach

K. Mark Weaver, Robert D'Intino, DeMond Miller and Edward J. Schoen

Introduction: development of a new venture model

The purpose of this chapter is to present a model representing a new venture approach to building an entrepreneurial focus for a university. The model builds on core business development factors and describes how the support and cooperation of the leadership of a university help to create the necessary conditions to introduce a new program and university focus on entrepreneurship.

Rowan University (Glassboro, NJ) is the model discussed in this chapter. University leadership (president, provost, deans of Business and Engineering) and the College of Business's entrepreneurship chair recognized that an entrepreneurial focus with an interdisciplinary approach is one desirable way to build its competitive advantage. They acknowledged the need for an entrepreneurship program that integrates the best parts of the university into a long-term plan to capitalize on existing opportunities and create an environment that foments new opportunities.

The adoption of a new venture development model provides the necessary first steps towards achieving the goal of building an entrepreneurial university. The model considers the needs, motivations, resource availability, implementation and product extensions needed to create an approach to university decision making that is consistent with venture feasibility approaches.

Need for an entrepreneurial focus

Many view the next major stage in the evolution of the US economy as the intensification and escalation of entrepreneurial efforts. Moving from an agrarian enterprise to an industrial and then a service economy, and the subsequent dependence on technology to supplant the labor force means an increased emphasis on intellectual property development and concomitant goods or services. Entrepreneurship appears to be the next threshold for the American economy (Aldrich and Ruef, 2006) to maximize fully the business advances and tools available to individuals (Shane, 2003) and, in particular, to early twenty-first century students. Perhaps a realization of business development and enhancement demonstrates that a comprehensive university has also evolved, one that cultivates students who no longer only seek employment but who also seek how to employ others. The provost of the case study university considered the development of an entrepreneurial minor available to business majors as an 'early stage product' to be followed by a more focused concentration that would be available to all majors. Such a concentration would provide students from majors across the campus with opportunities to apply knowledge and skills gained within their discipline to learning entrepreneurial perspectives and gaining opportunities to solve problems through the creation of new product and service ventures.

Rowan University is one of four public colleges and universities located in South Jersey: two are liberal arts colleges with Rutgers-Camden and Rowan University as the only comprehensive post-secondary institutions in the area. These institutions compete for the best and the brightest students graduating from New Jersey's high schools. A focus on entrepreneurial studies was viewed by the institution's leadership as an attractive approach to increasing the uniqueness of the academic program and thus, the institution's competitiveness with regard to the enrollment of academically talented students from the region.

In addition to giving the university a competitive edge, the university identified entrepreneurial development as a core part of a long-term strategy to improve the region for all individuals living in Southern New Jersey. South Jersey has not enjoyed the surge in development of high-tech enterprises experienced in North Jersey or Southeastern Pennsylvania and its economy has suffered as a result. The development of the South Jersey Technology Park (SJTP), located at the university, is one element of addressing the region's needs for growing businesses and job creation. The mission of this unique high-tech community is to foster the development of advanced methods of research; commercialize ideas and products; and facilitate technology transfer, education and entrepreneurship in the fields of engineering, the sciences, computer science and business. The ultimate goal of this initiative is to develop an engine to drive significant economic development in the region.

Motivations for forming new initiatives and programs
Successful entrepreneurs have the ability and willingness to recognize and capitalize on opportunities (Venkataraman, 1997; Corbett, 2007). Because that ability transcends one's academic discipline and because opportunities arise in virtually all fields, the chance to develop and apply entrepreneurial skills must be offered to all interested students, regardless of their field of study. Shane (2000) pointed out that a variety of knowledge from different disciplines can help develop the opportunity recognition process. The guidelines for developing new academic programs are similar to the steps followed in developing a new service. At Rowan University, a program or minor proposal must fulfill specific requirements such as demonstrating market demands, sufficient resources to support the program, essential quality, and coherence of the curriculum. In addition, one key strategic objective within the university's Five-Year Plan: 2002–07, offered a very real motivation to develop such a program: 'proposed new programs will be evaluated on the extent to which they will serve to enhance the reputation and quality of the University or existing programs'. Over the past five years, the university has risen steadily in the recognition of its academic quality as measured by such indicators as scholarly aptitude test (SAT) scores, class rank of entering freshmen, and the university's rankings in such periodicals as the *US News & World Report*.

Rowan University elected to employ the project-based learning (PBL) model in the campus-wide implementation of its entrepreneurship program (described more fully in the PBL section). In product development terminology, a new service/product (the academic program) is more likely to succeed when there exists an efficient business model that not only gives customers (students) what they want, but also affects a positive response for the organization (the university). For the entrepreneurship concentration, the ideal vehicle is the venture- or project-based learning model, through which students from multiple disciplines work together in teams to assess opportunities and to develop plans necessary to convert the opportunity into successful enterprises. As an example of this approach, two engineering students, in collaboration with business students, developed an attachment to permit snowboarders to ride traditional ski lifts more comfortably. Collectively, the group determined the potential demand for and price of the product, developed financial projections for the production and distribution of the product and selected the optimal type of material for production.

In order to motivate key actors, a cohesive approach was used with many disparate units, and the entrepreneurship program was developed in several general stages:

- perform a review of courses included in successful entrepreneurship programs across the globe;
- determine the manner in which those subject areas could be taught on a project basis;
- develop a project-based entrepreneurship specialization (including curriculum and ancillary activities) for business students;
- ascertain how the entrepreneurship curriculum could be offered to non-business students and how course prerequisite obstacles could be overcome;
- develop a pilot project with the College of Engineering;
- build interest and develop 'champions' in the other university colleges and departments through entrepreneurship boot camps;
- obtain the support of the other college deans; and
- obtain the support of interested faculty throughout the campus.

One of the most challenging new service/product features to establish was the prerequisite course portion of the product mix (discussed in a later section). In this case, the proposed new 'product' was a combination of nine courses that did not require any business prerequisites for non-business majors. This heresy was based on the principle that an additive model of learning as opposed to a duplicative model should be developed. In accordance with university regulations, the new academic program required acceptance by multiple university committees through many review processes without student input, an undertaking much like the new product approval process in a company wherein a new development is reviewed and approved by a technology committee, even if the new product is clearly more functional for end users.

The university provost provided leadership and support in establishing this program which included: providing an opportunity for the endowed chair/professor to discuss the merits of the entrepreneurial concentration with the deans of all colleges; placing the proposal on the Board of Trustees Academic Affairs Agenda for a full discussion; supporting the program's approval in numerous venues; and deliberating with the university Senate to effect changes in the general education program to make it far more flexible and reduce the number of required courses. This change, in particular, made entrepreneurship education a reality for students pursuing majors in the other colleges.

Marshalling the resources to create the entrepreneurial focus

The resource issue is a common barrier that many new ventures cannot overcome, primarily due to the lack of a broad view of the available resources. Finding and properly using the human, physical and financial resources are critical requirements to build a venture for success. The university took a broad view of resource availability by evaluating the physical, financial and human resources at their disposal. The coalescence of several significant events during the 2000–02 academic year helped form the resource base for a university-wide entrepreneurship program. First, the university embarked on a successful effort to purchase/acquire options to buy nearly 600 acres of property strategically located adjacent to campus and with excellent major highway access to the Philadelphia International Airport, Philadelphia, Camden, Trenton, Washington DC and New York City. This land provided the future physical space for the South Jersey Technology Center, in addition to providing space for new academic buildings that would allow the university to grow significantly.

Second, the New Jersey Economic Development Authority awarded the university a $6 million grant to construct the South Jersey Technology Center, the only high-tech center in the seven southern counties of the state. The Technology Center was envisioned as a site for companies to pursue the commercialization of products they have created, to provide faculty and students the space to conduct more federal- and state-funded research projects, to provide additional laboratories to permit the College of Engineering to expand its interdisciplinary, project-based curriculum, and to house a business incubator under the auspices of the College of Business for emerging, technology-related companies. Capital infusion is a key aspect of the resources that are required to move toward the goal of an entrepreneurial university.

Third, the College of Engineering, gaining a national reputation for its innovative, interdisciplinary project-based undergraduate curriculum and having graduated its first class in May 2000, received ABET (Accreditation Board for Engineering and Technology, www.abet.org) accreditation and was positioned to expand its outreach efforts to the regional business community. This accreditation was instrumental in attracting faculty, students and the financial resources needed to move the entrepreneurial efforts forward.

Fourth, the Colleges of Engineering and Business agreed to combine their expertise to offer South Jersey manufacturing and businesses a set of unique services that unite management expertise with engineering research and development. Under this agreement, the College of Engineering provided technical assistance with projects ranging from developing a new product to revising a process or applying new technology. Existing companies or entrepreneurs gained access to specialized training and expert assistance by working on their project with Rowan faculty and engineering students in state-of-the-art facilities. The Management Institute, which served as the training division of the College of Business for the past 25 years and which has recently been moved into the newly created College of Professional and Continuing Education to consolidate those services throughout the university, trains employees in areas such as designing the manufacturing environment, quality controls, lean manufacturing, and six sigma (Pyzdek, 2003), and assists companies in applying for training funds to improve employee skills, successfully obtained over $5 million for training from the New Jersey Department of Labor over the past five years. The cooperation of these different units of the university provided both human resources and financial support for innovative projects.

Fifth, business students worked with the engineering students to make sure that there is a focus on the market for the project. The cooperation of these different units of the university provides both human resources and financial support for innovative projects.

And sixth, another key resource issue that confronted the entrepreneurship program was determining where to position the resources, similar to the situation confronted by new ventures when deciding how to allocate the often limited funding. In 2001, the provost initiated a review of the 18 centers and institutes at the university to evaluate their fiscal viability and internal business controls and their centrality to the university's mission. The provost charged the directors of existing centers to develop guidelines regarding the development, review, continuance and/or dissolution of centers and institutes.

The university had been subsidizing the centers and institutes at a cost of about $2 million per year. This funding included release time/adjunct replacement for tenured faculty, salaries for staff, operational expenses and overhead. Given a mid-year decrease in state appropriations in 2001 and an expectation of further decreases in 2002–03, it was essential to determine the impact of existing centers and institutes in supporting the university's fulfillment of its mission as well as their fiscal viability. A review of account balances showed a number of centers and institutes with deficit spending. Four centers and institutes were closed or tabled, with a non-renewal of some personnel contracts, which produced a saving of funds for diminished university resources. The approved guidelines differentiated among centers/institutes that were completely self-sufficient or partially supported by the university. All were required to break even or generate revenue and demonstrate a centrality to the university's mission. Each unit was expected to provide indirect costs toward such overhead expenses as space, bookkeeping and utilities, with funds generated from external grants and contracts where appropriate.

The Center for Innovation and Entrepreneurship (CIE), a proposed centerpiece of the new entrepreneurial focus, was required to fulfill all of the new guidelines developed by the provost. The chair demonstrated a capacity to generate revenue from external grants, and the dean of the Business College made the hiring of additional entrepreneurship faculty a priority in the college's faculty-staffing plan. Moreover, by conducting boot camps with faculty and academic administrators across the university, the endowed chair/professor attained support for the entrepreneurial focus; that is, he had demonstrated that such a center could serve all students and faculty. In addition, undergraduate interns from the concentration would serve companies in the region directly from the new center and the new Technology Center. Their support of local businesses would serve to increase the university's reputation as a contributor to the economic well-being of the state. Because the CIE met the self-supporting model required by the provost, the CIE was viewed as an entrepreneurial venture within the entrepreneurial university, and thus led to its inclusion in the implementation plan.

Developing an implementation plan
The university recognized that the expansion of the campus, the creation of the Technology Center and Business Incubator and the partnership between the College of Business and the College of Engineering provided a unique opportunity to promote significant economic growth in the region by helping develop businesses, create jobs and transform new technologies into commercial enterprises. The university also understood that entrepreneurship education would have to transcend all six colleges of the

university: Business, Communication, Education, Engineering, Fine and Performing Arts, and Liberal Arts and Sciences. The Rohrer Professor of Entrepreneurial Studies was a resource that could help develop the interdisciplinary linkages required to succeed in building the entrepreneurial university model.

A critical component of developing the university-wide entrepreneurship program was routinely consulting with the Rohrer Professor of Entrepreneurial Studies, who apprised important constituencies of the development of the entrepreneurship program. The chair met once each semester with the College Deans' Council to promote the participation of non-business faculty in various entrepreneurial events, advise the deans of the project proposals developed in the boot camps, to update the deans on the development of the entrepreneurship specialization and to invite the participation of the other colleges by promoting entrepreneurship education as a potential concentration within diverse academic programs. A new technology entrepreneurship certificate program was the first to be developed from this process, and progress has been made on similar certificate programs for other colleges.

In addition, encouraged by the dean, the chair assisted faculty in the other colleges in developing and submitting grant proposals to support various economic development projects in South Jersey, worked with the president's office to develop proposals for financial support from the local congressional delegation of economic development projects, and engaged in outreach efforts to regional business organizations (Chamber of Commerce of Southern New Jersey, Delaware River Port Authority and Philadelphia Entrepreneurs Forum) to obtain support for entrepreneurship initiatives that would be based at the university.

New product extensions to the entrepreneurial university model
Having developed the internal bridging and linkages that were critical to fostering an entrepreneurial environment within the university, the next phase of the development is to identify core competencies and areas of competitive advantage within the South Jersey region. Burke (2002) recommends that universities' planning changes need to become more connected to their external environment. An analysis of current and potential university stakeholders can identify future outreach partners and consulting clients.

A key component of this extension effort was the formation of the Entrepreneurial Forum of Southern New Jersey (EFSNJ, www.efsnj.org) to promote entrepreneurial innovation and business growth in the South Jersey region. The following are examples of how the Forum and outreach efforts were seeds for growing new programs:

1. *Camden/Parkside Project*: Assisted Camden/Parkside area to focus on business development, skills development and job creation.
2. *Echelon Mall Evaluation Project*: Provided the information and tools to assist the Township and Economic Development Committee in evaluating alternative redevelopment approaches for the mall and the surrounding business zone.
3. *Haddon Heights Business and Professional Association*: Facilitated the development of a strategic plan and assisted in successful grant developments for enhancement and restoration of the Station Avenue shopping zone, resulting in a grant for $250,000 for streetscape and beautification.

4. *Harrison Township Economic Development Council*: Engaged in the initial stages of development of a long-term strategic planning model for Harrison Township.
5. *Extension of the boot camp model*: Conducted boot camps to introduce educators to entrepreneurial concepts that can make their research and teaching more effective, increases their cooperation in economic development efforts and demonstrates how they can gain professionally/financially through participation of the SJTP and Incubator. Support of the State of New Jersey and local legislators increased as the outreach efforts increased and helped secure funding for the Incubator and the Technology Park's first building.

A second component in extending the new venture model was creating academic opportunities that expanded the market for the Center's programs. Two key areas were included: the creation of the general education course and the movement to a project-based learning model.

Creation of a general education course
The goal of increasing access to entrepreneurship education for students from a broad range of fields was advanced significantly by the university's decision to place a course entitled Entrepreneurship and Innovation (E&I) under the 'general education' umbrella. This decision was based on a combination of pragmatism, sound pedagogy, and perceived benefit to the university.

Students pursuing non-business majors were offered access to the entrepreneurship program through the E&I course, which was listed as a social and behavioral science course with general education status. Other universities have developed programs to link entrepreneurship with liberal arts, but general education status for entrepreneurial courses is a comparatively rare and groundbreaking phenomenon. The successful case for conferring general education status on the E&I introduction course draws upon analyses undertaken by the Association of American Colleges and Universities and the Carnegie Foundation for the Advancement of Teaching. This analysis addresses gaps in general education and liberal arts courses. Traditional general education courses typically stand as the introductory courses for liberal arts majors and as such are understandably less likely to facilitate the cross-pollination of ideas across disciplines. In contrast, by emphasizing integrative learning, the E&I course is inherently multidisciplinary and has the integration of concepts from divergent sources as its subject focus.

Offering the E&I course to afforded non-business students, irrespective of major, provides students with a chance to develop their entrepreneurial talents. There is ample evidence based on career surveys that indicates that significant numbers of students from non-business disciplines and diverse career paths are likely to be self-employed in the future. For example, self-employment figures include:

*   12.5 percent of geoscientists (Farr and Shankin, 2004);
*   40 percent of music majors (ibid.);
*   13 percent of psychology graduates (ibid.);
*   11 percent of economists (BLS, 2004);
*   one-third of writers and authors (ibid.); and
*   over half of all artists and related workers (Farr and Shankin, 2004).

The E&I course content addresses six traditional concerns of entrepreneurship courses reframed for an audience of non-business students:

- *Entrepreneurship domain* Entrepreneurship occurs in small business, high-technology–high-innovation environments, corporate environments, social enterprises and international enterprises.
- *Entrepreneurial thinking*   Emphasizes thinking about understanding and developing opportunities.
- *Problem solving* Offers an overview of strategic and scenario planning that introduces students to means of developing strategy, scenarios, tactics, tools, skills and requisite timing to execute plans.
- *Creativity*   Underscores the importance of creativity by validating the proposition that creativity can be learned and clarifies the underlying logic, specific knowledge, tools and skills for achieving creativity.
- *Opportunity recognition*   Illustrates the importance of perception, including new ways of seeing and hearing in order to discover and create unique opportunities.
- *Entrepreneurial careers*   Expands the student's appreciation for the multiplicity of venues and circumstances to which the entrepreneurial process can be applied.

The student's initial encounter with the discipline reveals the convergence of the generative creative process and the entrepreneur's innovation response. It does so in the context of the student's effort to plan his or her life work and future career. Students who test the waters of this new curriculum are immersed in a learning experience that conveys unmistakably the essential character and multiple forms of entrepreneurial pursuits.

Key student learning outcomes include:

- understanding the essentials of entrepreneurship;
- learning how to use the motivations, skills and strategies of successful entrepreneurs;
- developing decision-making knowledge and skills;
- developing creativity and innovation knowledge and skills; and
- learning opportunity recognition for new products, services, and customers.

From the conception of the E&I course, designers were clear that conventional didactic pedagogy was not likely to stimulate a wide range of students with dissimilar interests to accomplish the course's ambitious learning objectives. Rather, the use of original and inventive learning exercises would be central to teaching methodology. Learning activities and resources draw upon authors specializing in creativity such as James Adams (*Conceptual Blockbusting*, 1986), Michael Gelb (*How to Think Like Leonardo da Vinci*, 1998), Chic Thompson (*What a Great Idea!*, 1992), Roger von Oech (*A Whack on the Side of the Head*, 1990) and of course, Edward de Bono (for example, *Lateral Thinking*, 1970 and *Serious Creativity*, 1992). This type of pedagogy relies upon helping to change the way students perceive, analyze and approach problems, problem solving and opportunity recognition.

Chief among the extrinsic benefits was sensitivity to the need to improve continuously the metrics by which university and individual programs are measured. In an era of heightened concern about the time it takes to fulfill graduation requirements, the ability to include such a course among general education distribution requirements adds flexibility. Another benefit may be an increase in student retention and graduation rates across programs. Curricular flexibility in defining courses that can be included under the general education tent would place more attention on satisfaction of persistence-related needs and student competencies. The addition of even one course focusing on the application of entrepreneurial knowledge to liberal studies is a critical strategy to improve job placement rates after graduation and respond to the need to prepare students for a more flexible, self-controlled career path.

Knowing one has support for a concept does not ensure that one can effectively navigate the gauntlet of university curriculum approval. There are at least six secrets to making the case that entrepreneurship belongs in general education:

- The first key to success is to focus on the universal and generic underpinnings of entrepreneurship and to remain free of traditional business school biases toward the for-profit sector over other contexts.
- The second key to success is to make an unambiguous case for the goodness of fit between the E&I course content and outcomes and the currently accepted general education cannon.
- A third factor that can effect approval is the proposal's use of the appropriate pedagogy and an appreciation for the learning theory that guides instructional techniques.
- Fourth, preliminary and judicious diplomacy were required. The CIE reached out and provided support and technical assistance to other areas of the university, local economic development councils and non-profit organizations to generate non-traditional support.
- Fifth, munificent efforts to create good will and a positive image for entrepreneurial courses and the CIE were seen as essential to success.
- Sixth, a series of initiatives to attract champions outside the College of Business to generate the required faculty support was undertaken.

Other campuses seeking to incorporate entrepreneurship into their curriculum can correctly argue that entrepreneurship energizes and revitalizes a general education program, because it emphasizes creativity and innovation and focuses on integrative learning to pull together the various styles or modes of thinking in a range of subjects. It also can provide a path to enhancing student career prospects by addressing entrepreneurial alternatives. As noted above, students are increasingly choosing self-employment, business creation and entrepreneurial careers within established organizations. Nonetheless, securing campus support for designating entrepreneurship a general education course within the social and behavioral sciences bank of the model was not an overnight phenomenon. Rather, the multiple success measures employed by the authors led to implementation of the course and success in enrollment.

Student project-based learning approach
PBL involves student learning with live-client projects in contrast to more defined problem-based learning. PBL often involves building a product or solving a specific course-related problem. The design of a PBL course engages students in actual complicated client

projects, which motivates students to learn more effectively through working on more complex tasks (Blumenfeld et al., 1991). We note that two popular variations exist within PBL. Student management consulting projects, generally offered in business schools, perform a management consulting engagement (Block, 1999) with a live client from a business, government, or non-profit organization. Student service learning (Kenworthy-U'ren and Peterson, 2005; Papamarcos, 2005) approaches are very similar, except that service learning projects are usually performed for non-profit or government clients and have a focus on teaching students to become more involved in civic life and their communities.

From the perspective of a professor designing the specific components and tasks of a PBL course, there is little difference between business school consulting courses and service learning courses. We distinguish the following four closely related learning approaches to situate PBL in the broad education field of experiential learning:

- *Problem-based learning*   Individual students evaluate the project, make a diagnosis, design a problem-solving approach, collect data and perform analysis to solve problems or build products. During this process, students learn specific skills and challenge their abilities. Often used in medical and engineering courses.
- *Management consulting projects*   Student teams engage in management consulting projects for business, government, or non-profit organ clients. A business management approach is brought to the client and the consulting project.
- *Service learning*   Individual or student teams engage with non-profit or government clients to solve problems and complete projects for live clients. A more civic engagement and service perspective is brought to the client and the consulting project.
- *Project-based learning*   Student collaborative teams meet with a client, define the project, design an approach, collect data, perform analysis, and make written and oral recommendations to their client to complete their projects. Experiential learning is emphasized during the course, with a reciprocal relationship between course knowledge and project learning. A PBL project can be designed as a component within an undergraduate or graduate course.

For this chapter, we use the term PBL to include student consulting projects and service learning projects as part of the PBL model. Two PBL components include: a client need or project, while student outcomes include a final student team-written report and oral presentation.

University examples of students learning with PBL
A PBL approach is used by college and university professors from many academic disciplines. This subsection will briefly describe various examples of PBL learning by students studying science and engineering, medical and legal education, graphic arts, liberal arts, social science courses, research methods and business and entrepreneurship education.

PBL is popular with introductory electrical engineering courses (Valim et al., 2006); civil engineering professors and students (Chinowsky et al., 2006); NASA engineering management courses (Kotnour and Vergopia, 2005); environmental engineering courses (Van Der Vorst, 1996); and chemical engineering (Newell et al., 1999, 2001). PBL components are also included as part of undergraduate physics and chemistry courses.

Using PBL provides the following three positive outcomes: first, increased student retention through more focus on student needs and competencies; second, development of critical thinking skills are learned as students work on projects; and third, preparation of students for a more flexible and self-controlling career path.

PBL approaches are also presented in courses teaching computer graphics (Marti et al., 2006); environmental sociology; research methods (Chinowsky et al., 2006); and interdisciplinary projects in international settings (Vaz, 2000). Numerous other academic disciplines are also using PBL educational approaches in their courses.

Within university business and entrepreneurship courses and degree programs, individual students learn using a combination of their own personal cognitive efforts in conjunction with the instruction of their business and entrepreneurship professors and the learning that takes place in interactions with their class members.

Rasmussen and Sorheim (2006) reported the results of PBL in five Swedish universities with a focus on entrepreneurship education. They found that students increased both motivation and the competence to manage projects through experiences with PBL courses. Okudan and Rzasa (2006) described an entrepreneurial leadership course in a Pennsylvania university with very positive outcomes. All of their student teams using PBL completed their assignments to manufacture products and sell them for a profit. Regarding student motivation, they reported that some students who did not graduate that term decided to enroll in their university entrepreneurship minor.

A boot camp approach to introduce university faculty to PBL

We propose that PBL will more effectively prepare students for entrepreneurship careers and future leadership roles in society because PBL has been a longstanding proven educational approach that requires students to solve problems, and promote active learning, critical thinking, analytical decision making, consideration of multiple points of view, research and summarizing skills, intellectual growth and team learning. PBL fits well in established business entrepreneurship courses, as well as the newer social entrepreneurship and environmental entrepreneurship courses currently offered at an increasing number of colleges and universities.

The unresolved question for introducing PBL approaches into university courses is how to prepare the professor for a new, more complex set of challenges and opportunities. One successful solution to introduce an entrepreneurship focus throughout the university is to offer faculty PBL boot camps to prepare faculty to design and manage PBL components in their regular course curriculum.

Faculty PBL boot camps get interested faculty to buy into a PBL educational approach and resolve multiple questions about learning philosophies, goals, methods, evaluations and assessment measures, and outcomes. Well-designed PBL boot camps for faculty demonstrate how PBL moves students outside their classroom and into the larger world of business and other organizations and provides many benefits for students, faculty, their colleges and their communities. A PBL boot camp can share information across academic disciplines, create 'win' opportunities for faculty and condense the preparation time for faculty to introduce PBL into their courses. The boot camps teach faculty how to help students learn to integrate their textbook and course learning with actual problems and projects and in the process discover how to use their newfound knowledge, skills and abilities to make a difference in the world.

A PBL boot camp illustration

A representative two-day (12-hour) faculty boot camp would include the following topics:

- introduce the goals of PBL;
- describe the learning theory foundations of PBL;
- introduce service learning and business consulting theory and best practices;
- understand client ethics and disclosure documents;
- learn how to locate and identify good projects for successful win–win conclusions for students, clients, and faculty;
- evaluate whether a project can be completed in one term;
- learn to manage unprepared clients;
- prepare students to act in a professional business manner;
- build and sustain field contacts; and
- provide a 'train-the-trainer' collaborative learning experience for faculty participants.

The boot camp introduces theory, information, and resources to help make the faculty's job easier when managing projects with student teams. The sequence presented includes who, what, where, when, why, and how, and essentially shows how the faculty member can best manage project-based education and learning within his or her current courses and time constraints.

The faculty boot camp subjects include:

- problem solving;
- consulting;
- service learning;
- project design, recommendation, and implementation; and
- project feedback and review.

Student learning from engaging in courses with PBL include:

- functioning well in multidisciplinary project teams;
- identifying, formulating and solving problems;
- communicating more effectively to both technical and general audiences; and
- using conceptual and analytical problem-solving tools.

Three books are suggested for inclusion in a PBL boot camp: *Flawless Consulting* (1999) by Peter Block; *High-Impact Consulting* (2002) by Robert H. Schaffer; and *The Performance Consultant's Fieldbook* (2006) by Judith Hale, along with other print and media resources.

A coaching perspective is presented in the context of student learning made within university term-time constraints with incomplete information and data. Faculty members must understand that they will have many opportunities to teach and coach as students work to complete their projects. PBL is presented in a broad organizational context because clients can include local business firms, new entrepreneurs, non-profits, college and government departments and social entrepreneurs and their social enterprises.

Faculty participants are asked to write down their own ideas and plans for project-based learning during the boot camp, as well as one take-away goal. The CIE served as the coordinating mechanism for the faculty PBL projects and for the university's economic development outreach initiatives. The 'so what?' for the workshop is to help participants better understand and manage their own student projects to foster project-based learning. By the conclusion of a boot camp, faculty should be able to:

- understand the concept of PBL and consulting;
- understand project development and management ideas and goals;
- learn about skills and resources to help manage consulting projects;
- gather momentum for new course projects;
- work on new PBL initiatives for a future course; and
- develop an action program for future implementation.

Outcomes of faculty PBL boot camp learning
We have learned through our PBL teaching experiences to take a more nuanced approach to PBL than through traditional management consulting or service learning projects. A major faculty concern is how to include a PBL component in a course while still covering the major subject content. One challenge that emerged from our experience presenting three faculty boot camps was learning how to design and manage 'smaller' projects that may constitute only 15–20 percent of the total course evaluation instead of 50–100 percent in a more traditional consulting or service learning course. Much more work will be required to fine-tune this more nuanced perspective on PBL and provide a way for many more professors to include PBL in their courses.

PBL is also an answer to questions involving US national concern about how to educate students to apply their formal knowledge to address multistep complex problems and learn how to complete business and social projects. College graduates who have successfully completed PBL projects early in their lives will have the skills and competence to contribute to their work organizations and their communities. PBL is becoming an important educational approach to help faculty improve student outcomes. This chapter provides learning theory and practice to help faculty better understand the promise and potential of PBL to provide many benefits for students, faculty, colleges and communities.

Summary and conclusions
Rowan University made commitments to the entrepreneurial university model through its decisions related to: securing funding, inclusion in the university's 10-year strategic plan, hiring the entrepreneurial chair, including the chair in the meetings of top-level decision makers, supporting the formation of the Center for Innovation and Entrepreneurship, assisting in developing the new Technology Commercialization Center and Incubator, agreeing to host the Entrepreneurial Forum of South Jersey and in the leadership's willingness to foment change within traditional university practices. Additionally, key leaders assisted the new chair in breaking through traditional barriers while maintaining the core set of governance guidelines while assuring a quality education.

Universities attempting such an approach must recognize that the entrepreneurial university is not one that begins with significant technology licensing programs, or a nationally known entrepreneurship program or a new marketing slogan. Infusing the entrepreneurial focus into all parts of a university requires the ability to develop discipline-specific champions who can show, for example, what an entrepreneurial art professor or student looks like, how the students will benefit, how the region will gain on the economic development front and how the initiative's funding sources benefit from their venture investment.

Success lessons learned
- A leadership team of university faculty and administrator influencers and champions is critically important for successfully creating an entrepreneurial university environment.
- A supportive campus environment for entrepreneurship education can be built step by step following the plan described in this chapter.
- A new venture development approach can be applied to a university campus environment.
- The motivation and anticipated goals to be achieved by becoming an entrepreneurial university should be clearly stated.
- New entrepreneurial initiatives and programs building on a university's internal strengths and resources should be planned; for example, a favorable geographical location or specific academic disciplines.
- Building entrepreneurial initiatives and programs should be linked with regional economic development and creating of high-paying jobs.
- Entrepreneurial courses and academic programs should be infused with a project-based student learning approach.
- Courses and projects should be designed with multidisciplinary student and faculty teams.
- An entrepreneurial university should be created through marshalling all the creativity and flexibility that would be needed to create any new innovative venture.

Conclusion
The combination of a supportive environment and the introduction of the no-prerequisites policy with a project-based learning model combined to create an environment for growth and sustainability of a broadly defined entrepreneurial program. The additive model of learning discussed previously was a key underlying philosophy among the faculty and administrators that helped develop the Rowan model. Together, a general education course championed from the bottom up, a no-prerequisites policy for non-business students and the formation of multidisciplinary teams of students and faculty created extremely valuable learning experiences for Rowan University students as well as to create value in the economic development efforts of the university.

Others considering such a model must create champions external to the College of Business and recognize that bright students, working with other bright students, can create a whole that is more than the sum of the parts. Rowan University is unlikely to return to the more traditional model; as faculty come and go, the hope is that the university community's passion and commitment to an entrepreneurial university model that recognizes value in differences will spread to other universities.

Bibliography

Adams, J.L. (1986), *Conceptual Blockbusting: A Guide to Better Ideas*, Reading, MA: Addison-Wesley.

Aldrich, H.E. and Ruef, M. (2006), *Organizations Evolving*, 2nd edn, Thousand Oaks, CA: Sage.

Block, P. (1999), *Flawless Consulting: A Guide to Getting Your Expertise Used*, 2nd edn, San Francisco, CA: Pfeiffer.

Blumenfeld, P.C., Soloway, E., Marx, R.W., Krajcik, M.G. and Palincsar, A. (1991), 'Motivating project-based learning: sustaining the doing, supporting the learning', *Educational Psychologist*, **26** (3&4): 369.

Bureau of Labor Statistics (BLS), US Department of Labor (2004), *Occupational Outlook Handbook, 2004–05 Edition*, Economists, www.bls.gov/oco/ocos055.htm; Writers and Editors, www.bls.gov/oco/ocos089.htm, 9 August 2004.

Burke, W.W. (2002), *Organization Change: Theory and Practice*, Thousand Oaks, CA: Sage.

Chinowsky, P.S., Brown, H., Szajnman, A. and Realph, A. (2006), 'Developing knowledge landscapes through project-based learning', *Journal of Professional Issues in Engineering Education and Practice*, **132** (2): 118–24.

Corbett, A.C. (2007), 'Learning asymmetries and the discovery of entrepreneurial opportunities', *Journal of Business Venturing*, **22**: 97–118.

De Bono, E. (1970), *Lateral Thinking: Creativity Step by Step*, New York: Harper & Row.

De Bono, E. (1992), *Serious Creativity*, New York: HarperBusiness.

Farr, M. and Shankin, L. (2004), *Best Jobs for the 21st Century*, 3rd edn, Indianapolis, IN: JIST Works.

Gelb, M.J. (1998), *How to Think Like Leonardo da Vinci*, New York: Delacorte Press.

Hale, J. (2006), *The Performance Consultant's Fieldbook: Tools and Techniques for Improving Organizations and People*, 2nd edn, San Francisco, CA: Pfeiffer.

Kenworthy-U'ren, A.L. and Peterson, T.O. (2005), 'Service-learning and management education: introducing the 'WE CARE' approach', *Academy of Management Learning and Education*, **4** (3): 325–35.

Kotnour, T. and Vergopia, C. (2005), 'Learning-based project reviews: observations and lessons learned from the Kennedy Space Center', *Engineering Management Journal*, **17** (4): 30–38.

Marti, E., Gil, D. and Julia, C. (2006), 'A PBL experience in the teaching of computer graphics', *Computer Graphics Forum*, **25** (1): 95–103.

Newell, J.A., Farrell, S.H., Hesketh, R.P. and Slater, C.S. (2001), 'Introducing emerging technologies into the curriculum through a multidisciplinary research experience', *Chemical Engineering Education*, **35** (4): 296–9.

Newell, J.A., Marchese, A.J., Ramachandran, R.P., Sukumaran, B. and Harvey, R. (1999), 'Multi-disciplinary design and communication: a pedagogical vision', *International Journal of Engineering Education*, **15** (5): 376–82.

Okudan, G. E. and Rzasa, S.E. (2006), 'A project-based approach to entrepreneurial leadership education', *Technovation*, **26** (2): 195–210.

Papamarcos, S.D. (2005), 'Giving traction to management theory: today's service-learning', *Academy of Management Learning and Education*, **4** (3): 325–35.

Pyzdek, T. (2003), *The Six SIGMA Handbook, Revised and Expanded: The Complete Guide for Greenbelts, Blackbelts, and Managers at All Levels*, 2nd edn, New York and London: McGraw-Hill.

Rasmussen, E.A. and Sorheim, R. (2006), 'Action-based entrepreneurship education', *Technovation*, **26** (2): 185–95.

Schaffer, R.H. (2002), *High-Impact Consulting: How Clients and Consultants Can Work Together to Achieve Extraordinary Results*, San Francisco, CA: John Wiley.

Shane, S. (2000), 'Prior knowledge and the discovery of entrepreneurial opportunities', *Organization Science*, **11** (4): 448–69.

Shane, S. (2003), *A General Theory of Entrepreneurship: The Individual–Opportunity Nexus*, Cheltenham, UK and Northampton, MA, USA: Edward Elgar.

Thompson, C.C. (1992), *What a Great Idea!*, New York: HarperPerennial.

Valim, M.B.R., Fariness, J.-M. and Cury, J.E.R. (2006), 'Practicing engineering in a freshman introductory course', *IEEE Transactions in Education*, **49** (1): 74–9.

Van Der Vorst, R. (1996), 'The local company project: involving local companies in undergraduate environmental engineering', *European Journal of Engineering Education*, **21** (2): 161–8.

Vaz, R.F. (2000), 'Connected learning', *Liberal Education*, **86** (1): 24–31.

Venkataraman, S. (1997), 'The distinctive domain of entrepreneurial research', in J.A. Katz (ed.), *Advances in Entrepreneurship, Firm Emergence, and Growth*, Vol. 3, Greenwich, CT: JAI Press, pp. 119–38.

Von Oech, R. (1990), *A Whack on the Side of the Head*, New York: Warner Books.

9 Teaching entrepreneurship through science-oriented teams and projects: three case studies

Jed C. Macosko, A. Daniel Johnson and Sarah M. Yocum

Introduction

Teaching students to be entrepreneurs poses a challenge from a pedagogical perspective. For students to become entrepreneurs, they must learn how to identify and pursue opportunities that create change and result in sustainable value for society. Part of this process involves students learning factual content knowledge about how to launch a new enterprise; however, students' ability to *apply* their knowledge will largely determine whether they are successful, especially during a venture's earliest phases. So how do we best assist students in developing these *applied* thinking and problem-solving skills? Numerous studies have shown that students gain such skills more quickly when their instructor creates an 'active learning' environment that focuses specifically on developing these abilities (Halonen et al. 2002, p. 284).

In this chapter, we briefly describe the pedagogical underpinnings of active learning, list five teaching strategies that promote active learning, and provide case studies of team- and project-based classes that used science-rich problems to move students out of their comfort zones and into active acquisition of entrepreneurial skills. We believe that active learning – particularly when stimulated by science-oriented projects – allows students to develop thinking skills most essential to early-stage entrepreneurship. Moreover, we have observed that students who learn these early-stage entrepreneurial skills are more likely to pursue the later stages of the entrepreneurial process (refining the venture, performing a financial analysis, developing marketing and operational plans and so on).

How can active learning help us teach entrepreneurial skills?

Active learning is the key unifying feature of internships, service learning, and similar experiences; it is largely why students gain so much from these opportunities. Unfortunately, many instructors are ill-prepared to use active learning pedagogy in their classrooms because they were trained and feel comfortable in a passive didactic (that is, lecture-dominated) style. In such a setting the primary emphasis usually is on content acquisition; the tacit (and faulty) assumption is that thinking skills will develop on their own. Neither of these two instructional approaches (didacticism and active learning) is inherently better than the other, and both have their place in the modern college classroom. However, they are not interchangeable; at certain times one approach will achieve the instructional goals and meet students' learning needs better than the other. To understand which is more appropriate in a given situation, it is useful to step back and understand how we learn. From that perspective, we can better understand how specific teaching techniques and strategies foster active learning, and by extension, development of students' applied thinking skills.

Constructivism is the dominant model for understanding the process of human learning. It emerged from work by John Dewey, Jean Piaget, and David Ausubel, and has been confirmed by empirical research in cognitive neuroscience and behavior (Dewey 1916, p. 6; Gardiner 1994, p. 9; Taylor et al. 2002, p. 231). According to the constructivist model, thinking patterns and content knowledge cannot be transferred intact and unchanged from one person to another, because a learner is not a blank slate. Instead, as information is transmitted, the receiving learner constructs his/her own unique mental models that reflect his/her life experiences and prior knowledge. Each mental model consists of both content knowledge and the thinking process skills required to access, manipulate and apply those concepts.

The constructivist model further posits that the *process* through which learners interact with newly acquired information dramatically affects how they can access and use that information. When individuals are challenged by a cognitive problem they first attempt to solve it using their pre-existing mental models. If they are successful, new knowledge or skills they gain while working through the problem become closely associated with that one particular mental model only. This cycle of associating new content and thinking process skills with existing mental models occurs routinely and is an essential component within the overall learning process. It also is the dominant mode of learning fostered by passive, didactic instructional situations such as lecturing. However, information gained this way tends to remain highly compartmentalized and is not applied readily to other situations.

Faculty members often see the limitations of this particular learning pattern. Most college students have constructed some form of mental model that allows them to identify relevant facts, retain them for a short time and recognize correct and incorrect statements relating to those facts on a multiple choice test. It is the same mental model they used throughout high school and to take entrance exams for the college of their choice. Yet when an instructor asks students to recall a moderately complex concept from a course taken the preceding semester (or even a lecture covered by a prior exam) and apply it to a novel situation, for many students the relevant content knowledge and thinking skills are unavailable. Other students may recall the information erroneously, show significant misunderstanding of the details, or misapply the necessary skills. A few students will successfully resolve the problem, but reluctantly or with great difficulty, especially if the novel situation is complex and/or ambiguous.

The constructivist model also describes a second form of learning, which is sometimes referred to as 'deep learning'. Learners will strongly resist developing new mental models until they are faced with a question, problem or situation that all of their current mental models utterly fail to solve. Once all existing mental models have failed, students (either unconsciously or consciously) begin actively assembling new 'provisional' mental models and testing them against the current challenge. While these provisional models are in play, students are extremely receptive to new content knowledge and can master new thinking process skills very quickly. Potentially relevant content knowledge and process skills associated with *other* pre-existing mental models also can be incorporated into these new provisional mental models. Once a new mental model has been constructed that can solve the current problem satisfactorily, the other provisional models are abandoned. If this newly acquired model is used in the future to solve other problems successfully, the content knowledge and thinking skills that are part of it are reinforced and become stronger still.

In practice, faculty can foster mental model-building by consciously challenging students so that their existing mental models fail to accomplish the required task. Students who are immersed in this active learning environment are much more willing and able to solve complex questions such as the task of applying knowledge to a novel situation as discussed in the last paragraph. The central tenets of constructivism do not apply to individuals only. Argyris and Schön (1978) divide the levels of organizational learning into single- and double-loop learning, which are similar to shallow and deep learning which occurs in individuals.

When instructors look critically at their teaching goals from a constructivist's point of view, it becomes easier to see when passive didactic versus active instructional strategies are more appropriate. Didactic methods are the better choice when the instructor's goal is mainly content dissemination. For instance, a lecture would be appropriate for teaching students the finer legal distinctions between for-profit and not-for-profit foundations. The effort students would need to expend to discover and summarize this information on their own is not an effective use of time. However, if the goal was for students to learn how to conceptualize a successful not-for-profit, a skill they might use now or in the future, active learning would be appropriate. Students could identify unmet needs and opportunities, find solutions that would meet those needs and make use of those opportunities, and possibly draft a business plan for a hypothetical or actual not-for-profit that would address these situations.

In another example, suppose the instructional goal is for students to learn different ways to secure sources of venture capital (VC). The instructor might initially explain or lecture about what VC is and how the industry is organized. But if the instructional goal is to build thinking skills and provide knowledge for accessing VC in the future, active learning would provide a better instructional tool. A didactic lecture about VC would be of limited longer-term value, because the basic facts and principles can be memorized, regurgitated and probably forgotten. Students might never actually try to apply that knowledge to a real situation. No long-term learning might occur. However, if students are charged with identifying VC firms in their region with the appropriate missions to fund specific venture ideas, and to identify the necessary contacts that might be used for an introduction to VC partners at those firms, they will have experienced the process, although at possibly a simpler level, that they might use in their future entrepreneurial career.

While it is possible to create a deep learning challenge in a passive instructional setting, deep learning is more likely to occur when students are actively engaged in the process. In an active learning environment, the instructor's role becomes that of a facilitator of the learning process, not the principal source of authority or information. The instructor's primary goal should be to provide learners with achievable challenges, that is, challenges that go beyond students' current mental abilities and skill sets, but which students still have a reasonable chance of accomplishing. A well-designed challenge does much more than just promote the formation of new mental models; it also encourages students to revisit and test the connections between their pre-existing mental models, thus strengthening and consolidating prior knowledge as well. Once a student succeeds in meeting a challenge it builds their confidence in their mental models and thinking processes, and increases their motivation to take on more advanced challenges (Pintrich et al. 1994; Lawson 2002, p. 76).

Facilitating learning is like any other facilitative process; the individual leading it must pay close attention to the current status of the group and provide required resources in a timely manner. Selected examples of facilitation are described in the sections that follow, however, a detailed review of this process is beyond the scope of the current chapter; those wanting to learn more about learning facilitation techniques should consult McKeachie (2002, p. 30), and Michaelsen et al. (2002, p. 59).

What teaching strategies promote active learning?

By default (and habit) most instructors tend to rely on unidirectional methods such as lectures, assigned readings, and perhaps some expository writing or a course project (Boyer Commission 1998, pp. 5–6; NRC, 2003 p. 14; Tanner and Allen 2006, p. 1). This is unfortunate because there are numerous methods that better challenge students' current mental models and encourage them to become more engaged in the learning process. The following list is merely a sampling of possible alternatives (for further information about these and other instructional methods, the reader should consult McKeachie, 2002, Michaelsen et al., 2002, Bain, 2004, and Herreid, 2006):

- *Directed discussion*   Discussions are easily adapted to the group's skill level, but can be difficult to conduct in larger courses. A highly functioning discussion group is not dominated by the instructor asking questions. Rather, the instructor's questions are just a catalyst for discussion of larger issues. Students spend most of the time addressing questions and comments to each other, not to the instructor.
- *Case-based learning*   Students discuss a fictional or factual narrative that illustrates specific concepts. A large number of business-related teaching cases are available, and new ones can be developed or adapted quickly. Lack of sufficient content coverage is a common complaint against cases, but if the instructional goal is to develop thinking and ability to apply content knowledge to new problems, this should not be a significant weakness.
- *Problem-based learning (PBL)*   This teaching method is used widely in law and business schools, yet is underutilized for teaching undergraduates. Case- and problem-based learning appear similar because both use historic or fictional cases for instructional purposes. The critical difference is in how the cases are employed. In traditional case learning, the case is used as a catalyst for a group discussion led by the instructor. In PBL, instructors still facilitate the learning process, but the cases do not provide sufficient content to solve the challenges presented by the case. As a group, students must identify the critical learning issues for which they must find answers in order to resolve the case. Individuals are assigned to locate and master the specific content knowledge needed to resolve case issues and to bring that knowledge to class to share with their peers. PBL is a powerful method for building functional content knowledge, improving thinking process skills and training students to work in cooperative groups.
- *Team-based learning*   This hybrid strategy for simultaneously teaching both content and thinking skills was developed by Larry Michaelsen (Michaelsen et al. 2002). Students are assigned to learning teams, and are jointly responsible for each other's progress. The method is suited to large and small classes. If well executed, it promotes high levels of active learning while continuing to provide content

Table 9.1   Summary of teaching strategies

Method	Well suited to teaching	Level of direct facilitation Req'd	Typical emphasis	Degree of student freedom
Directed discussion	Content	Moderate	Predefined or historic question	Topic: low Direction: moderate
Case based	Process skills	Low to moderate	Predefined or historic question	Topic: low Direction: low
Problem based	Both	Moderate	Situations requiring reasoned decision	Topic: moderate Direction: high
Team based	Both	High	Depends upon course topic	Topic: moderate Direction: moderate
Project oriented	Process skills	Low	Specific question or problem to solve	Topic: low Direction: very high

coverage. As described below, one of the authors offered a freshman seminar that successfully utilized this learning strategy to teach entrepreneurship (an in-depth description of the case appears later in this chapter).

- *Project-oriented learning*   This strategy combines elements of team-, discussion-, and problem-based learning. Students are presented with a real business problem or situation that must be solved. The specific parameters of the problem are not fully defined; clarifying them is part of the students' learning process. Students also must decide how to proceed in order to solve the problem. Through group discussions, students develop an initial plan for solving the challenge problem, which becomes the roadmap for their course project. The instructor provides general guidance as the group project develops and keeps students on task to accomplish their stated goals in the time allowed. The instructor can choose to provide critical resources (such as reference materials, access to an outside expert in the field or funds to purchase materials) if needed, but ideally students will provide most or all of the necessary intellectual and physical resources. Success or failure is entirely up to the students; from the start, students must know that the instructor will not 'save' a faltering project. In practice, students can learn many of the same skills through project-oriented learning as they would gain during an internship. Below, we describe a junior/senior seminar course that was offered by one of the authors that used this method successfully.

Table 9.1 summarizes the major features of each of the preceding methods.

Harnessing life's molecular machines: an example of a team-based, active learning course
Team-based learning was employed for a freshman seminar offered in January 2007 by one of the authors. This seminar, 'Harnessing Life's Molecular Machines: From AIDS Tests to Hydrogen Cars', reflected the professor's growing awareness of the naturally occurring nanotechnology found in every living cell and the limitless potential that these molecular machines offer to society. The course objective was to use the novelty of these machines and their potential in marketable devices as possible venture ideas for students to experience the entrepreneurial process – especially the early stages of the

entrepreneurial process of identifying and assessing venture ideas to determine whether the venture ideas could be venture opportunities. Because the students were freshmen without the content knowledge related to cellular mechanisms, a blended approach, which integrated active and didactic learning in a team-based assignment approach, was needed to simultaneously deliver the content and provide the impetus for experiencing the entrepreneurial process.

On the first day of this freshman seminar, the 15 students were divided into five groups that served as learning teams for the semester. Each group of three students was assigned different ways of utilizing molecular machines. For example, one group investigated how these machines could be used in cutting-edge medical devices; another group explored how such machines could be used in alternative energy applications; a third group researched how the machines could be used in low-cost technology appropriate for developing countries.

Throughout the semester, these groups were given many team-building opportunities, which allowed them to develop from mere groups of students into successful learning teams. For example, students were assigned weekly reading quizzes and were awarded additional quiz points if their group achieved the highest combined score. The learning teams avidly competed with each other for the bragging rights that winning these points afforded them. Also, groups were required to jointly present three projects in the beginning, middle and end of the semester. This assignment proved to be an effective team-learning exercise, particularly for teams that had one or more members who were less comfortable delivering oral presentations and who had to rely on learning these skills from other members of their team.

Surprisingly, halfway through the semester, the students' focus shifted from building biotech devices to teaching other students about molecular machines, particularly junior high and high school students. Initially, only one group had been assigned the task of exploring how educational materials related to molecular machines could be commercialized, but, after learning about these nanomachines, other groups also began examining how to popularize them for young people. In fact, one group, which initially had been exploring molecular machines as alternative energy tools, created a business plan for an educational entertainment company as one of their team projects. They submitted this plan as an entry for a $1,000 seed money competition on campus, which they received later in the semester.

The shift from making devices to popularizing the science of molecular machines further assisted the ongoing team-learning process. With the initial research topics, it had been difficult for some students to envision starting their own company. But with their new focus – creating the 'Pokemon of molecular biology' – they had no trouble seeing how they could contribute. This vision for starting a company was infectious and spread from the three students who had entered the seed money competition to five others in the class. Months after the semester had ended, six of these freshmen continued to work together to write a better business plan, raise private funding, and develop new education materials. As sophomores, these six students enrolled in an independent study course with the same instructor and submitted two more funding proposals for a total of over $250,000.

From an active learning standpoint, the class was a success. Three-quarters of the 12 students directly participated in the formation of the educational entertainment company, and the other quarter participated indirectly – each student was on a learning team with at least one of the company's founders. Six of the 12 students who took the class are involved in the company and are continuing to build on their knowledge of molecular machines and on their thinking skills as they 'chart' the course of the new company. But the real success of the class can be gauged from the students' comments, selected from their final reports on their experiences in the seminar.

On the class:

Seminars like this one are why I chose to come to Wake Forest over other schools.

[This was] a wonderful experience that I look to take with me throughout the rest of my life.

[T]hree of our original fifteen students had dropped the class, at least one of whom could not believe how hard it was. . . . I pity the few that dropped the class, I am proud to have taken it, and cannot wait to apply what I have learned.

On the teams:

I'm learning that two heads are often better than one and that more than two heads is even better.

I feel as if I have found a group of people and a goal that spark my interest and creativity.

[A]s the classroom discussion seemed to revolve more and more around this new start-up company I felt more and more involved.

On the company:

The chance to work with peers on such a large-scale task, and actually get grant money and get legitimate businessmen to believe in our idea, is a once in a lifetime opportunity.

[T]he plan we produced became my work of pride for the year.

I would have never guessed that I would become part of a team of ten students and one professor that would start up and run a company.

On other ventures:

Without Professor Macosko . . . I would not have this valuable connection in the biology department, nor . . . the chance to really make a difference to multiple villages in Africa.

[T]his class . . . has inspired me to go out and literally live the motto of *pro humanitate* and better the conditions of the world.

[T]hanks to this class, I have been very inspired to try to start my own company in college.

On entrepreneurship:

I am now considering a minor in entrepreneurship and I am very excited to learn about business and the effort it takes to start and run a company.

[A]s a Biology and Spanish major, I never would have taken a business class during my four years here, but now I am learning about how business plans are written, how companies are organized, and the financial problems that arise when trying to start up a company.

[T]he start-up company BioBotz . . . not only stimulated my interest in the matter, but four other classmates', further influencing us to pursue minors in entrepreneurship.

Overall, team-based learning was a good fit for this science-rich freshman seminar. As one electrical engineering professor remarked about his use of this active learning strategy, 'Team-based learning seemed to be an effective and enjoyable way to get students to learn difficult material' (Weeks 2002, p. 1). Implementing this strategy amounted to placing students in groups and allowing those groups to mature into teams by assigning challenging, open-ended projects that inherently required a high degree of cooperation. Specific application of team-based learning will vary depending on content and class size, but in this freshman seminar it proved an extremely robust strategy for imparting an entrepreneurial mindset to students in a highly content-driven setting.

One benefit of a science-based course with an entrepreneurship experience is that students are provided with a chance to explore a scientific area of study that could provide technologies that can be building blocks for venture opportunities with greater competitive advantages over venture ideas that are typically generated in an entrepreneurship class focused only on the entrepreneurial process. In those more typical classes, students are asked to generate entrepreneurial ideas and then to examine their feasibility. In most cases, student ideas result from their everyday experience – bars, restaurants, book exchanges, apartment locators and so on. Because these ideas are familiar to all college students, there is little specialized knowledge and, therefore, little competitive advantage.

The adaptable textbook project: an example of a project-oriented, active learning course
In January 2007 one of the authors offered a junior/senior seminar course entitled, 'Building a Better Textbook'. The idea for the course originated from his frustration with current introductory biology texts. These 900-plus-page encyclopedic tomes are fact-rich but provide little guidance on how concepts are connected. This encourages shallow memorization at the expense of deeper, more functional understanding. The goal of the course was for students to develop a prototype chapter for a more streamlined textbook that focused on conceptual understanding instead of fact accumulation, was student centered, and could be tailored to fit different course structures.

Ten energetic students representing disciplines from business to humanities were recruited for the course; only one was a science major. At the first class meeting the instructor presented the students with the entrepreneurial problem of designing a new model for biology textbooks and outlined three general goals for the semester. First, the group would conduct a market survey to determine students' and instructors' needs. Second, they would use their findings to create a prototype textbook chapter that could be used for future fundraising. Third, they would test their prototype with an actual class of biology students. In essence, students were charged to explore the entrepreneurial process from venture idea for a new biology textbook model to research on market needs of students and faculty to designing a product to carrying out product testing with the target audience.

At the second meeting, students posed and discussed a number of specific questions related to the challenge problem: how do we conduct the needs assessment? Who should participate? How will we collate and present our findings? What will be the topic of the chapter? What concepts should it include? By the end of the second weekly meeting, students had set deadlines for completing the market survey and the prototype chapter.

Almost immediately, the students coalesced into a cohesive, productive team. By the third week of class, the group was deciding for itself what needed to be done next in order to reach each of the goals. Participants split most of the work into smaller, well-defined projects, and self-assigned teams of two to three the responsibility for completing specific tasks. For example, two teams developed separate needs surveys for faculty and students. Two other teams administered these surveys to 253 local college students and to 51 faculty instructors both locally and nationwide (using an online survey system identified by one of the participants), then compiled the responses into a formal market survey report. Several key decisions about the structure of their prototype chapter were based on these data. Other members of the group arranged for professionals in the book publishing industry to come and share their insights with the group.

The students chose to write their prototype chapter on basic genetics, a topic that all felt was particularly difficult to understand. In the development process, they conducted competitor research. They selected and read chapters from widely used college biology textbooks and a popular science guide to genetics, then examined how the writing styles, organization, conceptual flow, and other elements contributed to instructional effectiveness. Many of the best practices the group identified ultimately appeared in their prototype chapter. A final draft chapter was finished in early April, just in time for testing. Copies of the chapter were given to a class of introductory biology students at Wake Forest University (Winston-Salem, NC), and the students were asked to compare it to their current textbook using a combination of both paper and online surveys. The test group rated their peers' chapter as significantly easier to read, with a clearer writing style and physical layout. There was sufficient content but not too much, and the supplemental instructional aids were useful, without being overwhelming. Clearly, the students in this course had successfully solved the challenge problem posed at the start of the course.

Although the chapter was a success, the question remained: did the students in the seminar course benefit from this experience? For their final assignment, participants were asked to reflect on the experience. Excerpts from their responses tell the story best.

> At the beginning of the course, I had no idea that we would come as far as we did and create such an amazing and useful product.

> All of us traveled through uncharted territories and encountered obstacles that were solved as a team. We all worked as a focused group striving toward a common goal, but equally as important, you let the class make the majority of the decisions . . . you gave us a great deal of ownership of the venture, which was one of the key factors why the prototype chapter was completed on time, met our objectives, and was well-received.

> I was able to build connections both inside and outside the classroom, and I seem poised to maintain them now too. I found that I worked more diligently when I was divided into these small groups as I felt more responsibility and ownership.

> The greatest strength of the course was its incorporation of students with very different academic backgrounds, and along with that different strengths and weaknesses.

This class provided me a great amount of fun and useful teamwork experience for the real world.

Over the course of the semester I've learned many things about working in a group and my own overall contributions that I can provide. I think that I was able to take away skills of cooperation and time management with this project.

The class was the most refreshing class I have had in a long time, yet I feel one of the most productive as well.

What I personally gained from participating in this class [was a] tremendous sense of satisfaction and added confidence.

Our small team did whatever it took . . . 'wanting to' vs. 'having to' work on a project makes all the difference in the world.

In retrospect, project-oriented learning is not for the timid. It requires instructors to relinquish an exceptional amount of control over their course. At the same time, it is not a replacement for true experiential learning experiences (internships, for example). Compared to didactic methods, this approach requires much greater instructor flexibility, and requires instructors to spend considerably more time monitoring students' progress. Instructor oversight still occurs as well, but it is happening largely behind the scenes without the students' knowledge. For example, in this particular course the students were unaware that their instructor independently contacted faculty colleagues to ensure that they would complete the students' book use survey. The willingness to take risks is at the very heart of entrepreneurship. Moreover, as the participants in this course demonstrated, students' desire to succeed can be a powerful tool for creating an active learning environment.

'Let's build a biotech company': one participant's reflections on a project-oriented learning course

In fall 2004, Dr Raymond Kuhn was starting a typical semester of Immunology at Wake Forest University. But, Dr Kuhn threw in a side note in his opening lecture and mentioned starting a biotechnology company around some basic, but key practices, in the immunology industry. If interested, students were asked to set up a short interview with him, and write a short application essay. The interview consisted of students talking about their backgrounds, likes, dislikes, and goals. Not once in the interview did Dr Kuhn ask students if they knew anything about biotechnology, business, starting companies, balance sheets, or any other of the million morsels of knowledge needed to actually launch a viable company. Looking back, he was simply composing a team of students with a common trait: the desire to build something worthwhile.

Dr Kuhn also placed flyers around campus calling on students to see him about starting a biotech company. Only one student responded to the flyer independently. All the other students that submitted applications were reacting to the excitement verbally conveyed to them by other students. Ultimately eight students were selected to participate in the seminar course: 'Building a Biotechnology Company'. The academic backgrounds of the students varied. Only two students were biology majors; other students' concentrations were accounting, business, economics, and communications.

It is important to point out the process by which these students were selected. A native interest was piqued in each student, which motivated them to pursue the particular project. An inherent passion to build value lies within each student; the objective or target merely changes.

The first meeting of the course consisted of Dr Kuhn describing a potential product, a diagnostic kit for studying fish disease. The students were charged with creating a viable company around the concept of a diagnostic kit.

The most poignant memory of that meeting was Dr Kuhn's statement, 'Everyone in the class gets an A'. By saying this, he changed the motivating factors for the course. Rather than worrying about whether the course would hurt our grade point average, we worried about not performing in front of our peers. The fear of failure is a powerful motivator. Failure in the eyes of the industry, the community and peers is far more damaging to a person's pride and psyche than just getting a bad grade for a course. By saying those seven words, he increased our accountability to ourselves and each other, which further fueled the passion to succeed. He then proceeded to hand out a short list of problems to be solved in order to form a biotech company.

The problems ranged from basic (but all-important) legal structure of the company, to intellectual property protection to marketing strategies to product production to financing the venture. Sitting around a large table in Winston Hall the students began discussing strategies for finding the answers to each of the proposed problems. In a matter of hours the students had split into research teams, decided to bring in guest 'keynote' speakers, and had selected officers. The speakers' areas of expertise ranged from marketing strategy to startup experience; from venture capital to public relations. Each speaker was chosen to give the students some real-world perspective on how a company is formed, grown and run successfully.

By listening to the real-life stories of these people and their businesses, the students adapted and created their own strategies for a viable business. Importantly (and to the credit of Dr Kuhn), only speakers with a history of successful problem solving were chosen to speak. Entrepreneurial environments have enough hardships to overcome; students learn to be critical and analytic as part of the learning process. Students need encouragement and positive motivators to keep moving forward.

It is important to note that the *students* decided how the class would be structured. Dr Kuhn was (as described earlier) a catalyst. He subtly interjected when the need arose or when pointed questions and advice were asked of him, but largely let the seminar run its course. Onlookers were surprised at the remarkable capability of the students. It goes to show that when passion is put to work, babysitting is not needed.

Background research was done in sub-teams in members' own time. Each class was three hours long. A guest speaker would come for the first hour, with 30 minutes for questions. Afterwards one team would present on its previous week's research on a given subject, and then the team would decide what needed further attention. The following week, the process would start again.

With hindsight, Dr Kuhn either masterfully designed the course to include all majors (not just biology) or it was a supremely fortunate accident. Real businesses are composed of managers and employees from many different backgrounds, tolerance levels, and methods of learning. Real businesses must utilize and devise the best solution to problems, which often requires a combination of different viewpoints and ideas.

The key to successful project-oriented learning lies in the motivation to discover and learn. Harry A. Overstreet said, 'First, arouse in the other person an eager want. He who can do this has the whole world with him. He who cannot walks a lonely way' (Carnegie 1936, p. 34). Dr Kuhn did just this. He proposed a project that provided each student an opportunity to incorporate his or her own ideas and strategies with those of others and apply it to something that mattered. When solutions are applied to things that actually matter, validation is reciprocated in exchange for all the hard work it took to reach a solution. The students, community, potential customers, and the industry were all engaged in the students' effort because each party was to benefit from its success in some way.

By the end of the semester, after hours of basic research in the library and interviews with countless members of the business community, the product concept morphed. Rather than marketing the diagnostic kit to university professors and researchers, the product could be marketed to the aquaculture industry. The students had discovered that this basic diagnostic product, designed in the proper form and marketed to the appropriate industry, could actually reap a substantial profit. There was a real need for something like this! It was essentially a semester of 'research' at the end of which a company was incorporated, a business plan was drafted, and the time had come to implement our own business strategies. By this point in time the company had also raised $11,000 in seed capital.

John Dewey once stated 'The desire to be important is the deepest urge in human nature' (ibid., p. 18). Working on a real-world problem increases the degree of accountability to the project. This accountability naturally motivates the students. When students realize that their work has true value and the value is recognized and rewarded with a stamp of approval from potential customers, the reward is priceless.

I am eternally grateful for the entrepreneurial exposure I gained in my senior year in the biotech seminar class. That experience changed my life and paved the discovery of the career path that I still walk today. It was in this class I discovered my passion for entrepreneurship, my own talents, and most importantly, gained confidence in my and my peers' aptitudes. Learning these skills at a young age gives students a phenomenal edge over the rest of our job-seeking competition. Young entrepreneurs have the ability to move forward faster with an exponential learning curve as opposed to the typical college graduate. We are fearless (albeit mostly out of ignorance); but we learn fast and have countless more opportunities in which to use the lessons we have learned. It is a sink or swim learning environment. You must start paddling immediately. The world will not wait. You have no choice but to learn.

I shall never forget the moment I knew this entrepreneurial lifestyle was for me. At the end of my senior year, I was standing in an elevator with two venture capitalists in the Babcock Graduate School Elevator Business Plan competition. I had two minutes to convince these venture capitalists that my company was primed for investment. While having no background in business and zero experience with venture capitalists, my mind raced and the words poured out. Apparently, they were the right ones. We were placed sixth out of 81 applicants – the only team with undergraduate members.

Today the company, now called Aqualutions LLC, has raised over $45,000 in direct capital through business plan competitions and other sources. It has also maintained a close working relationship with Wake Forest University and Dr Raymond Kuhn, who raised an additional $75,000 for the company through a grant. The company has two product offerings and is now working on the proof of concept trials. Along with Dr Kuhn, three of the original students remain as the core team.

Conclusion

In these three science-based entrepreneurship seminars, students worked together as a team and created new mental models in order to solve problems that were intractable under their old set of models and assumptions. They created their own questions, figured out where to get data to help provide perspective, engineered some new entity (an educational program, a textbook, or a biotech company), tested it, and refined it. This constructivist learning process is similar to what an entrepreneur would do in creating a new product or service, thus these students experienced an early stage of the entrepreneurial process.

   The key feature of these three seminar classes was an emphasis on science and solving science-related problems using an entrepreneurial model. While team building was not a primary goal for any of the courses, in all three we saw students coalesce into highly functional interdependent groups. The three courses created an active learning environment that was essential to the acquisition of new mental models. The strategy of combining a science-rich project and learning teams can be used to help students learn, and learn to apply, entrepreneurial skills.

References

Argyris, Chris and Donald A. Schön (1978), *Organizational Learning: A Theory of Action Perspective*, Reading, MA: Addison-Wesley.
Bain, Ken (2004), *What the Best College Teachers Do*, Cambridge, MA: Harvard University Press.
Boyer Commission on Educating Undergraduates in the Research University (S.S. Kenny, B. Alberts, W.C. Booth, M. Glaser, C.E. Glassick, S.O. Ikenberry, K.H. Jamieson, R.M. O'Neil, C. Reid-Wallace, C.-L. Tien and C.N. Yang) (1998), *Reinventing Undergraduate Education: A Blueprint for America's Research Universities*, New York: Carnegie Foundation for the Advancement of Teaching.
Carnegie, Dale (1936), *How to Win Friends and Influence People*, reprinted in a revised edition (1981), New York: Simon & Schuster.
Dewey, J. (1916), 'Method in science teaching', *General Science Quarterly*, **1**, 3–9.
Gardiner, Lion F. (1994), *Redesigning Higher Education: Producing Dramatic Gains in Student Learning*, San Francisco, CA: Jossey-Bass.
Halonen, Jane S., Felicia Brown-Anderson and Wilbert J. McKeachie (2002), 'Teaching thinking', in McKeachie (ed.), pp. 284–90.
Herreid, Clyde F. (ed.) (2006), *Start With a Story: The Case Study Method of Teaching College Science*, Arlington, VA: NSTA Press.
Lawson, Anton E. (2002), *Science Teaching and Development of Thinking*, Belmont, CA: Wadsworth/Thomson Learning.
McKeachie, Wilbert J. (ed.) (2002), *McKeachie's Teaching Tips*, 11th edn, Boston, MA: Houghton Mifflin.
Michaelsen, Larry K., Arietta B. Knight and L. Dee Fink (2002), *Team-Based Learning: A Transformative Use of Small Groups*, Westport, CT: Praeger.
National Research Council (NRC) (2003), *Bio2010: Transforming Undergraduate Education for Future Research Biologists*, Washington, DC: National Academies Press.
Pintrich, Paul R., Donald R. Brown and Claire E. Weinstein (1994), *Student Motivation, Cognition, and Learning: Essays in Honor of Wilbert J. McKeachie*, Hillsdale, NJ: Lawrence Erlbaum.
Tanner, K. and D. Allen (2006), 'Approaches to biology teaching and learning: on integrating pedagogical training into the graduate experiences of future science faculty', *CBE–Life Sciences Education*, **5**, 1–6.
Taylor, Peter C., Penny J. Gilmer and Kenneth G. Tobin (2002), *Transforming Undergraduate Science Teaching: Social Constructivist Perspectives*, New York: Peter Lang.
Weeks, William (2002), 'Team-based learning in: "El Eng 447: Information Theory and Coding Theory"', www.ou.edu/pii/teamlearning/docs/Course%20by%20Wm%20Weeks.pdf, 6 November 2008.

PART III

INTERSECTIONS AND PRACTICE

10 Balsamic vinaigrette: entrepreneurship in the arts and sciences
*Kelly G. Shaver**

Introduction

Ask the president of a liberal arts college 'What does this place *do* for its students?' There is a long list of excellent answers, none of which includes the words 'provide job training'. One good answer might be to encourage life long interest in learning, by placing a high value on informed discussion, showing students the differences between supposition and fact and teaching them to find and use the latter. Another answer might be to encourage independent judgment by presenting contrasting – and often equally well-researched – views on important life questions. In this sense, the liberally educated student may prefer 'it depends' as his or her answer of choice, but will also be able to indicate the factors that should be considered in reaching one decision or the other. A third answer might be to provide a connection to the world's intellectual traditions through general education requirements that lead students to study several topics – outside of an academic major or minor – in detail. Merely scratching the intellectual surface fails to provide sufficient background for understanding.

Compare these objectives of a liberal arts education with several descriptions of the nature of entrepreneurial behavior. One major current textbook on entrepreneurship notes:

> [S]eeking opportunities, taking risks beyond security and having the tenacity to push an idea through to reality combine into a special perspective that . . . can be exhibited inside or outside an organization, in profit or not-for-profit enterprises, and in business or nonbusiness activities for the purpose of bringing forth creative ideas. (Kuratko and Hodgetts, 2004, p. 3)

Another current textbook definition notes that entrepreneurship is 'the process of creating something new with value by devoting the necessary time and effort, assuming the accompanying financial, psychic, and social risks, and receiving the resulting rewards of monetary and personal satisfaction and independence' (Hisrich and Brush, 1985, p. 18 as cited in Hisrich and Peters, 2002, p. 10). Moreover, although the research literature in entrepreneurship has often concentrated on the presumed personal characteristics of the people involved (Shaver, 1995), today's view takes a perspective that has been part of social psychology for over half a century, since Fritz Heider first argued that behavior was a joint function of the person and the environment (Heider, 1958). In the entrepreneurship literature this view is best captured by Shane and Venkataraman (2000), who note that both opportunities and individuals are required. For these authors and many others, entrepreneurship 'involves the study of the *sources* of opportunities; the *processes* of discovery, evaluation, and exploitation of opportunities; and the set of *individuals* who discover, evaluate, and exploit them' (ibid., p. 218).

From the perspective of social psychology, the difference between the liberal arts and sciences as currently construed and entrepreneurship as just described is a difference only in *content*. Curiosity as a psychological *process* will run its course in exactly the same way whether its objective is a scientific discovery or a new business opportunity. The content domains may be different, but the way they are approached is the same. This is true for other psychological processes as well. The process of evaluation is inherently comparative. Features are identified, strengths and weaknesses enumerated and conclusions are drawn. This happens whether the content under scrutiny is the market potential for an invention or a debate over the historical significance of a cultural event. The process of creativity is inherently inventive. Cognitive boundaries are softened, fresh categories emerge and elements are combined in new ways. Again, this happens whether the result is a painting, an imposing metal sculpture, a novel, or a way of capturing images without film. Given these similarities in process, one might ask why entrepreneurship is not already an important component of the liberal arts and sciences. The remainder of this chapter will suggest a few reasons why this might be so and propose ways in which the desirable goal of greater integration might be encouraged.

The basic ingredients

Everyone knows that vinaigrette consists of oil and vinegar. Is this metaphor an apt description for the possible combination of entrepreneurship and the liberal arts? Let us see. Whenever one begins talking about the liberal arts, or liberal education – even as contrasted with professional training of one sort or another – one is tempted to begin with ancient philosophy. I confess: I will yield to this temptation. The first line of Aristotle's *Metaphysics* is 'All men by nature desire to know' (Aristotle, as translated by Ross, 1952a, p. 499). But very quickly Aristotle's argument draws a distinction between art and experience. In this view, art is an understanding of universal truths, whereas experience is knowledge of practical realities at an individual level. Where *action* is concerned, experience is key: 'the physician does not cure *man* [but rather an individual named person] who happens to be a man' (ibid., p. 499). But where *wisdom* is concerned, art is key, because understanding *why* something is so requires a knowledge of the causes of things, which knowledge can be obtained only at the level of universals. In Aristotle's opinion, knowledge is preferable to practice, theoretical understanding is better the farther removed it is from day-to-day necessity and the teaching of knowledge is a proper job for scholars, not practitioners. Indeed, in his *Politics*, Aristotle notes:

> There can be no doubt that children should be taught those useful things which are really necessary, but not all useful things; for occupations are divided into liberal and illiberal [with the latter including] *all paid employments*, for they absorb and degrade the mind. (Emphasis added; Aristotle, as translated by Ross, 1952b, p. 542)

To place Aristotle's distinction into a modern context, 'liberal' education provides food for the mind, whereas pre-professional education (described in more detail below) serves only the body. The study of philosophy, art and mathematics sharpens the intellect and contributes to wisdom. They represent the purest form of human educational endeavor precisely because they are ends in themselves. True, they contribute to one's sense of cultural place, and to one's sophisticated awareness of the relationship between the individual and the state. But the development of personal identity and the exercise of responsible citizenship are as highly regarded in the present-day liberal arts community as they were in Aristotle's time. Consequently, these additional effects of liberal education raise few eyebrows in the academy.

The valued life of the mind – as contrasted with the appetites of the body – is also an integral part of Plato's description of the ideal State (Plato, as translated by Jowett, 1952). Although recognizing that a self-sufficient society must have its merchants, retailers and 'hirelings', their everyday pursuit of things material has dire consequences:

> For I suspect that many will not be satisfied with the simpler way of life. They will be for adding sofas, and tables, and other furniture; also dainties, and perfumes and incense, and courtesans, and cakes, all these of not one sort only but in every variety . . . and gold and ivory and all sorts of materials will have to be procured.
> . . . Then we must enlarge our borders; for the original healthy State is no longer sufficient. Now will the city have to fill and swell with a multitude of callings which are not required by any natural want. . . . Then a slice of our neighbours' land will be wanted by us for pasture and tillage, and they will want a slice of ours, if, like ourselves, they exceed the limit of necessity . . . And so we shall go to war, Glaucon, shall we not? (Ibid.: pp. 318–19)

The Platonic view of mercantilism as base and intellectualism as elevated is, for many, part of the metatheory of the liberal arts. As noted by Deckert (1976) the lower parts of the soul have to do with appetites and desires, the middle part is the spirited (emotions such as anger and pride) and the highest part – the rational – enables knowledge and understanding. The most advanced person is, therefore, the one 'who places highest value on the ideals of goodness, truth and beauty' (ibid., p. 41). Without suggesting that Plato's version of human nature is true, Deckert argues that 'liberal arts education is an effort to move the student up the Platonic value scale' (p. 41). In a society that values achievement and mercantile success (yes, even back in the cultural upheavals of the 1970s), the liberal arts goal of leading students *away* from these values must necessarily be a covert enterprise. The result is that

> [T]he liberal arts college sublimates; the true mission of the liberal arts becomes a hidden agenda [when] the cherished desire of the faculty is to convert the student. To turn the student on to the life of the mind and spirit in such a way that he will never again be totally satisfied, fulfilled, happy with mere material affluence or even with honor and prestige. (Ibid., p. 43)

To the extent that Deckert's view of the liberal arts faculty remains accurate, one can expect quiet, inertial, resistance to proposals to infuse aspects of the liberal arts curriculum with entrepreneurship. Few endeavors could be farther from the Platonic ideal than one considered to be devoted to the creation of wealth. In this context it matters not that the entrepreneurial processes involved in the creation of new social values are exactly the same as those underlying the creation of new commercial ventures.

In modern writing on the topic, liberal education is often contrasted with 'pre-professional training'. At the undergraduate level, such training is often associated with schools of architecture, business, education, or engineering, but it would also include both pre-law programs and pre-med programs. Whatever its particular content might be, pre-professional training is seen as preparing students to provide food for the body, but not necessarily for the mind. Interestingly, some commentators see the rise of specific pre-professional programs as evidence of the *failure* of the liberal arts. For example,

Powell (1983) notes that the liberal arts in America have maintained a very conservative educational tradition: 'In totally irrational ways, the practical has been excluded from the liberal arts curriculum so that students are deprived of the full fruit of their education' (p. 227). A student who masters the art of writing poetry has also learned a means of communication that could inform his or her later work in journalism. A student who delights in the process of scientific discovery has also learned a methodology for generating or testing inventions. A student who knows how to manage and analyze social science data to test a theory has also learned a way to narrow complex issues of public policy into answerable questions. Powell argues that by refusing to acknowledge that education in liberal arts and sciences might actually be *useful*, the conservatives among these faculties have helped to create a demand for the very pre-professional education they decry.

It is probably not a mistake to suggest that the Aristotelian and Platonic view is shared by more than a few present-day academics. These people would regard physics as more pure than engineering, because the latter is concerned with practicalities such as making sure that a suspension bridge built simultaneously from both shores will actually meet in the middle. They would favor an artist whose work 'makes a statement' over one whose work is merely 'a commercial success'. They would prefer religion to psychology, because the former better prescribes how people *ought* to live, whereas the latter merely collects data about how people *actually* behave. We have come a long way from the days when dissenters from the accepted view in universities were tried for heresy and burned at the stake.[1] Nevertheless, there is still concern in bastions of liberal arts and sciences that education for virtue requires that any form of financial gain be renounced. The origins of the former are intellectual, the origins of the latter are practical. The two traditions are as separate as oil and water. Or in the present metaphor, oil and vinegar.

At this point the Aristotelians might cheerfully proclaim that I have endowed purely intellectual pursuits with the emollient properties of oil – while relegating practical pursuits to the status of a *sour* liquid without which people can live quite well, thank you. However, one of the lessons learned from introductory philosophy courses is that one needs to be wary about agreeing too quickly to an argument by example. Because sometimes, as here, there is a catch. Oil can be pressed from olives (a fruit) and vinegar can be distilled from wine (made from fruit). So the origins may not be as different as the defenders of liberal arts would claim: both olives and grapes are fruit. A still more troublesome truth, as far as the liberal-arts-as-oil view is concerned, is the fact that grapes are sweet right off the vine, whereas olives are inedibly bitter right off the tree (Townsend, 1978).

The process: shake things up
The point here is not to argue for the vinegar *over* the oil, any more than it is to argue the reverse. Rather, the point is that in today's university, the two can be used to create a mixture that everyone might enjoy. But doing so requires vigorous shaking – and not just metaphorically, because bringing entrepreneurship and the liberal arts together is, in most universities, more than a novel idea. The barriers to success are both intellectual and institutional.

First, the intellectual barriers. To the extent that liberal arts faculties subscribe to the Aristotelian view of education, or devote their professional lives to moving students 'up the Platonic value scale', they are not likely to be receptive to the suggestion that a materialist pursuit such as entrepreneurship become part of their own course offerings.

For people trained in business, the resistance is difficult to understand. After all, few English majors go on to write the Great American Novel, but rather find jobs in journalism or publishing that will pay them for their skills. Some art majors, after graduation, find poverty a virtue while waiting to be 'discovered', but many more become designers and graphic artists working for large and small companies. Some history graduates go on to careers in academia, but a substantial fraction find their way into law school or public policy. The connection between excellent liberal arts training and later success in business appears so likely that one wonders why any liberal arts faculty fail to see it. The issue is even more sharply drawn for those of us with training in psychology who believe, with Maslow (1968), that the basic needs for food, shelter and safety must be satisfied before one can turn to the self-actualization that is high on the Platonic value scale.

Upon reflection, however, the answer seems almost too obvious. For a liberal arts faculty member who subscribes to the Platonic ideal, the one argument least likely to be convincing is one based on economic interest. For such an individual, economic arguments are to be eschewed, whether they are applied to undergraduates or to the faculty member. One could even claim that to keep their personal behavior consistent with their teaching, Platonic faculty members would have to avoid doing anything for the purpose of *self*-interest. Thus the world view of an entrepreneurship professor – whose academic metatheory is based on the assumption that people will act in their self-interest – is incompatible with the world view of one of Powell's 'highly conservative' liberal arts faculty members. So on a purely intellectual level, an attempt to spread entrepreneurship into the liberal arts may produce a lot of controversy, not all of which will be easy to articulate or resolve.

Next, the institutional. Even for those liberal arts faculty who are *positively* disposed toward incorporating elements of entrepreneurship into their courses, some vigorous institutional shaking will still be needed. Universities typically have mental models for how to foster collaboration among faculty, with one of the more prominent being the 'interdisciplinary program' (see Chapter 11 in this volume by Janssen, Eeckhout, Gailly and Bacq for an extended discussion of the nature of interdisciplinary approaches). Whether the traditional approach to interdisciplinary education will ultimately prove to be a positive example remains to be seen.

To understand how an interdisciplinary program might be successful (or not), it must be considered against the background of the typical university or college structure. This structure begins at the top with a board of trustees to whom the university or college president reports. The president's responsibilities concentrate on maintaining and increasing the financial support needed to keep the institution healthy, while setting the broad agenda for the university as a whole. Under the president is a chief academic officer (often a provost) who is primarily responsible for the day-to-day operations of the institution. Direct reports to this provost may be limited to the leaders of various academic divisions, or they may also include administrative directors of finance, development, or auxiliary enterprises. Academic divisions are usually led by deans and associate deans. In universities with small professional schools (such as business schools), the organizational superstructure for the professional schools may end with an associate dean. In institutions with larger professional schools, these may also have the equivalent of the department chairs that are the final 'content' officers for faculties of arts and sciences. Decisions flow up in this structure; money flows down.

Regardless of the strength of faculty 'self-governance', none of this will come as a surprise to any faculty member. Moreover, faculty members who change institutions from public to private (or vice versa), or from large to small (or vice versa), will find in their new homes an academic landscape very much like the one they recently left. Indeed, if ever there were an industry sector in which management success at one 'company' should predict management success at another company, higher education has to be at the top of the list.

So what happens when an interdisciplinary program is created, either because of pressure upward from interested faculty, or because of pressure downward from administrative officials? Whatever the source of instigation, the 'life cycle' of an interdisciplinary program may also be quite similar across institutions. At its beginning, an interdisciplinary program is likely to have two defining characteristics. First, it is likely to be *problem-* or *phenomenon-driven* and second, its intellectual content is likely to be found at the intersection of two or more traditional disciplines. American Studies, Black Studies, Environmental Studies, International Relations, Neuroscience and Public Policy are all examples that possess these two defining characteristics. All of these interdisciplinary endeavors have other features in common:

- there is typically an internal 'champion';
- the initial organizing of the program is likely to be done by a committee;
- at least in the early stages, there will be no faculty *slots* devoted to the program;
- because resources are finite, there will be opportunity cost to every traditional *department* that elects to take part;
- having students is very good, having publication outlets is even better; and
- if it is to be successful, the program will have to create a structure for self-governance (for example, hiring, merit increases and promotion, tenure) that looks very much like the structures found in the 'home' academic units of the participating faculty.

New interdisciplinary programs are often greeted with applause by both faculty and administrators who hope the programs will break down the barriers across academic units, get researchers out of their departmental 'silos', and provide students with a stimulating discussion of problems or phenomena as they might be addressed in the real (read 'nonacademic') world. Such external examples abound: cross-functional teams within a corporate structure, matrix organizations in the nonprofit sector, or think-tanks that use experts from many areas to write reports designed to influence public policy.

In all too many instances, however, interdisciplinary programs will not survive (let alone prosper) unless they can attract at least two very scarce resources. The first of these is internal to the university, the second is external. Within the university, putting lots of enthusiastic students in interdisciplinary courses is rarely sufficient to ensure legitimacy. Indeed, there are academics who would regard a classroom full of excited students with suspicion, fearing either that the subject matter was simplistic or that the instructor was known to be an easy mark. To achieve internal legitimacy, an interdisciplinary program requires faculty slots to call its own. This means it has to have its piece of the institutional pie, its own procedures for evaluating faculty activity and a way to make its own in-person case to the administration. Outside the university, an interdisciplinary program needs appropriate publication outlets for its faculty. Consulting opportunities are good, endowment support is wonderful, but for faculty members publications, not greenbacks, are the coin of the realm. Some interdisciplinary programs will be blessed by the fact that the home disciplines of its faculty participants take an ecumenical approach to scholarship. Others may have to be involved in the creation of journals at the same time they are creating programs.

For those of us interested in broadening the reach of entrepreneurship into the liberal arts and sciences, the example of most interdisciplinary programs provides a dose of caution to accompany the enthusiasm. It is one thing to make the (to some audiences difficult) intellectual case that the skills that are essential to successful entrepreneurial behavior are the same skills that contribute to becoming a liberally educated person. It is another thing entirely to negotiate one's way through the sometimes Byzantine organizational structure and function of the modern university. Here some personal examples are instructive. My Venture Launch course to be taught at William and Mary (Williamsburg, VA) in the Spring of 2004 was part of an intended business concentration in entrepreneurship, developed with funding from the Kauffman Foundation. The concentration – which potentially could have involved four separate courses – had the backing of the assistant dean for the BBA program. A formal proposal for the concentration had been submitted to the Business School's Curriculum Committee for its review, in the hopes that it would recommend approval to the faculty of the School. Even if there had been approval, however, it would not have been forthcoming before a December School faculty meeting. And that meeting would have taken place approximately a month after students had registered for the Spring Semester. Indeed, to be included in the Spring schedule, courses had to be submitted by mid-October. Because of the mismatch in schedules, three of the core courses (the fourth was an internal modification of an existing course) had to be listed with the temporary 'topics' numbers traditionally used for courses introduced before their formal approval is complete. Unfortunately, because of accreditation pressures, many schools of business place strict limits on the number of 'topics' courses for which students may register (assuming they can even find full descriptions of the content).

Bad as the situation sounds, the scheduling nightmare can in other liberal arts colleges be even worse. If the school of business is large enough to have departments, new course proposals often must be submitted to, and approved by some department prior to consideration by the School's Curriculum Committee. In universities where committees consider the budget ramifications of new programs, and the liberal arts and sciences faculties retain final control over all curricular matters, approval by a school of business would be followed by discussions in a Budget Committee, a university-wide Curriculum Committee, and then a vote in a Faculty Senate. It is no wonder that new program proposals can take in excess of a year to receive their final approval (assuming that no substantial revisions were required at any point in the process). Full approval of the College of Charleston's (Charleston, SC) Entrepreneurship Concentration took more than 10 months – which to some folks will sound like the academic equivalent of the world land speed record. The length of this process takes on new meaning when one knows that the Nanjing Auto Group in China started with bare ground, built an entire manufacturing plant, and rolled out MGs that meet European emission standards in *slightly over eight months*! It is a dramatic understatement to say that the academic approval process militates against innovation.

Approval, however, is not a guarantee of success, as two more challenges face those who would develop interdisciplinary endeavors. The first of these is the challenge of putting students into classes. Students have to know the courses are available and they have to find them in a registration system. In the era of the World Wide Web, social networking, and print-on-demand, it might surprise some readers to learn that many college and university catalogs have lead times measured in months. It is possible to have a program approved in May that cannot appear in a catalog in time for an academic year beginning in August. Because catalogs are printed only once a year, this means that a program approved in one academic year will be *available* the next, but not publicized until the year after. And unless the program has its own listing – and its own course designation in the university's registration system – students will need to search in multiple places to find the necessary courses.

The second challenge centers on issues of faculty function and evaluation. In many online registration systems, a cross-listed course (available to departmental students under one designation and to the interdisciplinary students under another) often has two different 'course registration numbers' (CRNs). Each CRN has its own prerequisites, class limit, and enrollment listing. This means that the instructor will receive two class rolls, two grade sheets and most likely two sets of student course evaluations for a single classroom full of students. If an interdisciplinary course is team-taught by professors from different departments or schools – as described in Chapter 14 in this volume by Mars and Hoskinson – these issues of evaluation are supplemented by legitimate concerns about the way in which teaching credit is apportioned.

Grades, credits, prerequisites, cross-listings, joint appointments; these are the in-the-trenches realities of interdisciplinary endeavors, no matter how many potential stakeholders express unqualified support for the idea. So unless the entire *institution* is committed to such a program and is willing (and able) to *modify* its internal systems to facilitate the program, the work faculty members do to build entrepreneurship into their courses will be just the beginning of their exercises in creativity. In short, for such a program to succeed, the 'institution shaking' has to originate at the top.

The result: tasty!
If the oil and vinegar can be shaken enough, the result will be a blend that the participants, at least, will find tasty. Regardless of their home disciplines, faculty members who collaborate in the classroom often find the experience a renewing one. As one's research progresses through the years, one's domain of expertise is likely to become much deeper, but less broad. As one moves from teaching first-year undergraduates to final-year doctoral students, the questions become more technically challenging, but in some ways less intellectually captivating. Doctoral students, like teenagers, know which questions are either already answered or off-limits. By contrast, first-year undergraduates, like four-year-olds, are likely to ask 'Why?' about practically anything. One of the significant benefits of cross-disciplinary collaboration – especially in the classroom – is that each faculty member can behave once again like a curious but uninformed first-year student.

The typical result is a level of intellectual excitement that invigorates teaching and enhances learning. Highly capable students can certainly benefit from a liberal arts education of even the most extreme Platonic character. They are comfortable with reasoning by universals and can engage in spirited discussions of what constitutes truth, beauty, or justice. For the rest of us, however, some connection to the practical can be important. In attempting to define what is good, or what is moral, an abstract comparison of utilitarianism to retributivism can carry us only so far. Asking what an entrepreneur should *do* about an employee who has embezzled to purchase medicine for a spouse provides a different way of looking at the implications of moral theories. To return to the beginning, the cognitive skills involved in creativity, evaluation and judgment are the same whether the content is abstract or practical. It is in this sense that balsamic vinaigrette as a whole is an improvement over either of its constituent parts alone.

Notes

* Development of this chapter was facilitated by support from the Ewing Marion Kauffman Foundation.
1. See www.ox.ac.uk/aboutoxford/history.shtml.

References

Deckert, M. (1976), 'Liberal arts: a Platonic view', *Liberal Education*, **62**, 40–47.
Heider, F. (1958), *The Psychology of Interpersonal Relations*, New York: Wiley.
Hisrich, R.D. and Brush, C.G. (1985), *The Woman Entrepreneur: Starting, Financing, and Managing a Successful New Business*, Lexington, MA: Lexington Books, as cited in R.D. Hisrich and M.P. Peters (2002), *Entrepreneurship*, 5th edn, New York: McGraw-Hill/Irwin.
Kuratko, D.F. and Hodgetts, R.M. (2004), *Entrepreneurship*, 6th edn, Mason, OH: Thomson/South-Western.
Maslow, A. (1968), *Toward a Psychology of Being*, 2nd edn, New York: Van Nostrand.
Plato, *Republic,* Book II, trans. by Benjamin Jowett, in R.M. Hutchens (ed.) (1952), *Great Books of the Western World*, Vol. 7, Chicago, IL: Encyclopaedia Britannica, pp. 295–441.
Powell, J.M. (1983), 'Professionalism and the liberal arts in the American university', *Liberal Education*, **69**, 225–32.
Ross, W.D. (1952a), Aristotle, *Metaphysics*, Book I, from *The Works of Aristotle*, trans. into English by W.D. Ross, published by Oxford University Press, and reprinted in R.M. Hutchens (ed.) (1952), *Great Books of the Western World*, Vol. 8, Chicago, IL: Encyclopaedia Britannica, pp. 499–626.
Ross, W.D. (1952b), Aristotle, *Politics*, Book VIII, From *The Works of Aristotle*, trans. into English by Benjamin Jowett, under the editorial supervision of W.D. Ross, published by Oxford University Press, and reprinted in R.M. Hutchens (ed.) (1952), *Great Books of the Western World*, Vol. 9, Chicago, IL: Encyclopaedia Britannica, pp. 445–548.
Shane, S. and Venkataraman, S. (2000), 'The promise of entrepreneurship as a field of research', *Academy of Management Review*, **25**, 217–26.
Shaver, K.G. (1995), 'The entrepreneurial personality myth', *Business and Economic Review*, **41** (3), 20–23.
Townsend, D.M. (1978), *The Cook's Companion*, New York: Routledge.

11 Interdisciplinarity in cross-campus entrepreneurship education*

Frank Janssen, Valérie Eeckhout, Benoît Gailly and Sophie Bacq

Introduction

During the last 30 years, the scientific community has shown a growing interest for entrepreneurship, driven by the increasing dynamic role of small and medium-sized enterprises (SMEs) in job creation and innovation and boosted by the emergence of new business environments, new technologies and globalization (Fiet, 2001). Parallel to this, a growing number of entrepreneurship education programs (EEPs) have appeared, first in the United States where, today, more than 2,200 courses are offered at over 1,600 schools (Katz, 2003; Kuratko, 2005), and then, more recently, in Europe, where most programs have been created in the last decade (Klandt, 2004).

The educational system, in particular universities, now plays a significant role in the emergence and diffusion of entrepreneurial culture (Fayolle, 2000). It strongly influences how students are able to detect, evaluate and capture attractive value-creation opportunities. Education is therefore a core element in the development of entrepreneurial spirit and initiatives. This, coupled with the growing importance of SMEs in their socio-economic environment, has pushed a growing number of European universities to develop EEPs.

Today, entrepreneurship also tends to be recognized as an academic field (Bruyat and Julien, 2001; Cooper, 2003). It has an important scientific community that has produced a significant body of research (Acs and Audretsch, 2003; McGrath, 2003). Some authors tend to think that it is a blossoming field that cuts across different disciplines (Acs and Audretsch, 2003). It can also be argued that the field is inclusive and eclectic (Low, 2001) and that it cannot be reduced to a single definition (Verstraete and Fayolle, 2004). It is certainly larger than the single 'business creation' perspective. According to Kuratko (2005, p. 578), '"an entrepreneurial perspective" can be developed in individuals. This perspective can be exhibited inside or outside an organization, in profit or not-for-profit enterprises, and in business or non-business activities for the purpose of bringing forth creative ideas'. From an educational point of view, this means that entrepreneurship education cannot limit itself to firm creation, but has to be broadened to the development of an entrepreneurial spirit that consists of, in business or in any other human activity, identifying opportunities and gathering different resources in order to create richness value that meets a solvable demand (Albert and Marion, 1998).

Nascent or mature, entrepreneurship as an academic field is by nature interdisciplinary and therefore requires adapted teaching methods. Several universities have tried to develop such educational approaches, dedicated to the specific objectives and requirements of their EEP. However, only a few of them appear to have adopted educational approaches that are truly interdisciplinary. Indeed, universities are often locked into their disciplinary structures in which entrepreneurship classes are school specific and only offered to students from one or sometimes two disciplines. Apart from business schools, entrepreneurship courses are sometimes offered by engineering schools. Nevertheless, truly interdisciplinary EEPs have emerged in a few universities. These programs act as pioneers and are likely to have contagion effects on other university education programs. Greene et al. (2004) underline that EEPs have often played the role of experimentation fields for several pedagogical approaches, such as virtual business simulation games, practitioners' testimonies and interdisciplinary education, which tend to be more common in traditional management education programs today.

In this context, the aim of this chapter is to discuss the link between entrepreneurship and interdisciplinary teaching approaches, through the case analysis of an interdisciplinary EEP run since 1997 at the Université Catholique de Louvain (UCL), in Belgium. Hence, this chapter attempts to provide an answer to one of the criticisms towards entrepreneurship education literature recently stressed by Béchard and Grégoire (2005). These authors underline the necessity to develop research and expertise at the intersection between entrepreneurship and education science, whereas the literature in entrepreneurship education seldom borrows concepts or theories from disciplines other than management (Gorman et al., 1997).

The chapter proceeds as follows. First, we present a conceptual model developed in order to assess the interdisciplinary level of EEPs. Second, we describe an existing interdisciplinary, inter-school EEP, run since 1997 at UCL. Third, on the basis of the interdisciplinary framework, we assess the interdisciplinary aspects and student satisfaction, and discuss the entrepreneurial impact of the interdisciplinary EEP. A final section concludes.

A conceptual model of interdisciplinary teaching

With regard to interdisciplinary education, the lexical diversity as well as the lack of either a generic definition of interdisciplinarity or a reference operational framework have led Rege Colet (2002) to propose a model that supports the application of interdisciplinary principles to education and enables us to assess those practices. The author defines an interdisciplinary teaching approach as the implementation of a learning experience where disciplinary skills and knowledge are confronted by a specific situation or problem defined in a non-disciplinary way, in order to foster the acquisition of an integrated body of knowledge[1] (Rege Colet, 2002). Let us stress that interdisciplinary education differs from multidisciplinary approaches. On the scale of relationships between disciplines, multidisciplinary approaches pertain only to the juxtaposition of several disciplines, whereas interdisciplinary pedagogy implies the integration of these disciplines.

In examining current definitions of interdisciplinary education, Rege Colet observed that such definitions are based on three principles that form what she calls 'the conceptual base for interdisciplinary approaches'. First, there is the principle of conceptual, theoretical and/or methodological *integration* of two or more disciplines put together. Second, in order to reach this integration, the *collaboration* principle of the different disciplines' representatives is necessary, which implies the coordination and cooperation between the scientific competencies. Third, the expected result of integration and collaboration takes the form of a *synthesis*. These three principles are therefore interrelated, particularly the synthesis, which is a consequence of the two first principles.

Rege Colet's own model, which is graphically represented in Figure 11.1, is based on

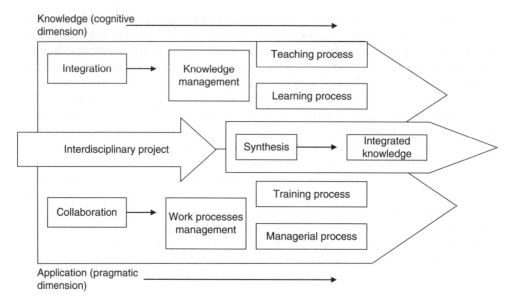

Source: Rege Colet (2002).

Figure 11.1   Conceptual model of an interdisciplinary teaching approach

these three principles. First, the integration principle defines the interrelation and the organization of the respective disciplinary bodies of *knowledge*. Second, the collaboration principle addresses the interaction and the management of the work *processes* that prevail between the stakeholders of the interdisciplinary project. Third, the synthesis principle covers the combination of the two first principles – that is, the resulting learning experience and impact. This last principle represents the connection between the objectives (that is, disciplinary integration) and the means (that is, collaboration). Moreover, any project contains a cognitive dimension, as in the integration principle, and a pragmatic dimension, required by the collaboration principle. These two dimensions are interrelated and their interactions produce synthesis. Finally, disciplinary integration pertains to a knowledge organization issue and collaboration pertains to work organization.

True interdisciplinarity implies a balance between the level of organization of the bodies of knowledge and the level of organization of the work processes. Two sorts of displacement are possible: either the organization of work dominates the organization of knowledge, or the organization of knowledge dominates the organization of work. In the first displacement from balance, the integrated content is neglected in favor of teamwork, project regulation and negotiations with the institution. Under these circumstances, the process can at best be multidisciplinary, as the different disciplinary bodies of knowledge are juxtaposed one to the other. In the second displacement from balance, the construction of an integrated conceptual referent is achieved at the expense of practical considerations. The process then becomes the extension of a paradigmatic work and becomes similar to a disciplinary approach. When real teamwork is lacking and disciplinary divisions prevail, disciplinary cooperation, confrontation and enrichment cannot take place.

As for the cognitive processes that may be involved, Bloom's (1979) taxonomy is often used in the interdisciplinary education literature in order to describe cognitive processes. This taxonomy uses six levels of analysis to express the level of learning difficulty. The construction of integrated knowledge implies a learning experience and cognitive processes of the highest levels of Bloom's taxonomy: that is, analysis, evaluation, and synthesis. In order to reach these levels, learning activities and working methods become more important than content (Petrie, 1992). Answering to this level of requirement, interdisciplinary teaching becomes instrumental and, in a converging approach, disciplines are mobilized to address a situation or a problem at hand.

In that sense, interdisciplinary approaches favor round trips between the purpose and the process.[2] Real-life problems often appeal to several disciplines. Therefore disciplines make sense only if they converge in order to bring out significant learning. This convergence process allows the discipline to go beyond the classification and simplified representation of the complexity of reality to the generation of a significant learning experience grounded in genuine problems or situations (Rege Colet, 2002).

The results are no longer central, but the process is – the purpose being to build coherence between the aims and the means mobilized to find a solution, not an optimal, but a satisfying one. A project cannot be separated from its environment and, as a result, from an educational point of view, an interdisciplinary approach becomes necessary.

Therefore, project- and problem-based learning approaches, in which the process occupies a central place, appear to be natural choices. The choice of the teaching method could be conditioned by the interdisciplinary nature of the entrepreneurship field. However, it could also result from the field itself. Whatever, there seems to be an overlapping between the approaches imposed by the nature of the field and the educational choices that pertain to interdisciplinarity. In other words, it seems that the best entrepreneurship education can only be interdisciplinary.

In the next section, we illustrate the close link between interdisciplinary teaching approaches and entrepreneurship through the analysis of a cross-campus EEP developed at UCL.

Example of a cross-campus interdisciplinary entrepreneurship education program
In this section we first present the relationship between the university and entrepreneurship at UCL and second describe the EEP run at UCL since 1997.

University and entrepreneurship: building a relationship around interdisciplinarity
Unlike many other EEPs, the EEP launched in 1997 at UCL has emerged from cross-campus initiatives and demands. The specifics of this interdisciplinary program result from the comprehensive offerings of the university and from its links with its local economic environment.

Entrepreneurship education at UCL is one of the multiple facets of broader and older questions about the relationship between the university and its economic environment. This questioning is based on the three fundamental missions of a university. UCL wanted to play a role in the entrepreneurship domain, not only through its *teaching mission*, but also in the context of its *research mission*, particularly through creating economic value from research results. In the context of its *mission of service to society*, UCL wanted to contribute to the socio-economic development of the region where it is located, the

Walloon Region, in the southern part of Belgium. The *Global Entrepreneurship Monitor* annual reports on Belgium (GEM, 2002 and 2003)[3] confirm that the Walloon Region is a poor performer in terms of entrepreneurship. Several of the leading local industries (steel, coal, textile and so on) had experienced a steep decline since the early 1980s, and helping to 'boost entrepreneurship' in its environment was perceived as a valuable objective by the university.[4] As a result, UCL has set up entrepreneurship support systems, working at three levels: managing intellectual property rights, financing new ventures and venture creation support.

First, in order to help to protect the university's intellectual property, on the one hand, and to manage and facilitate technological transfer from the university to *extra muros*, on the other, in 1982 UCL created a company dedicated to these goals, called Sopartec. To date, Sopartec manages about 80 patent families. Second, UCL has set up a device, managed by Sopartec, facilitating the access to funds for entrepreneurial project bearers from the university. Either the university directly reinvests funds that have been raised by the valorization of past research in new entrepreneurial projects, or it helps to find public and private funds. Moreover, the university has participated in the creation of a venture capital fund, called VIVES. Third, besides an incubator, created in collaboration with the Walloon Region, a business center has been offering information and support services since the late 1980s.

In the area of entrepreneurship education in itself, the Louvain School of Management (LSM) has been offering various courses in entrepreneurship and SME management since the early 1990s. In 1997, at the engineering and law schools' request, an interdisciplinary program in entrepreneurship and firm creation, called CPME,[5] was launched in collaboration with the LSM. Thanks to the rector's support, this education program has benefited from the financial support of several firms and from the University Foundation. In order to distinguish itself from other programs intended for venture creators or designed for management students, and to emphasize its complete character, UCL has decided to offer it as an optional program to students in engineering, bio-engineering, law and management who are between their undergraduate and their graduate cycles of studies. This choice resulted from a desire to bring together students from different schools around one common entrepreneurial project. At the beginning, it meant that the students had to work in teams containing representatives of at least three of the four above-mentioned orientations. The interdisciplinary option has been the result of three elements: a faculty demand external to the LSM, a will for differentiation, and a collective, rather than individualistic, view of entrepreneurship.

Although mainly aimed at an interdisciplinary audience, the EEP could have limited itself to disciplinary teaching. However, entrepreneurship appeals to disciplines as divergent as economics, management sciences, law.[6] Therefore, entrepreneurship education should necessarily be interdisciplinary. It also should focus on the different functions of organizations simultaneously rather than in parallel.

Next, we illustrate the close link between a university and entrepreneurship through the analysis of the interdisciplinary cross-campus EEP developed at UCL.

The CPME program at UCL
This subsection details the interdisciplinary program in entrepreneurship and firm creation, CPME, which was created by UCL in 1997. We present the program's objectives,

target audience, format and content, learning objectives and the corresponding peda-gogical approaches.

The program's initial objective was 'to train students to deal with the issues related to new business creation', and 'to provide potential student-entrepreneurs with the analysis and problem-solving tools and concepts that will help them along their process of new business creation'. Since then, the goal pursued by the program has been broadened in order to include entrepreneurial skills and activities in their widest sense and, more generally, the development of entrepreneurial spirit.

The program has been integrated into the engineering, bio-engineering, law and man-agement curricula. The target audience of the CPME program is students in the process of completing a degree in one of these four disciplines. The CPME program is not a sepa-rate degree. Its courses replace some compulsory courses and seminars of the bachelor's and master's degrees.

Since September 2007, the CPME program has undergone some changes. It has been offered to all of the 10 schools of UCL: the Economic, Social and Political Sciences School, the Law and Criminology School, the Engineering School, the Bio-engineering, Agronomy and Environment School, the Psychology and Education Sciences School, the School of Theology, the School of Sciences, the Liberal Arts School, the School of Philosophy and the School of Medicine. However, in 2007–08, only the first six schools joined the program.[7] Other schools are planning to offer it to their students, in particular the School of Medicine and its Department of Physiotherapy and Physical Education.

In terms of format and content, the CPME program is spread over the last three years of its parent bachelor's and master's degrees. About 30 students are selected each year, leading to a total number of about 80 students over the three cohorts of students, taking into account those who have failed or left the EEP. Students are selected through a written application and an individual interview on the basis of their motivation. They start the program with a self-assessment seminar concentrated on one weekend. The first-year courses total 135 hours and include three courses, of 45 hours each, that cover the main aspects (legal, financial, economic and managerial) of entrepreneurship. About 20 percent of the classes are co-taught by the teachers coming from different disciplines. Students' final evaluation is based on an interdisciplinary oral presentation and a paper containing all these aspects in one single work graded by all teachers. Teachers quickly bring the students to address real-life problems. This early exposure to real-life problems forces them to test their ability to leverage their disciplinary knowledge as well as to apprehend how those disciplines interact and overlap in a business context. The second year includes two courses that represent a total of 100 hours and are dedicated to an SME analysis and to an international entrepreneurship class. For the SME analysis class, students have to choose an SME, analyze it in all its aspects, and to present it in class in the presence of the entrepreneur. This class also has interventions from faculty, SME specialists and entrepreneurs, case studies and fieldwork. The international entre-preneurship class focuses on familiarizing students with other entrepreneurial cultures through collaborative work with students from foreign universities[8] on international venture projects or on international new venture creation simulation games. These courses are more interactive, as students have to collectively address various business problems within a given cognitive context. Finally, the last year is mainly devoted to the completion of a master's thesis project addressing the creation of a new venture, and to a 30-hour class addressing business planning methodologies. Through the joint development of their new business project, students must identify, analyze, combine and develop on their own the relevant specific knowledge. The master's thesis project must be completed by an interdisciplinary group consisting of three students from different schools.

Since September 2007, CPME courses have been concentrated on the two last years of studies, that is, the two years of the master's degree, as a consequence of the Bologna Reform. The former first- and second-year courses are now taught in the first year. The second year of the EEP still centers on the master's thesis project. Instead of 30 students, 50 students are now accepted each year.

In terms of learning objectives, the CPME program targets both training and support objectives, through which the program addresses both cognitive (integration principle) and non-cognitive (collaboration principle) skills. *Training* programs target students who aspire to launch entrepreneurial activities, but who would not have identified a specific business opportunity yet. Such EEPs or courses aim at providing students with specific tools and abilities, in order to allow them to develop entrepreneurial attitudes and aptitudes, and to be prepared to start or buy a new business or to develop new activities within existing businesses in a more or less distant future. *Support* programs target students who would already have identified a potential business opportunity and who are looking for personalized support and advice to help them to capture that specific opportunity and build their project.

An adapted pedagogical approach corresponds to each of those categories. Training programs, while also requiring the learning of the models, concepts and theories of entrepreneurship, must go beyond traditional knowledge 'transmission-reception' teaching approaches. Indeed, they must confront students with reality in order to develop their entrepreneurial attitudes and skills (Saporta and Verstraete, 2000). Active involvement of the students and problem-based approaches appear adequate in such EEPs in order to achieve the right confrontation between theoretical concepts and practical business problems. Finally, such programs, like any learner-centered program, tend to require more extensive teaching resources and supervision and are better suited for smaller groups of students than traditional academic programs. Support programs typically require a more individualized approach, fine-tuned for the specific characteristics of the business opportunity identified by each student or team and involving a significant amount of coaching, networking and data gathering. This type of learning experience can, for example, be achieved through a student's final thesis or a business plan competition.

The CPME program clearly focuses on problem-based learning and interactions between students and teachers. The first two years provide students with specific skills, as well as relevant concepts and tools, through problem-based learning activities, combining interventions from academic experts and entrepreneurs, case studies, fieldwork and business games. During the third year, students receive dedicated and individual coaching and support for the completion of their master's thesis project which has to be about the creation of a new venture, which can be any kind of organization (commercial, social and so on).

In summary, the CPME program begins with the learning of theoretical concepts, continues with projects and problem-based approaches and ends with a master's thesis project for which each student receives personalized support.

For each class, students have to complete projects and essays in interdisciplinary groups and are evaluated on the basis of class participation. The spatial and temporal framework has been adapted to the interdisciplinary class requirements: shifted schedules, specific classrooms and equipment exclusively reserved for CPME students and for which they are responsible. These settings have been specifically designed to foster students' autonomy, responsibility and professional approach. The classes are taught in the evening in a dedicated building and students have an exclusive 24-hour-a-day access to the program facilities, including computer and telecommunication equipment, meeting room, logistic support, and so on. Those facilities are managed by the students themselves, with the different cohorts sharing responsibilities. This collaboration and the access to an exclusive space generate a 'club' effect among students who develop their own learning community, cutting across the different cohorts and across their original disciplinary affiliation. Moreover, sharing a physical space fosters the exchange of knowledge and experience among students and creates a bonding effect that provides a sense of security. This helps students in their attempt to face the challenges and uncertainties of entrepreneurship.

As announced in the name of the program, the approach used within the EEP is interdisciplinary. The next section presents an assessment of the interdisciplinarity of the EEP and of its impact.

Assessment of the EEP
In this section, we first describe and analyze the interdisciplinary aspects of the program's design on the basis of the conceptual framework developed by Rege Colet. Second, we look at the interdisciplinary index of the CPME program on the basis of Rege Colet's assessment tool. Third, we evaluate the students' satisfaction. Fourth, we assess the entrepreneurial impact of the EEP. This analysis will enable us to draw some lessons, concerning strengths and weaknesses, that we shall support through the students' point of view on the EEP and, particularly, on its interdisciplinary nature.

Interdisciplinary integration and collaboration aspects of the program
The interdisciplinary character as well as the length of the program are features that differentiate it from many other EEPs. Aspects of the CPME program's design are inherent in its interdisciplinary nature. Throughout the program, students must complete numerous group projects, including their master's thesis project, involving students from distinct disciplinary affiliations. But the interdisciplinary dimension of the program's design is much deeper, represented in its objectives, pedagogical approach, target audience, governance, and the students' assessment. Those aspects are discussed below.

The CPME program addresses the two types of objectives of Rege Colet's model – cognitive and pragmatic. Indeed, along its first learning objective (training), the CPME program addresses cognitive abilities, such as the review of the relevant concepts and tools and problem-solving activities. These abilities refer to the integration principle in the sense that they aim at integrating various bodies of knowledge. Moreover, along its second objective (support), the EEP also addresses pragmatic abilities, such as providing dedicated coaching and support to students for the completion of their master's thesis project. These pragmatic abilities refer to the collaboration principle in the sense that they aim at gathering the various stakeholders of the program in the support and assessment of the master's thesis project. In non-cognitive terms, this EEP also aims at developing autonomous and responsible citizens as well as collaborative leaders. Following Rege Colet's model, we first address the knowledge organization, and then the various aspects of work organization.

Beyond being rooted within the disciplinary structures and processes of the university, it is through its pedagogical approach that the EEP aims to be truly interdisciplinary. The team of teachers and coaches, the students' projects, the learning and assessment activities, and the examination and master's thesis jury all feature a strong interdisciplinary dimension. The sequence of learning activities and content is designed to drive students to progressively free themselves from their disciplinary point of view and adopt a wider perspective, allowing them to understand entrepreneurship as an integrated body of knowledge. The initial classes start with the basic disciplines (management, law, and so on), then rapidly bring the students to address real-life problems. This transition forces students to apprehend how disciplinary bodies of knowledge interact and overlap in a business context. Although the first classes typically involve teachers sharing specific issues, concepts and tools with students, they are followed by more interactive sessions where the teachers limit their intervention to the presentation of business problems that students have to address collectively within a given cognitive context. Finally, through the joint development of their new business project, the students' growing autonomy goes hand in hand with a level of coaching and support that is increasingly personalized around the specific expectations, objectives and abilities of the student groups. Furthermore, the involvement of the teachers becomes in itself entrepreneurial, having to respond to changing demands, deal with projects with uncertain prospects and sometimes explore uncharted territory.

The CPME program also shows various interdisciplinary aspects in terms of work organization, such as target audience, governance and student assessment. First, in terms of target audience, as mentioned above, the aspiring entrepreneurs are selected from within different schools early in their program, that is, at the end of the first cycle of studies. This allows students to be trained in parallel with their disciplinary specialization, rather than subsequently. This feature distinguishes this EEP from other experiences which rely on entrepreneurial education offered in the context of postgraduate, lifelong learning or executive education programs.

Second, in terms of governance, the program is managed by a Scientific Committee that includes academic representatives from all the schools involved. This governance body meets once a month. Moreover, the program's structure and contents have been validated by each of those schools and are recognized as an integral part of their respective bachelor's and master's degrees. This full recognition is demonstrated by the fact that the EEP master's thesis project, although managed by the interfaculty Scientific Committee of the CPME program, actually replaces the master's thesis required in each discipline's master's degree program.

It should be noted that this strong integration of the EEP within the respective disciplinary programs, in terms of both student audience and governance, is quite unique given the deep and secular trends of most universities. To us, it seems particularly revealing of the dynamics of opening of UCL. Such dynamics are propitious to the emergence of a true interdisciplinary teaching and learning experience.

Third, we investigate the students' progress through the interdisciplinary master's thesis project. Like any teaching program that goes beyond the simple acquisition of disciplinary concepts and tools, the student assessment process is by nature difficult to implement, be it in terms of the definition or the measurement of evaluation criteria. As an academic program integrated into the bachelor's and master's degrees, the CPME program must, however, include a formal assessment that has to be consistent with the requirements of the respective disciplines, and recognized as such by the respective academic authorities. This interdisciplinary assessment of the student's learning represents a particular challenge given that the respective disciplines tend to rely on different assessment criteria, measurement methods, scales or philosophies. The assessment must therefore take into account not only the integration principle of the EEP (assessment of the acquisition of an integrated body of knowledge) but also its collaboration principle. Indeed, it must also aim at assessing how well tasks, responsibilities and deliverables are shared and coordinated among the members of each entrepreneurial team. Both principles are often intertwined, as each member tends to take responsibility for the issues related to his/her disciplinary affiliation, but also for the implications of those issues and their resolution on the other dimensions of the projects and for the resulting interactions with the other team members. Depending on the characteristics of the entrepreneurial projects, the tasks and issues at hand might be strongly unbalanced towards the disciplinary expertise of some of the team members (for example, in a high-tech project, unbalanced towards engineering, or in a service business involving complex contractual agreements, unbalanced towards legal aspects). However, it is the collective work that is judged, as individual team members are evaluated on the basis of the quality of their team's work. This leaves the responsibility for the balance of the workload and quality of deliverables to the team members themselves. Individual assessment is therefore used only for an assessment of the disciplinary skills involved in the EEP and of the students' ongoing participation in the learning activities. Importantly, it is the quality of the teamwork that is evaluated, not the economic potential of their entrepreneurial project. Indeed a group might do a good job by correctly concluding that the entrepreneurial opportunity they had considered has limited or no potential, given its features, resource requirements, competitive environment or market. The result of the project in itself cannot constitute the unique assessment criterion. It is the ability of the team to reach this conclusion, to argue and to synthesize it that is assessed, as it reflects their ability to adopt the integrated point of view required in an entrepreneurial context.

The master's thesis project that the students have to complete at the end of the program provides a good illustration of this collective interdisciplinary assessment and its degree of complexity. As each group includes members from different disciplines, it is mentored by a team of academics including members of the corresponding faculties. Thus, there are typically three thesis advisors (instead of one in traditional projects), from three different schools of the university. This multi-advisor structure, with which academics are sometimes uncomfortable, can generate two types of *negative side-effects* that might harm the collaboration principle underpinning the EEP. Some could feel that their contributions are diluted or underrepresented in the project, and therefore could not contribute enough to its success. On the contrary, others could try to bias the project towards their own disciplinary interest or assessment criteria, threatening the overall balance and coherence of the project. It is the EEP manager's responsibility to ensure that those potential pitfalls are avoided across the portfolio of projects that is generated each year.

Detailed and quantifiable assessment criteria are therefore difficult to define and/or implement a priori, as the assessment of each project tends to be consensus based, with the program manager balancing the opinions of each of the thesis advisors involved. Although this approach appears relatively pragmatic, nevertheless it generates some discomfort among students faced with an assessment process that sometimes appears arbitrary, or at a minimum lacks transparency. This assessment issue is actually frequently raised in the feedback provided by the students, although it does not affect their overall (positive) perception of the EEP itself. We shall discuss this later.

The CPME program ultimately aims at contributing to the launch of interdisciplinary entrepreneurial teams, as student groups consist of future professionals, coming from different schools, who should be able to combine their respective expertise, learn to adopt each other's point of view and use each other's language. This learning process across multiple disciplines is a key element of the EEP, frequently stressed by the students and by the teachers. This again reinforces the interdisciplinary dimension of the EEP. The exposure to real-life business projects that could ultimately lead to entrepreneurial career opportunities for the students also contributes to this dimension, as students are forced to adopt interdisciplinary perspectives if they want to be able to deal with the complexity of real business problems. Doing this as an entrepreneurial team requires students to learn, on the one hand, how to reach a sufficient level of autonomy and professionalism and, on the other, how to trust, leverage and recognize the specialized skills of each member of the group. The entrepreneurial projects that are progressively shaped by the students along the CPME program therefore constitute a cornerstone of the professional development objectives of the program.

For the teachers and program managers, these projects are the core around which the contributions of each discipline can be combined and integrated as the different facets of entrepreneurship. The projects also generate a stronger commitment by the students to achieve practical results, leading them to engage more proactively in the learning process. Let us stress again that the learning process *per se* can be considered as more important than the end product, as significant learning can be extracted even if the entrepreneurial project does not ultimately succeed. Of course, content is not totally irrelevant. For example, having the same interdisciplinary teams concentrate on managing the process of bronze casting would not teach them as much about new venture creation as would concentration on an entrepreneurial problem. Through this active learning process, students will have confronted the various aspects of entrepreneurship and its diversity of tools, terminology and perspectives by testing, exploring, challenging, assessing and ultimately validating (or not) their entrepreneurial project. This is achieved with the help of the tools and concepts provided and through interactions with their learning peers. Let us note that project-based learning is indeed a natural choice for EEP because the notion of a project is common to all types of entrepreneurial activities.

As it results from the principles of knowledge integration and of collaboration between the program's stakeholders, the synthesis principle can only be analyzed through the evaluation of the CPME program's interdisciplinary aspects as a whole.

Synthesis aspects of the program
The CPME program has been evaluated by adapting an assessment tool based on the interdisciplinary dimensions developed by Rege Colet (2002). This tool, approved by the

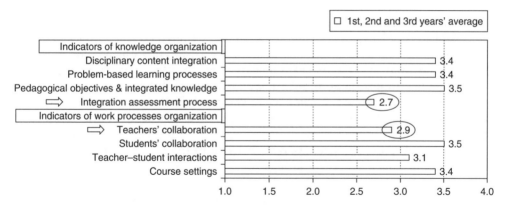

Figure 11.2 Evaluation of the interdisciplinary dimensions according to Rege Colet

original author, evaluates the level of integration, collaboration and synthesis involved in an interdisciplinary learning process, using Likert-scale surveys. The resulting data locate students' and teachers' perceptions regarding the degree of integration in the structure of the knowledge content, on the one hand, and the degree of collaboration in the work processes organization, on the other. In this approach, the integration principle is measured by four indicators: the level of disciplinary content integration, the level of integration in problem-based learning processes, the level of integration in pedagogical objectives and finally the level of integration in the assessment process. The collaboration principle is measured by four other indicators: teachers' collaboration, students' collaboration, teacher–student interactions and course settings. Each of the eight indicators consists of several items on which the questionnaire tests the level of agreement of the students (the four levels used in the original article are: completely agree, partially agree, partially disagree and completely disagree). Finally, an interdisciplinary index is defined as the ratio of the scores (total of the scores obtained for each indicator) along the integration and collaboration dimensions. A truly interdisciplinary program should be balanced along those two dimensions, that is, achieve an interdisciplinary index of 1 (Rege Colet, 2002).

This test, conducted with the first-, second- and third-year student cohorts in April and December 2004, confirmed that the CPME program is actually quite interdisciplinary, with interdisciplinary indices of, respectively, 1.08, 1.17 and 0.99 for the three years of the program. The balance between the organization of the knowledge content and of the work processes, during the three years, appears therefore to be well perceived by the students (see Figure 11.2).

The test also provides detailed information regarding the perceived strengths and weaknesses of the program in terms of the teaching strategy's coherence. Those results were consistent with the student satisfaction surveys discussed in the next subsection and identified specific dimensions on which to act in order to improve the quality of the EEP as a whole. Again, and not very surprisingly, despite a very positive report regarding the interdisciplinary quality of the program, room for improvement was noted in terms of collaboration between the teachers and in terms of clarity of the student assessment process. As highlighted above, collaboration between teachers and consensus about the assessment process are contingent on the willingness and ability of teachers and speakers from distinct disciplines to work together, exchange information and experience as well as communicate and act as a team. All of these are aspects that do not tend to emerge spontaneously from an academic environment.

Note that this evaluation of the interdisciplinary dimensions was developed and conducted with the intention of providing the teachers and the EEP manager with feedback that could be used to assess and regulate the quality of this complex interdisciplinary program.

In the next subsection, we look at the students' satisfaction with the EEP.

Students' satisfaction
Parallel to the evaluation of the interdisciplinary dimensions mentioned above, surveys have been conducted during five successive years (2000, 2001, 2002, 2003 and 2004), on the initiative of the EEP manager, in order to collect students' opinion on the program. Note that the surveyed students were, prior to the survey, preselected on the basis of their interest in entrepreneurship.

A first qualitative survey, including open and semi-structured questions, was sent to the first three cohorts of students, those who completed the program in 2000, 2001 and 2002. Based on this preliminary survey, a questionnaire with 57 closed-ended questions and three open-ended questions (related, respectively, to the key strengths of the program, its key limitations and some suggestions) was defined and sent by mail to the students of the 2003 and 2004 cohorts. All of the students completed the first survey and 54 percent replied to the postal questionnaire.

Those surveys provide very encouraging results: they indicate that 98 percent of the students are 'quite satisfied' or 'very satisfied' with the CPME program as a whole. The two main advantages noted by the students related, on the one hand, to the interdisciplinary approach of the program and, on the other, to the high level of interactivity in the learning process. Those two features of the EEP are not only sources of motivation a priori, but also appear as the main drivers of student satisfaction a posteriori, indicating that their expectations regarding the interdisciplinary approach and interactivity have been met. In particular, students report a high level of satisfaction regarding the interdisciplinary dimension of the program content, the teaching team, the student groups, the guest speakers and the evaluation jury.

Compared to traditional courses, the EEP requires extra efforts from the students who have to dedicate two evenings a week to their entrepreneurship classes for several years and to provide a lot of additional work for their different assignments. This means that these students are probably more motivated, but also probably more demanding than 'regular' students. In terms of evaluation, we can assume that the process is more similar to adult education programs, grouping people with different backgrounds and expectations, than to traditional disciplinary student evaluation. However, compared to adult education evaluation, the fact that the students have different educational backgrounds is not perceived as a problem, because interdisciplinarity is at the core of the program. As a result, students are not dissatisfied because of different initial levels of knowledge among their peers. This highly motivated audience constitutes one of the sources of success of the CPME program (Table 11.1).

With regard to factors that students believe could be improved, the answers to these

Table 11.1   *Students' satisfaction survey: some results (% of students who agree partially or completely)*

Some results: May 2006	1st year	2nd year		3rd year
		Business students	Others	
At the time of my enrollment, I had a project of venture creation	31	33	33	18
The program of this year reinforces my motivation to create or take over a business in the medium term	81	57	87	83
Content and training activities				
The progression of activities through the year is adequate	78	100	67	83
The practitioners' contributions are of sufficient quality	81	86	100	83
The teaching methods tally with the program's objectives	78	86	93	92
The interdisciplinary teamwork is useful	94	86	93	100
Learning evaluation				
The evaluation criteria of the teamwork are clearly explained	33	43	47	82
The 'content' dimension of the teamwork is sufficiently taken into account in the evaluation	76	60	69	83
The 'process' dimension of the teamwork (stages, methodology, progression, etc.) is sufficiently taken into account in the evaluation	31	67	42	83

surveys mention the coordination among the teachers and the assessment process. Students seem to wish for a stronger collaboration between teachers, as well as greater transparency in terms of assessment. They report that the links between the different classes should be made more explicit, indicating that the integration between the various classes could be improved. They also tend to perceive that the collective assessment process lacks transparency and is somewhat unfair. In particular, as mentioned above, a small weight is attached to the individual contributions relative to the collective results of the group. Furthermore, the interdisciplinary dimension of the program makes it difficult to select detailed and explicit assessment criteria and thresholds that would cope with the diversity of the students' projects in terms of scope, content and disciplinary knowledge. In particular, the respective expectations of the teachers coming from various disciplines, and how they are combined towards a consensus, appear sometimes unclear to the students, or at least are not communicated clearly enough. The weakness of the program thus seems to be in the collaboration principle. However, recall that the interdisciplinary dimension is present at the level of the program content, the teaching team, the student groups, the guest speakers and the assessment jury. These multiple sources of interdisciplinarity probably partially explain their concern.

We have also assessed the CPME program in terms of the professional development of our alumni. Finally, in the last subsection we discuss the issue of the entrepreneurial impact of the EEP.

Entrepreneurial impact of the EEP

Due to an explicit regional economic concern, in the early stages of the CPME program, at least from a formal point of view, its aim was limited to entrepreneurship in its most restrictive meaning, that is, new firm creation. In this perspective, such an education program could only be targeted at potential firm creators and would be conditioned and measured by a single success imperative: the number of new firms created. This approach is largely predominant in university entrepreneurship courses and/or education programs.

In order to assess the direct entrepreneurial impact of the CPME program, we conducted a survey in 2005 (Heylemans, 2006). The sample consisted of students who took the CPME program between 1997 and 2005 (our first students graduated in 2000). A total of 124 questionnaires were sent. Eighty-four percent of the questionnaires reached their destination and 16 percent were returned because of address changes. The results show that 63.8 percent of former CPME students think that the EEP has had an impact on their entrepreneurial intentions. Before starting the program, 58.7 percent of students considered themselves likely to create a business. After they had taken the EEP, 79.3 percent estimated that it was more than probable. The EEP has also had a positive impact on their estimated capacity to set up a business: 89 percent of students felt that they were capable of setting up a business at the end of the EEP, against 63.8 percent before starting the program.

With regard to the impact of the EEP on student motivation to start a business, the results show that 75 percent of the students want to become entrepreneurs after their first, second or last year in the CPME program, whereas only 35 percent (on average) claimed to have a project of venture creation in mind at the time of their entry into the program (see Table 11.1).

Among the alumni of the CPME program, some have already started a business. The survey showed that 11 percent of the students who graduated between 2000 and 2005 have created a firm. Privileged sectors are retail, accounting, leisure, the Internet, tourism and telecom companies. This rate is even more impressive when it is compared to the results of surveys that have been conducted by 'traditional' European students. These show that the great majority are, above all, interested in job security and that the risk aversion rises with the education level (Boissin and Aimin, 2006; Guyot et al., 2006). Moreover, our results do not reflect the number of spin-offs that CPME students have helped to set up, or their entrepreneurial activities among existing organizations.

However, this also means that many alumni of the EEP have made 'traditional' career choices, joining existing organizations. Those choices correspond in general to their disciplinary origin. They would probably have been made even if students had not followed any venture creation program.

Over time, we have identified various potential explanations of this apparent discrepancy. These are related to delayed effects, selection bias and technology intensity. These explanations have largely contributed to the evolution and the enlargement of the original objectives. We discuss these below.

First, delayed effects result from the fact that European university education seems to encourage students to regard venture creation with caution, highlighting the pitfalls of naive 'dot-com type' projects. Some students wish to develop entrepreneurial activities in a more or less distant future, but decide first to work for large organizations. For those students, the entrepreneurial impact of the EEP in terms of future intentions (Kolvereid and Moen, 1997; Noel, 2001) is not yet visible, and can only be observed from a long-term perspective. The students' 'cautious patience' and the 'observation delay' of the EEP's impact is consistent with several empirical studies which have shown that a strong functional or sector-based professional experience actually improves the subsequent survival prospects and increases the growth potential of the entrepreneur's venture (Dunkelberg and Cooper, 1982; Hambrick and Mason, 1984; Storey, 1994; Westhead and Birley, 1995; Dahlqvist et al., 1999). This explanation is consistent with students' motivations and tends to demonstrate that the assessment of the entrepreneurial impact of an EEP should include data collected several years after its launch (Block and Stumpf, 1992). Informal studies quoted by Vesper and Gartner (1997) have indicated a strong correlation between the participation in an entrepreneurial course and the likelihood of launching one's own business in a more or less distant future. This conclusion is probably reinforced in the case of students attending a complete EEP rather than an isolated course. The survey among our alumni also shows that 70 percent of the students who graduated between 2000 and 2005 and have not yet created a firm wish to do so within seven years maximum.

An inadequacy between our selection methods and our objectives could constitute a second potential explanation for the discrepancy. A selection bias in the students attending the EEP, diverging from the initial new business creation objective, could be another potential mitigating factor of the entrepreneurial impact of the program. Anecdotal evidence suggests that some 'résumé-driven' students apply for the program not because they want to become entrepreneurs, but because they realize that attending this program would boost their perceived value on the job market, either because of its interdisciplinary dimension or because of the positive perception often associated with entrepreneurship by recruiters. Dealing with this selection bias would require the EEP managers to be able to select students with the right entrepreneurial aptitudes more effectively at the beginning. Academic research (Brenner et al., 1991; Chell et al., 1991; Filion, 1997; Chen et al., 1998) tried to identify factors that could be associated with entrepreneurial aptitudes: individual characteristics (desire for independence, result-orientation, internal locus of control, flexibility, leadership, and so on), entrepreneurial motivations (need for achievement, search for autonomy, and so on), external factors that can stimulate the appearance of entrepreneurial skills (socio-cultural environment, family context, professional experience, education, and so on). Similarly, typologies of entrepreneurs have been suggested. However, these a priori factors have to be put into perspective as the entrepreneurial process remains multifaceted and contingent, and cannot be reduced to a predefined model that could be used to identify future entrepreneurs. Indeed, some psychological tests or typologies that had been developed to identify entrepreneurs have been severely criticized (Chell, 1985). The same applies to typologies and traits that only constitute ideal types. The entrepreneurial aptitudes of a student remain difficult to assess a priori in a systematic manner. Moreover, even this audience of résumé-driven students can play a role in the diffusion of an entrepreneurial culture within their future organizations or within society at large and therefore contribute somewhat to the objectives of the EEP. The promotion of an entrepreneurial culture should also involve the education of students whose career will have indirect entrepreneurial features. Therefore, the goal of an EEP is not only to create entrepreneurs, but also to educate students who will work with entrepreneurs, whether as employees, consultants or managers and, more widely, who can contribute to the emergence of a more entrepreneurial environment. Finally, students who, after exposure to an EEP, decide that this life is not for them will probably avoid opening businesses that could be doomed to failure. Learning what you are not made for can be as important as learning what you do well.

Finally, a third potential explanation is the technology intensity of the program, as technology-oriented start-ups such as university spin-offs were probably overrepresented in the early versions of the program. Indeed, as part of the interdisciplinary master's thesis requirements, all project groups had initially to include a student from the engineering school. As a consequence, due to this school's internal requirements, most of the master's thesis projects had a strong technology dimension. In particular, a large proportion of them related to the commercialization of intellectual property and technologies developed within the university. This technology bias excluded de facto a wide range of entrepreneurial opportunities in other potential domains of creation – for example, in the retail or service sectors – that could otherwise have been pursued in the context of the EEP. To deal with this 'technology' issue, the rules defining the structure of the master's thesis groups have been made more flexible. Students are now allowed to form groups according to their own interest in the topic and not on the basis of their scientific discipline, even if it involves no or limited technology and therefore offers limited room for an in-depth contribution from an engineering student. Yet, all groups must remain interdisciplinary, that is, include students from at least two different schools.

The evaluation process has contributed to the evolution of the program. Under the simultaneous influence of students and professors, beyond new business creation in a restrictive sense, the goal pursued by the CPME program has been broadened to include entrepreneurial skills and activities in their widest sense, such as intrapreneurship, working for an SME, not-for-profit venture, spin-offs, and, more generally, the development of an entrepreneurial spirit. This consists of, 'in business, as well as in all human activities, identifying opportunities, gathering resources of different natures, creating wealth that encounters solvable demands' (Albert and Marion, 1998, p. 28). This also clearly shows that entrepreneurial impact assessment of EEPs needs to look beyond the measurement of the number of firms created by the EEPs' alumni.

Conclusion

In their introduction to the *Academy of Management Learning and Education* special issue on entrepreneurship education, Greene et al. (2004) stress the fact that entrepreneurship classes have often played the role of testing grounds for teaching methods that tend to be generalized today to traditional business courses. Entrepreneurship is a good training ground for universities wanting to develop interdisciplinary teaching approaches, because entrepreneurship as a theoretical body of knowledge is by nature an interdisciplinary field, and because entrepreneurship education is well suited to the teaching approaches related to interdisciplinary content.

The case study of a university EEP presented in this chapter illustrates how interdisciplinary university programs can, at bachelor's or master's degree level, already help students to build bridges between academia and the 'real' world, as well as between themselves and their future professional development. It allows students to be exposed not only to interdisciplinary content and problems but also to interdisciplinary teamwork managed, in the case of the CPME program, around their entrepreneurial master's thesis project. For institutions, these interdisciplinary programs amplify the university's strength as a locus of varying knowledge and culture that blend to create new knowledge. Therefore such programs can build bridges between the local socio-economic environment and university. For teachers, programs such as this interdisciplinary EEP provide fertile ground for the development of new educational approaches and skills that can spill over to other (disciplinary) programs of the institution. This reinforces interdisciplinarity as one of the core assets of the university, where various experience, theories and knowledge can confront and feed each other. As Joseph Schumpeter emphasized decades ago, most innovations do emerge from the creative combination of existing knowledge.

Furthermore, and as stressed by the students, the interactive and embedded learning approach developed in interdisciplinary programs such as the EEP presented here is one of its most attractive features. This approach is now being reinforced within academic institutions and developed throughout the university as a way to address new problems within normal disciplinary contexts. Paradoxically, as the approach moves into the traditional disciplines there could be decreasing student interest in an EEP, as its way of operating becomes less novel. Alternatively, the generalization of active and contextualized teaching methods could lead more students to be attracted by interdisciplinary programs like the UCL EEP, because they would already have been accustomed to its methods.

The interdisciplinary dimension of an EEP also generates specific 'cultural' challenges in an academic environment where such connections are seldom rewarded, despite their being very time consuming. The broader academic environment is still not very propitious for interdisciplinary EEPs. On the one hand, it is extremely difficult to pry professors from their disciplinary framework. Indeed, international assessment and evaluation systems do not generally include pedagogical efforts, notwithstanding the fact that interdisciplinary teaching is more demanding. Moreover, university promotion systems favor research and, in particular, strictly disciplinary research, and it is quite hard to define and apply common assessment criteria to interdisciplinary work. In sum, the major difficulties in launching these kinds of programs are linked to the fact that they have to subsume academic imperatives from distinct schools. Interdisciplinary governance bodies and dialogue with faculty authority are therefore essential elements.

Finally, the intrinsic value of an EEP should be considered in the light of its overall objectives. Those objectives should definitely relate not only to the number of start-ups created in the short term, but also to entrepreneurial activities, intentions and attitudes in their widest sense. This includes new business development, involvement in SMEs, and all the activities directly or indirectly related to entrepreneurship. The objectives of an EEP should therefore also be conceived from a cultural perspective, as a contributor to the emergence of an environment that stimulates and values entrepreneurship. In other words, as David Birch declared in an interview (Aronsson, 2004), the role of entrepreneurship education is to stress the social and economic role and importance of entrepreneurship, as well as to make the public and the political leaders aware of it in order to generate a favorable environment.

Notes

* The authors would like to thank Kelly Shaver for his very useful comments and suggestions.
1. Translated from French.

2. We are not saying that contents do not count, but that 'goals for students are much more process oriented' than content oriented (Petrie, 1992, p. 320).
3. These are the only two reports specifically analyzing the Walloon Region. Although the data for 2003 show some improvement, later reports about Belgium as a whole conclude that the situation is still troublesome.
4. There was no scientific evidence for the lack of entrepreneurial spirit back in 1997. The first GEM report for Belgium was written in 2000.
5. CPME stands for 'Formation Interdisciplinaire en Création de Petites et Moyennes Entreprises' (Interdisciplinary Education Program in SME Creation).
6. Psychology and sociology are also integrated in some entrepreneurship courses.
7. These six schools represent 60 percent of the UCL students (Report of the Rectoral Council of the University of Louvain for 2006–2007, Chantiers et Défis 2006–2007, p. 66).
8. We have developed an international entrepreneurship course involving a student exchange in collaboration with some US universities. See Jones et al. (2008).

References

Acs, Z.J. and Audretsch, D.B. (2003), 'Introduction to the Handbook of entrepreneurship research', in Acs and Audretsch (eds), 3–20.
Acs, Z.J. and Audretsch, D.B. (eds) (2003), *Handbook of Entrepreneurship Research*, Boston, MA, Dordrecht and London: Kluwer Academic.
Albert, P. and Marion, S. (1998), 'Ouvrir l'enseignement à l'esprit d'entreprendre', in Birley, S. and Muzyka, D. (eds), *L'Art d'entreprendre*, Paris: Village Mondial, 28–30.
Aronsson, M. (2004), 'Education matters – but does entrepreneurship education. An interview with David Birch', *Academy of Management Learning and Education*, 3(3), 289–92.
Béchard, J.P. and Grégoire, D. (2005), 'Entrepreneurship education research revisited: the case of higher education', *Academy of Management Learning and Education*, 4(1), 22–43.
Block, Z. and Stumpf, S.A. (1992), 'Entrepreneurship education research: experience and challenge', in Sexton, D.L. and Kasarda, J.M. (eds), *The State of the Art of Entrepreneurship*, Boston, MA: PWS-Kent Publishing, 17–45.
Bloom, B.S. (1979), *Taxonomy of Educational Objectives: The Classification of Educational Goals*, London: Longman.
Boissin, J.P. and Emin, S. (2006), 'Les étudiants et l'entrepreneuriat: l'effet des formations', *Proceedings of the XVth International Conference in Strategic Management*, Annecy-Geneva, 13–16 June.
Brenner, O.C., Pringle, C.D. and Greenhaus, J.H. (1991), 'Perceived fulfillment of organizational employment versus entrepreneurship: work values and career intentions of business college graduates', *Journal of Small Business Management*, 29(3), 62–74.
Bruyat, C. and Julien, P.-A. (2001), 'Defining the field of research in entrepreneurship', *Journal of Business Venturing*, 16, 165–80.
Chell, E. (1985), 'The entrepreneurial personality: a few ghosts laid to rest?', *International Small Business Journal*, 3(3), 43–54.
Chell, E., Haworth, J. and Brearley, S. (1991), *The Entrepreneurial Personality: Concepts, Cases and Categories*, London: Routledge.
Chen, C.C., Greene, P.G. and Crick, A. (1998), 'Does entrepreneurial self-efficacy distinguish entrepreneurs from managers?', *Journal of Business Venturing*, 13(4), 295–316.
Cooper, A. (2003), 'Entrepreneurship: the past, the present and the future', in Acs and Audretsch (eds), 21–34.
Dahlqvist, J., Davidsson, P. and Wiklund, J. (1999), 'Initial conditions as predictors of new venture performance: a replication and extension of the Cooper et al. study', paper presented at the 44th World Conference of the International Council for Small Business, Naples (Italy), 20–23 June.
Dunkelberg, W.G. and Cooper, A.C. (1982), 'Patterns of small business growth', *Academy of Management Proceedings*, 409–13.
Fayolle, A. (2000), 'Editorial du dossier sur l'enseignement de l'entrepreneuriat', *Revue Gestion 2000*, 17(3), 74–5.
Fiet, J.O. (2001), 'The pedagogical side of teaching entrepreneurship', *Journal of Business Venturing*, 16, 101–17.
Filion, L.J. (1997), 'Le champ de l'entrepreneuriat: historique, évolutions et tendances', *Revue Internationale P.M.E.*, 10(2), 129–72.
GEM (2002), *The Global Entrepreneurship Monitor: Executive Report for Belgium*, www.gemconsortium.org/document.aspx?id=265, March 20, 2008.

GEM (2003), *The Global Entrepreneurship Monitor: Executive Report for Belgium and Wallonia*, www.gemconsortium.org/document.aspx?id=357, March 20, 2008.

Gorman, G., Hanlon, D. and King, W. (1997), 'Some research perspectives on entrepreneurship education, enterprise education and education for small business management: a ten-year literature review', *International Small Business Journal*, **15**(3), 56–77.

Greene, P., Katz, J. and Johannisson, B. (2004), 'From the guest co-editors: entrepreneurship education', *Academy of Management Learning and Education*, **3**(3), 238–41.

Guyot, J.-L., Lohest, O. and Giacomin, O. (2006), 'Le passage de l'auto-emploi, prise de risque: le cas des primo-créateurs en Wallonie', in *Données longitudinales dans l'analyse du marché du travail*, University of Aix en Provence, June.

Hambrick, D.C. and Mason, P.A. (1984), 'Upper-echelons: the organization as a reflection of its top managers', *Academy of Management Review*, **9**(2), 193–206.

Heylemans, A. (2006), 'L'impact des formations entrepreneuriales sur la création d'entreprise', Thesis, Louvain-la-Neuve (Belgium): Louvain School of Management.

Jones, S., Denslow, D., Janssen, F., zu Knyphausen-Aufseß, D., Lopis, J., Shinnar, R. and Toney, B. (2008), 'Teaching international entrepreneurship through student exchange: observations, obstacles and recommendations', *Journal of Entrepreneurship Education*, **11**, 99–115.

Katz, J.A. (2003), 'The chronology and intellectual trajectory of American entrepreneurship education: 1876–1999', *Journal of Business Venturing*, **18**, 283–300.

Klandt, H. (2004), 'Entrepreneurship education and research in German-speaking Europe', *Academy of Management Learning and Education*, **3**(3), 293–301.

Kolvereid, L. and Moen, O. (1997), 'Entrepreneurship among business graduates: does a major in entrepreneurship make a difference?', *Journal of European Industrial Training*, **21**(4), 154–60.

Kuratko, D.F. (2005), 'The emergence of entrepreneurship education: development, trends and challenges', *Entrepreneurship Theory and Practice*, **29**(5), 577–97.

Low, M.B. (2001), 'The adolescence of entrepreneurship research: specification of purpose', *Entrepreneurship Theory and Practice*, **25**(4), 17–27.

McGrath, R.G. (2003), 'Connecting the study of entrepreneurship and theories of capitalist progress: an epilogue', in Acs and Audrestch (eds), 515–31.

Noel, T.W. (2001), 'Effects of entrepreneurial education on intent to open a business', *Frontiers of Entrepreneurship Research*, Babson Conference Proceedings, www.babson.edu/entrep/fer.

Petrie, H.G. (1992), 'Interdisciplinary education: are we faced with insurmountable opportunities?', *Review of Research Education*, **18**, 299–333.

Rege Colet, N. (2002), *Enseignement universitaire et interdisciplinarité: Un cadre pour analyser, agir et évaluer*, Brussels: De Boeck University.

Saporta, B. and Verstraete, T. (2000), 'Réflexions sur l'enseignement de l'entrepreneuriat dans les composantes en sciences de gestion des universités françaises', *Revue Gestion 2000*, **17**(3), 97–121.

Storey, D.J. (1994), *Understanding the Small Business Sector*, London and Boston, MA: International Thomson Business Press.

Verstraete, T. and Fayolle, A. (2004), 'Quatre paradigmes pour cerner le domaine de recherche en entrepreneuriat', Proceedings of the 7ème Congrès International Francophone en Entrepreneuriat et PME, Montpellier (France), 27–29 October.

Vesper, K.H. and Gartner, W.B. (1997), 'Measuring progress in entrepreneurship education', *Journal of Business Venturing*, **12**(5), 403–21.

Westhead, P. and Birley, S. (1995), 'Employment growth in new independent owner-managed firms in Great Britain', *International Small Business Journal*, **13**(3), 11–34.

12 Lights, camera, action: advancing liberal arts values . . . entrepreneurially

Lynnette Claire

Introduction

Many of the chapters in this book have focused on spreading entrepreneurship throughout a liberal arts curriculum. This chapter describes a method of teaching entrepreneurship and increasing student self-efficacy in a business course by using non-traditional methods from other disciplines. The entrepreneur job shadow and documentary project, which results in an entrepreneur film festival, could be used in both liberal arts colleges and research universities, as long as the administration embraces innovative learning methods.

As a part of an introductory course in entrepreneurship, the entrepreneur job shadow and documentary project gives students an intimate experience with one entrepreneur and exposure to many others (through the film festival) to supplement what is learned in class. During the first half of a 15-week course, in addition to the job shadow and documentary project, students read about entrepreneurship, hear about entrepreneurs and entrepreneurship in class, engage in opportunity recognition exercises, and start developing the skills they will need to develop ventures of their own. The entrepreneur job shadow and documentary project provides a structure for students to explore their own growing understanding of the concept of entrepreneurship and what it may be like to engage in entrepreneurship.

The Entrepreneur Film Festival is the culminating event of the six-week entrepreneur job shadow and documentary project at Tacoma, Washington State, in which each student creates a 10-minute documentary of a local entrepreneur during at least eight hours of job shadowing. The entrepreneurship film festival is in its third year, with two festivals per year (one per semester). The festival is open to the public, which includes the student filmmakers, their peers and professors, the entrepreneurs featured in the films, and other interested community members. It has served as an excellent method for engaging students in exploring what entrepreneurship means, what it looks like, what the challenges and opportunities are, and what skills they would need to engage in it. Through the job shadow, the students find themselves developing a close relationship with their entrepreneurs and creating a short video case about one specific entrepreneur. The process of creating each film is time-consuming, painstaking, frustrating, and incredibly rewarding. In an average of 20 hours spent in editing each 10-minute film, the students relive their job shadow and think critically about what it means to be an entrepreneur.

The job shadow and documentary project brings together the arts, technology, communication and business to reinforce the liberal arts values of interdisciplinary connections, critical thinking, and lifelong learning. Additionally, the project contributes significantly to our entrepreneurship students' high rates of business formation through opportunities for 'deep learning' (Kreber, 2001, p. 225; Cooper and Lucas, 2006, p. 4) that increase students' self-efficacy (ibid.).

Table 12.1   Entrepreneur job shadow and documentary timeline

Week	Activity and items due	Points possible (200)
1	Reflection 1 (expectations) due	10
	Filmmaking 101	
2	30-second video due	8
	Locate entrepreneur	
3	Reflection 2 (identifying entrepreneur) due	10
	Choose film festival themes	
	Filmmaking 201 – guest speaker	
	Job shadow entrepreneur	
4	Job shadow entrepreneur	
5	Reflection 3 (reflections on entrepreneurship) due	10
	Job shadow entrepreneur/edit film	
	Create posters and send invitations to entrepreneurs	
6	Filmmaking 301 – guest speaker	
	Professor views draft films	
	Edit film	
7	Reflection 4 (technical challenges and art) due	10
	Edit film	
8	Film due	80
9	Entrepreneur Film Festival (2 nights)	16
10	Reflection 5 (learning outcomes) due	16
	Signed job shadow time log due (points reflect 8 hours of job shadowing—extra credit is possible)	40

This chapter begins with a description of the entrepreneur documentary project and the Entrepreneur Film Festival. The challenges of the project precede the benefits section. In the benefits section, the learning mechanisms are discussed as well as other goals such as building ties with our local community.

Entrepreneur documentary project
The entrepreneur documentary project takes place within an entrepreneurship class in a school of business and leadership. Students do not necessarily come into the class with filmmaking interest or experience. On the first day of class, the students learn that they will be expected to find a local entrepreneur and make a 10-minute documentary about him or her as an *individual* assignment (see Table 12.1). Student reactions to the project vary from delight to terror.

Students are advised to locate an entrepreneur doing something that interests them and initiate job shadowing that will result in a short film. If students have difficulty identifying an entrepreneur, they meet with the instructor to talk about their interests and the instructor identifies local entrepreneurs who may be of interest. The students are required to spend at least eight hours job shadowing and creating a film that is publicly available, so the entrepreneur needs to be willing to accommodate that.[1] Students are supplied with a job shadow time log form in which they note the date and times they job shadowed and what they did. Both the student and the entrepreneur are required to sign the form for the students to receive credit for the job shadow time.

For most students, filmmaking is a new activity. They are told that, although the class is not an art class, the documentaries should be high quality. If the documentary is not of sufficient quality, the instructor will send the film back to the student for more editing. To date, film quality has not been a significant problem. Innovation and artistry are desirable, not required, qualities. The films are required to be interesting, tell a story, demonstrate that the individual is an entrepreneur, and address one of the themes the class has chosen.

The class meets three days a week for 50 minutes each session. The day before the class chooses the themes for the films, the instructor shares with the class previous themes and asks the students to think about themes before the next class session. Popular themes include Entrepreneurial Triumphs and Challenges, A Day in the Life of an Entrepreneur, and The Entrepreneurial Beginnings. During the next class session, the students generate a list of possible themes for the films. Each student is allowed to vote for two themes of interest. This narrows down the list of themes and we talk through the remaining options, ensuring that everyone has one theme that he or she could conceivably use for his or her documentary. The themes help give form to the films by focusing their observations and analysis, as well as helping them compare entrepreneurs at the film festival.

The students receive three class sessions of instruction about filmmaking. Filmmaking 101 occurs during the first two weeks of the semester and begins with how to check out a camera from our media services department and how to turn it on. It includes using a tripod, lighting, framing, shooting interviews, the importance of B-roll (the visual images that will be shown while the entrepreneur is talking), and a general description of film editing. The instructor brings a camera, wireless microphone and tripod to class to emphasize the critical importance of these three items to creating a quality film. Much of the instruction is on the board, demonstrating basic composition concepts such as the rule of thirds, the concept of head room, and where to position a subject given the light source in the room.

Filmmaking 201 occurs during the third week of the term and includes examples of quality documentaries with tips about how to achieve semi-professional results. This session is conducted by a professional documentary filmmaker who explains what to avoid (panning, lots of zooming, fancy transitions, distracting objects in the frame) as well as what to focus on (details that people do not normally see, the non-focal person's story, still images). The filmmaker also explains how to use film editing software.

Filmmaking 301 is also conducted by the professional filmmaker – and often another person on the filmmaker's staff. In this session, held a week and a half before the film is due, the filmmaker critiques a student's film. This is usually someone who has put a lot of work into his or her film and is nearly done with the project. If no one volunteers, a film from a previous semester is used. The critique points out what is done well and where improvements could be made. One might think that the student whose film was critiqued has an unfair advantage, but the students have not perceived it that way. They are all grateful for the person who allowed his or her film to be critiqued and find the critique useful in saving them time in editing. The students also have technical support available in the library media center, which they cite as one of the key elements to a successful project.

Students are required to make a 30-second edited video with music on the soundtrack at the beginning of the project (due at the end of week two). The 30-second video on any topic of their choosing (one of the best was titled 'A Day in the Life of My Feet') takes some of the fear out of filming and editing the film. The 30-second films are shown in class and it usually inspires the students to improve the quality of their work. It also gets the students working on the documentaries at an earlier date.

As students shadow the entrepreneurs and edit their films, they write reflections: four during the process and one at the end of the process. The reflections are turned in as the project is occurring to give the instructor a sense of difficulties and concerns as well as to help students process the learning they are doing. The reflections motivate the students to move beyond what they did, looking deeper for lessons learned that could be applied beyond this one project. The first reflection is completed at the end of the first week of class and asks students to reflect on their expectations of the project: learning expectations as well as what they are looking forward to and what they are concerned about. The second reflection is due at the end of the third week of class. In this reflection, they share how they chose their entrepreneurs and describe their initial contact with the entrepreneur. They are expected to provide their entrepreneurs' contact information. This reflection is critical to help students stay on track to complete the project. During week five, the third reflection encourages them to think about what they are learning about entrepreneurship in general from a very specific experience. The fourth reflection comes during week seven and helps move the students fully into the editing phase. It asks them to consider the technical challenges and how art relates to learning. As a side note, students express the most frustration at this stage. It passes. The final reflection is after the film festival. This reflection asks them to think about what they learned from shadowing an entrepreneur and making a documentary, what they learned from watching their colleagues' documentaries, and how the experience has enriched their understanding of entrepreneurship and themselves. According to previous research (Kreber, 2001, p. 225; Cooper and Lucas, 2006, p. 4), the combination of experience and reflection are keys to 'deep learning'.

Entrepreneur Film Festival

The Entrepreneur Film Festival is held on two nights in a large lecture hall/theater on campus. Publicity is sent out in the form of posters and press releases three to four weeks before the event. Personal, hand-written invitations to the entrepreneurs have increased the attendance of the entrepreneurs at the festival.

The students assist with the festival, handing out programs, making popcorn and acting as ushers. Student attendance at the festival is required and many bring their friends. When the students' entrepreneurs attend the festival, the students usually sit with them and their families.

With eight to 10 films per night, an intermission is needed. The film festival is free, as are the sodas and popcorn (provided by the School of Business and Leadership). The instructor acts as the master of ceremonies between the films, providing transitions and providing interesting extra information (such as mentioning students who composed and performed soundtracks for their films). Although the festival has been held as a community event, it could be conducted as an entrepreneurial venture by the students.

Challenges

Technical challenges
As with most people interested in entrepreneurship education, I am well-schooled in entrepreneurship, but know little about filmmaking. Although I am employed at a small school with limited media resources, it has been possible to gain a basic understanding of filmmaking. Larger universities have staff who can help with the basics of filmmaking. However, even our small media department has someone who knows how to use the video-editing software and is willing to help the students and the instructor. If your university does not have a media support person with video-editing knowledge, there are students and other staff on campus who have expertise they may be willing to share (for instance, there may be a filmmaking club on campus).

Our university also belongs to NITLE (National Institute for Technology and Liberal Education), a non-profit initiative to promote innovative teaching at liberal arts colleges with 130 member institutions (www.nitle.org). Many of their programs are technical in nature. Even after one two-day workshop on filmmaking and editing, I felt far more confident in filmmaking. If your university does not have in-house expertise and is not a member of NITLE, there are two choices to gain basic filmmaking skills. One is to find a short course in your community (through a community college or an arts organization). The other method is to experiment: take a digital camera, film, then edit. Learning to edit on a Mac is easiest as its film editing program is the most intuitive. After learning that, Windows Movie Maker and off-the-shelf products such as Adobe Premier Elements are not much more difficult. Students who have never made a film before report that they are able to work effectively with off-the-shelf film-editing products.

Going beyond the basics, however, can be challenging as the entrepreneurship professor with expertise in filmmaking is probably fairly rare. I have relied on a local professional documentary filmmaking company, Wonderdog Media (www.wonderdogmedia. com), to supplement my knowledge. Most documentary filmmaking companies are passionate about what they do. I had no prior connections with Wonderdog Media and found them willing to help based on a cold call. There are also non-profit associations that may be able to provide assistance. For instance, in Seattle ReelGrrls (www.reelgrrls. org) exists as an after-school media and technology training program that empowers young women through creating films. Not only is an organization such as ReelGrrls an organization that may be willing to share its expertise, its alumni may also be resources. With the assistance of professional filmmakers and our own media staff, I have not yet had a student who did not master the film-editing software.

Equipment challenges
Perhaps at a larger university, the equipment challenges may not be so great (then again, they might). When I started this project in the Spring term of 2006, the media center owned three or four digital cameras, one wireless microphone, a handful of tripods, and four computer terminals with film-editing software. Sharing this equipment among 20 students who are creating films at the same time was a challenge. Encouraging students to exchange phone numbers and e-mail addresses and coordinate the equipment over weekends helped. We also have a form that allows students to see who is using equipment at any given time so that they may contact each other outside classtime via e-mail.

Encouraging students to begin earlier is a constant challenge, but those who start earlier avoid some of the stress of getting hold of equipment. I recently had a local company offer to loan its cameras for this project. Obviously, purchasing more equipment would solve the equipment crunch.

Perhaps the biggest equipment challenge is the film-editing software. Our computers with such software are located in our media center in the library. The library is not open 24 hours a day. If an institution had laptops with software (Macs would be ideal) that could be checked out to students for a few weeks, the problem would be eliminated. If students are using the university computers, they are often constrained by the computer on which the raw footage is downloaded; once the footage is on a specific computer, the student must return to that particular computer to edit it. Students are not accustomed to being physically constrained in this way. When the deadline is approaching, there is always one student who needs access to the same computer as another student in order to finish the project. One solution to this would be to purchase 20 gig flash drives to hold the raw footage. Then students could take their footage and semi-edited video with them from computer to computer. Although computer constraints can be frustrating at times, the students also form a tight-knit community due to shared need:

> I saw a lot of growth from the beginning to the end. It felt good when we were finally finished, because we each had a finished product that we spent hours upon hours working on. I think our class was down in the Media Center more than any other class and the employees that worked there. (Student reflection)

Potential challenges

At some universities, getting approval for this project, including the film festival, might be difficult. I am fortunate to be located in a strong liberal arts and low-bureaucracy environment where faculty are encouraged to follow their passions. I would expect that outlining the potential benefits of a project such as this would help ease the approval process.

Benefits

Critical analysis

From the beginning, the project forces critical analysis: the selection of entrepreneurs forces students to think about how they define entrepreneurship and who an entrepreneur really is. These definitions build on readings and class discussions about entrepreneurship and will vary by professor depending on how narrowly one defines entrepreneurship. The entrepreneurs the students shadowed have ranged from the international candy factory entrepreneur (our own local Willie Wonka) to retailers, accountants and high-tech entrepreneurs. This variety of entrepreneurs and the selection of their own entrepreneurs create learning opportunities:

> My peers also created excellent documentaries that helped reinforce the ideas we have discussed in class. For instance, there is no 'entrepreneurial profile'. All entrepreneurs are different and they all have different personalities. Also, entrepreneurs can be any age. The other important lesson I learned, is that there are entrepreneurial opportunities in all professions. (Student reflection)

The combination of both experiential learning (through job shadowing and the creation of the documentary) and the reflections (both the editing process and the written reflection) fuel the critical analysis that must occur in 'deep learning' (Kreber, 2001, p. 225; Cooper and Lucas, 2006, p. 4). To film the appropriate material for a documentary, the students constantly process the job shadow experience, asking questions about how the entrepreneurs' behaviors fit in the framework of the particular question being explored. In the editing process, the students re-analyze the images and words to create a short story on film. The reflections provide an important part of the critical analysis by providing opportunities for the students to reflect as they are participating in the project. According to Kolb (1984, cited in Kreber, 2001, p. 219), transformation takes place in the interplay between active experimentation and reflective observation.

Risk taking

Entrepreneurs take risks. Creating a business plan is not risky. Creating a film for public viewing is. This project models instructor risk taking and promotes student risk taking by engaging the class in a project in which not one ongoing class participant has expertise. It is also a project with many unknowns.

Students note that not every entrepreneur shadowed employs best practices or demonstrates leadership in his or her field. Students think critically in both the filming and editing portions of the project about what to include and what to exclude. Deciding what to leave out is as important as what to leave in. Choosing where to begin and end filming, the images to include, the music to add – these all affect the meaning of the film. As Rabiger (2001, p. 64) noted 'what emerges, after editing, is never actuality but an artfully constructed impression of it'. The ethical filmmaker must remain true to his or her subject and story. The successful filmmaker must tell a compelling story. One reason the films are due one week before the film festival is to ensure that students have exercised sound judgment during the creation of their films.

Holding a public film festival of student work, work by students who most likely are making their first films, is also risky. Making students aware of the risk – and your faith in them – helps them understand how people ameliorate risk as well as the necessity of taking risks that are worth taking.

Self-efficacy

Central to the individual's entrepreneurial behavior is the concept of self-efficacy (Cooper and Lucas, 2006, p. 12). Self-efficacy has been described as 'people's judgment of their capabilities to organize and execute courses of action required to produce given attainments' (Bandura, 1997, p. 6) and these beliefs are more influential to a person's likelihood of choosing a career path or making another decision than what is objectively true (Betz, 2000, p. 215, 2004, p. 343; Bandura and Locke, 2003, p. 87). The documentary film experience increases self-efficacy through two primary mechanisms.

First, the eight hours (or more) of job shadowing provides vicarious experience of entrepreneurship. Such vicarious experience has been found to increase entrepreneurial self-efficacy (Cooper and Lucas, 2006, p. 7). Student reflections indicate that their self-efficacy has been increased, as is demonstrated by the following excerpt from a student:

> I used to think of entrepreneurs as people who always find it easy to build up businesses and make lots of money, and that they must have a natural gift for doing that. Through this assignment, I understand that they are just normal people like everyone else, and being entrepreneurs is neither easy nor natural for them, in most cases. The one thing that they have in common is they love doing what they do, and I've learned that this is the most important motivation that keeps them going and eventually helps them succeed. It was very inspirational to see their stories on screen, and I now think that at one point in life, I would want to become an entrepreneur, just to be able to do what I really love to do but have not had the chance to.

Second, the film-editing process provides opportunities to increase self-efficacy, in part because editing raw footage into a 10-minute documentary requires students to engage deeply with their entrepreneur and his or her story. The students watch and listen to all their footage and narrow it down into pieces that may have a place in the story. Finding the story requires them to extract the entrepreneur's most important words and the most important images. Once they have story-boarded the film, the detailed editing commences. In this process, they listen over and over again to phrases, trying to find the ideal places to cut the entrepreneur's words. They listen carefully, reliving the job shadowing experience and finding more depth and meaning from the event. One student who is now a frequent contributor to YouTube commented, 'After the film and interview were over, I could not help but re-watch it over and over again. The sense of accomplishment exceeds many of the previous projects I endured over the course of my collegiate career'.

A final student reflection is included in this section on self-efficacy to demonstrate the variety of ways in which this project increased student self-efficacy:

> I was proud of myself for creating a successful movie. Previous to this assignment I had never even held a video camera. I had a lot to learn in a short amount of time, and I was very pleased with the results. This project is useful in many ways. It teaches students how to learn new tasks, seek assistance, and coordinate schedules in a way that is different from most projects. It forces students beyond their comfort zone. I remember feeling overwhelmed at times, but the project forced me to take responsibility and work hard to complete the assignment. To complete the assignment I had to improve my communication and planning skills. I needed to get equipment from multiple places and plan meetings with my entrepreneurs who have busy schedules. The project also forced me to ask for help.

Community goals
Like many contemporary universities, our university values community involvement. Because the students must create documentaries on local entrepreneurs, the project and resulting film festival fosters positive relationships between local businesses and the university. Aside from students and the entrepreneurs themselves, most of our film festival attendees come from the local business districts. One of the local business districts has posted web-friendly versions of district business films on their website. The local cable channel has approached the instructor about showing the documentaries on its network.[2]

Cross-disciplinary education and lifelong learning
Creating a film festival of student-created films seems a more likely assignment for a filmmaking class than a business class. The film festival project could be housed in the theater department or in a school of communications. Enfolded within a business course,

the creation of a documentary and the resulting public film festival is a tangible product of the university's commitment to interdisciplinary study.

Allowing students to explore their creative expression of a message has resulted in low performers excelling as well as students discovering creativity that had lain dormant. The selection of visual images and music to give life to the documentaries caused one student to reflect that 'presentation is almost as important as the content'.

The public film festival provides a significant incentive to create high-quality (or at least quality) work. The students are more concerned with their peers' and entrepreneurs' evaluation of their work than the instructor's evaluation. Student reflections reveal that seeing their work larger than life is a very satisfying experience for them: 'Seeing my film on a much larger screen really made a difference because it made me appreciate some of my sections more and helped me to see things that I would have changed' (student reflection).

In class discussion following the film festival, students often choose a favorite visual image (a sequence in which a bar owner mixes a drink – shot from directly overhead) or a favorite musical accompaniment (one time, student composed and performed). The aesthetic appreciation of the films goes deeper than simple viewing, as the students now understand the work that enters into even a 10-minute film.

It took a computer science colleague to bring to light the fact that the interdisciplinary nature of this project goes beyond the arts and film. This project fulfills his course objectives well: in addition to teaching students new programs and programming, he attempts to break down their fear of new programs. Few of the students in the entrepreneurship course have ever used film editing software. They plunge into it without a lot of instruction and discover that they really can learn a new program. Most students, in their fourth reflection offer some variation on one student's succinct comment: 'Editing has definitely been a challenge'. Teaching students how to continue lifelong learning is recognized as an important goal in many educational institutions. The final reflection of another student directly addressed how this project had contributed to his lifelong learning path: 'If it was not for this project, I would have never thought I could edit film to begin with; therefore, the knowledge I acquired is priceless because the innovations and creations that I will manifest in the future are only going to get better as times goes on'.

Conclusion

The entrepreneur job shadow and documentary project has exceeded the initial learning outcome expectations. It strengthens students' critical thinking skills, models and teaches risk taking, allows students to explore the importance of bringing disciplines together, and empowers them for lifelong learning. The increase in self-efficacy leads students to start ventures of their own, in addition to helping them understand entrepreneurship on a cognitive level. Lights, camera, action: learn!

Notes

1. Consultation with the University of Puget Sound Institutional Review Board indicated that human subjects approval was not necessary for this project or for this chapter. The chapter was determined to be a description of a teaching technique rather than an analysis of the content of the entrepreneur's or student's work. Readers considering this project at another institution are advised to ensure that their universities interpret the project in a similar manner.
2. Clearly, embracing this opportunity would require the permission of students and their subjects. The Institutional Review Board would also need to be consulted about the appropriateness of this action.

References

Bandura, Albert (1997), *Self-Efficacy: The Exercise of Control*, New York: Freeman.
Bandura, Albert and Locke, Edwin A. (2003), 'Negative self-efficacy and goal effects revisited', *Journal of Applied Psychology*, **88** (1), 87–99.
Betz, Nancy E. (2000), 'Self-efficacy theory as a basis for career assessment', *Journal of Career Assessment*, **8**, 205–22.
Betz, Nancy E. (2004), 'Contributions of self-efficacy theory to career counseling: a personal perspective', *Career Development Quarterly*, **52** (4), 340–53.
Cooper, Sarah Y. and Lucas, William A. (2006), 'Developing self-efficacy for innovation and entrepreneurship: an educational approach', *International Journal of Entrepreneurship Education*, **4**, 1–14.
Kreber, Carolin (2001), 'Learning experientially through case studies? A conceptual analysis', *Teaching in Higher Education*, **6** (2), 217–28.
Rabiger, Michael (2001), 'Documentary filmmakers decide how to present compelling evidence', *Nieman Reports*, **55** (3), 63–5.

13 Entrepreneurship simulation game seminars: perceived learning effects on natural science, liberal arts and business school students

Christian Lendner and Jutta Huebscher*

Introduction

It is now widely acknowledged that entrepreneurs contribute in a valuable way as innovators, employers and risk-bearers to the economy as well as to society as a whole. One major policy aim in fostering entrepreneurship is, therefore, the general support and training of would-be entrepreneurs. After a lengthy period of disagreement among scholars about the possibilities of entrepreneurial training, the general opinion is now that entrepreneurs can indeed be trained – at least to some extent, see, for example, Ronstadt (1987), Timmons (1990), Solomon and Fernald (1991) and Klandt and Volkmann (2006). Many universities have established professorships in entrepreneurship in their business school department, but it is common practice that entrepreneurship courses are available to, or are attended mainly by, business school students. In consequence, scientific evaluation of the effects of entrepreneurship education is also focused on data-sets provided by business students only. But from what we know about entrepreneurial development (which is often technology based, see Venkataraman, 2004), these courses should be reaching students of other disciplines as well, such as those in the natural sciences, engineering or the arts. It is mainly those non-business school students who might have the specialized knowledge necessary to generate new business ideas for their specific branch of industry. In comparison, business school students often state that they would like to start up a business of their own, but lack the right idea. So successful implementation of entrepreneurship education in disciplines outside of business school is of prime interest. In this chapter we suggest simulation game seminars as one viable way to achieve this goal.

By examining perceived learning among natural science, business school and liberal arts students, our data go much farther than studies using only the opinions of MBA or other business students. In doing so, we not only look at the knowledge content common in entrepreneurship courses, but we also test for the specific learning effects that should be achieved, especially by the simulation game method. Knowledge transfer in single aspects of subjects such as accounting or marketing occurs easily in traditional classes, but training in comprehensive qualities of entrepreneurs such as understanding of dynamic economic interrelationships is most important considering the severity of consequences of mistakes. Furthermore, simulation methods try to approximate more closely the complexity of real business. Computer entrepreneurship simulation game seminars aim at closing this methodological gap between entrepreneurial knowledge transfer and training.

Previous evaluation results

The first business simulation game was played in the US in the 1950s. It was introduced by the American Management Association and was designed for managers from big corporations (Li and Baillie, 1993). Because the method has been used for more than half a century now, one would expect two things: first, that it had been adapted to meet the needs of the specific subject being taught, in our case, entrepreneurship; and second, that research had been undertaken to determine whether this goal was being achieved. Interestingly enough, almost the contrary is true: empirical evidence on the usefulness of the simulation method for entrepreneurship education is scarce.

Available research on simulation game evaluation is divided into two main parts, Feinstein and Cannon (2002). One focus is the improvement of simulation game development, which is characterized by attempts to increase the verisimilitude of the games, that is, their level of realism. A problem here is that higher levels of realism may detract from educational efficiency, as students get lost in a myriad of details. The second focus of the evaluation literature is exactly the educational efficiency of simulation games. A necessary prerequisite for training success is the verification of the game, that is, the model must work as intended. Selecting a good game is essential because program and logic errors or poor equipment will diminish student enthusiasm. Only if the computer program actually works, can one proceed to ask the interesting questions: do students learn anything from the game? Is it valid? Can the conclusions reached from simulation be used in the real world? Only if this can be assured will the simulation game method provide entrepreneurship instructors with a valuable method for delivering the desired touch of reality in the transfer of knowledge.

We now briefly review the literature on the educational effectiveness of simulation games. In an early study, Wolfe and Chanin (1993) found that simulation game seminars impart conceptual knowledge to students. In a later work, Wolfe (1997) compared simulation with case studies and found that simulation works better than other methods. Li and Baillie (1993), however, present evidence that the case study method is as effective as simulation game seminars. In the special issue of *Simulation and Gaming* on simulations in entrepreneurship education, West and Wilson (1995) show that simulation leads to the development of pattern recognition and stereotypes. The research done by Washbush and Gosen (2001) also supports the thesis that the simulation experience does improve learning. This might be due to increased interest and motivation levels through the simulation game seminar as opposed to traditional classroom projects (Tompson and Tompson, 1995). This is in line with the result that students in complex game seminars rated their learning experience as more valuable than those in seminars in which easier versions of a game were used, Li and Baillie (1993).

Further results concern the learning environment in a simulation game. Wolfe and Chanin (1993) report that group play fosters higher learning levels than play by individuals on their own, but that self-assigned teams do not outperform randomly assigned teams. In a review of the games that have been used, it appears that superior students outperform less talented ones, a fact indicating that luck does not play too important a role. Finally, games that offer a wide range of user-choice in decision matters can increase motivation among students, Wideman et al. (2007).

There is much less literature about the specific learning content of simulation game seminars. Li and Baillie (1993) postulate that good games should force students to practice long-term planning skills with their decisions reflecting a balance between long- and short-term considerations. In a review of five studies on learning effectiveness of simulations in business policy courses, Wolfe (1976) concludes that students learn more about the basic need for strategy formulation and how to plan and how to forecast sales, than about appraising the past performance of firms. As for specific entrepreneurial training content of the games, Feldman (1995) states that a number of games do not relate to entrepreneurial processes such as market feasibility analysis, business planning or new venture finance. These are all features that entrepreneurship simulation games should have, but which they often lack.

In general, the review of relevant literature on the subject shows that simulation games indeed have a positive pedagogical effect. On the basis of the known research, it seems safe to say that students learn from seminars involving gaming simulations. These seminars all have in common that the students are involved in an iterative process, supported by the simulation game and directed by the lecturer, that increases knowledge about entrepreneurial matters in general. But the evidence on specific entrepreneurship learning effects, such as knowledge gains in new venture finance, business-plan writing or other entrepreneurial decision-making-related issues, is more scarce. In other words, what exactly participants learn in an entrepreneurship simulation game seminar has, up to now, not received much attention in the literature. Furthermore, the studies on the effectiveness of the business simulation method, which have been reviewed, are based mostly on opinions of MBA students and their perceived learning effects. Entrepreneurship courses, however, are also aimed at non-business school students. The majority of such students lack previous knowledge of business administration and entrepreneurial thinking and, therefore, comprise quite a different target group for simulations. It is one of the objectives of entrepreneurship seminars for non-business school students to offer them a 'crash course' in entrepreneurial matters. As far as we know, there has been no analysis, as yet, to measure whether learning effects obtained through simulation games are comparable for students of all disciplines.

Simulation game seminars as constructivist teaching instruments

Entrepreneurship lecturers often feel that classical teaching methods by lectures and reading assignments do not fit the complexity of their subject. To convey a touch of reality, they often decide on a combination of lectures and cases, and sometimes practical projects. The computer simulation method now allows students to experience first-hand actual entrepreneurial behavior in their day-to-day business under the same conditions of ambiguity and risk (Sexton and Upton, 1987). Getting students to experience entrepreneurial behavior during a simulation game is a teaching approach based on constructivist learning theory (Piaget, 1950). According to the theory, students gain knowledge by examining their own experience. The role of the teacher is limited to facilitating the active learning-by-doing process of the students. Ideally, this learning should also include a double-loop learning process (Argyris and Schön, 1996), in which students are encouraged to rethink concepts that have proven inadequate.

An entrepreneurship simulation game can be defined as a dynamic model of the real entrepreneurial process in which a balanced number of decision variables require integration of several subunits such as opportunities in the market or new venture finance for organizational start-up performance (Keys and Wolfe, 1990). The game provides first-hand experience with entrepreneurial management interdependencies and competition in one common marketplace. Participants create a company out of nothing by searching for and allocating the needed virtual resources, and by following the opportunities of the specific virtual market framework in their decision-making process (Klabbers, 1999). Entrepreneurship simulation games and the software that is used, respectively, should make a point of this latter issue. Entrepreneurial elements besides business-plan writing and new venture finance, include opportunity recognition in the virtual market of the game and winning over not-yet-controlled resources to be committed to the recognized opportunity. This concrete experience and its outcome are observed and reflected on by the participants in an iterative process with immediate feedback. The idea is to accelerate the frame of action of the long-run planning situation in order to mirror the whole entrepreneurial process (Keys and Wolfe, 1990). Simulation games are all quite similar in that they require input from the students who must first process the information. Then participants are confronted with a certain outcome of their decisions, both in absolute terms of profit, loss, liquidity status or market share, and in relation to other virtual competitors. The models of the standard business games are usually designed to show the general principles of management interdependencies and strategy. Entrepreneurship simulation games such as TOPSIM Start-up, however, go beyond general management and small business issues in the above-mentioned way through teaching opportunity recognition and assembling the needed new resources through business-plan writing and new venture finance. Available entrepreneurship simulation games differ, however, in the credibility of their scenario, in the appropriateness of their sophistication level, and in their technical reliability.

Simulation game seminars are an intrinsically motivating teaching method for problem-oriented learning in an authentic context (Gee, 2003). In line with the constructivist learning theory, the decision-making process of the participants is characterized by trial and error, which supports the development of logical thinking and problem-solving skills (Whitebread, 1997). But these are generally desirable characteristics of teaching methods.

Especially for the needs of future entrepreneurs, it creates a 'mistake-friendly' environment for understanding, selecting and appropriately developing a set of key entrepreneurial skills. Venture evaluation and its deeper integrated understanding are essential parts of an effective simulation game. Entrepreneurs and students are, moreover, forced to apply otherwise inert knowledge acquired in more or less theoretical classes (Kriz and Hense, 2004). This facilitates retention, understanding and further active use of that knowledge. Learning without reflection is therefore replaced by critical thinking. This is all the more important, as start-up reality requires decision making under uncertainty and tolerance for ambiguity. Finally, it is possible to describe simulation games as very realistic, because they usually require team-building processes such as those which are necessary in start-ups (West, 2007). TOPSIM Start-up, for example, can only be played if real teamwork takes place because of the time restrictions. The game teaches the importance of a unified purpose among the team founders and efficient peaceful resolution of the conflicts that are almost inevitable under conditions of uncertainty.

From a theoretical perspective, the objective of the seminar is not only the procurement of new knowledge about various start-up problems, marketing and finance issues, but also to foster a deeper understanding of change processes themselves. It could be argued that an entrepreneurship simulation game had been successful if the participants had not only contextualized their existing knowledge so that they had developed a feeling for when, and where, to use it (see Bransford et al., 2000), but also if gained an impression about the interdependencies of decisions of the competitors and their probabilities for dynamic change. Sensitivity to the fact that information on opportunities previously acquired might not always hold true is a very important training objective for entrepreneurs and other people acting in dynamic environments, especially as it is those dynamic relationships among competitors and one's own start-up that often opens up new opportunities. A very important teaching objective is, finally, an increase in interest for topics in entrepreneurship.

Many of the teaching objectives, however, have to be further differentiated according to the prior business knowledge of the participants. Whereas business students should have enough basic knowledge to be able to concentrate on entrepreneurial interrelationships in playing the game, non-business students are likely to need an overall introduction first. The objective for non-business seminars is, therefore, primarily to help students develop some concepts about basic entrepreneurship content. At the same time, building knowledge on interrelationships and general understanding should not be neglected. For the most part, teaching objectives are similar for students of the liberal arts, natural sciences and business schools, even though the importance of the different objectives may vary among the different groups.

Hypotheses

On the basis of all the teaching objectives of gaming simulation seminars described above, it is now appropriate to ask what the participants of the simulation games believe they might learn from taking part (for details of the software used, see the next section). Of all possible perceived learning effects, we concentrate our analysis on entrepreneurial content and interrelationships, as these are the most important training objectives for future entrepreneurs. This is essential training content because mistakes of entrepreneurs in the areas of opportunity recognition or business performance evaluation in a dynamic environment are particularly dangerous for the survival of the new venture firm. It is, therefore, desirable to produce learning effects especially in these, but also in general business areas.

The repetitive process of active application of, and reflection on, key business variables and entrepreneurial ways of thinking facilitate learning during the simulation. Having to make decisions in all aspects of entrepreneurial activity requires that participants think about these aspects, which sensitizes them to the topic and further leads to the necessity of building up new knowledge. We hypothesize that participating students of all educational backgrounds, therefore, learn new skills and abilities, such as business-plan writing, venture finance, and specific problems of start-ups such as opportunity recognition, controlling or marketing issues, as well as new understanding of entrepreneurial decision making. Simulation game participants of all university disciplines should therefore believe that abilities in the various tested fields have increased through participation in the entrepreneurship simulation game (H1). This prediction, of course, depends on the use of a computer simulation game with entrepreneurial problems, as opposed to management problems, considered in the software design.

Apart from postulating in H1 that all students in the seminar believe that they have learned something important, a differentiation by university discipline is appropriate for further analysis. Specifically, it is reasonable to argue that business school students can build on prior business knowledge, whereas students of the natural sciences or liberal arts usually cannot. As one of the main goals of the simulation seminar is the integration of knowledge, it seems logical to assume that participants who already have some basic knowledge are more apt to understand the various interdependencies of key business skills than participants who need to catch up on basic issues first. We hypothesize, therefore, that the perceived learning effects reported by business school students on interrelationships and other *complex business issues* should be greater than these effects reported by non-business school students (H2). Nevertheless, basic knowledge can be trained as well in a seminar involving an entrepreneurship simulation game, which should make the game equally attractive as a basic crash course and an overview of entrepreneurial issues for non-business school students. This leads us to the third hypothesis (H3), namely, that participating non-business school students will experience higher perceived learning effects than business school students in *fundamental business skills* such as controlling, marketing and so on.

Evaluation method
Between 2004 and 2006, we collected 2,161 anonymous opinions[1] of entrepreneurs and students about the quality of the simulation game method in 108 seminars on the basis of the simulation game software TOPSIM Start-up. As the evaluation results depend on the specific software used, we briefly present its main content and describe the organization of the seminars in which it was used.

The software TOPSIM Start-up allows participants in its different versions to virtually open and manage a surfboard production and store, sporting bike production and store, and an online shop or a fitness studio. This is the software version for training in services. All seminars, regardless of the version used, are organized in the same way using English or German as the computer simulation language and starting with the writing of a business plan for one of the opportunities available in the virtual market given by the software design. Participants search in a virtual Internet (a specific database attached to the game as well as the real Internet), for information about the virtual market and, thus, are taught how to detect opportunities in a market. The virtual market of the entrepreneurship simulation software is designed in order to reveal opportunities in the given businesses (surfboards, bikes or fitness studios). The software allows start-ups only in the areas of market opportunity and is, therefore, very entrepreneurial, as the market dictates the sort of business to be founded. The opportunity is to be discerned from a wide variety of information about locations, cost of labor and capital, cost and contingencies of machinery and so on. The combination of all these details in a business plan is needed by the participants to assemble resources to their cause, as they are to start a business in a field in which they have no resources and so have to convince the owners of the resources to employ them in the start-up. The difficulty here is to match the opportunity to the financial restrictions. Opportunity recognition and entrepreneurial new combination of not-yet-controlled resources takes up the first half of the entrepreneurship simulation seminar (which normally lasts for two days). Then the virtual businesses are founded, that is, the most important conditions are set, such as location, number of initial personnel, kind of machinery and potential subsidies. On the second full day, the firms start entrepreneurial competition in the virtual market for six time periods. First, the teams get new information, which might or might not correspond to the projections used for the business plan and which might reveal new opportunities. Then they prepare their decisions by calculating different scenarios in an Excel-based tool. After approximately an hour, each team decides on, and the simulation software calculates, market shares, profits, cost per unit and the virtual balance sheet. Participants get immediate feedback and the process starts all over again.

At the end of the seminar each team presents the performance of its firm in an annual meeting to the other teams and the lecturer. This debriefing phase at the end of the simulation is pedagogically valuable for two reasons. First, participants may profit from other teams' virtual experience and second, the lecturer may check and complete the conclusions reached. The main characteristic of TOPSIM Start-up in all its versions is that it is an entrepreneurship simulation and not just a management or strategy simulation. Opportunity recognition and business-plan writing, negotiation with venture capitalists and other owners of resources and the need to permanently improve and differentiate the virtual product separate it clearly from strategic choice games, even though strategic issues are included for reasons of completeness. It is one of the main virtues of the entrepreneurship simulation game method that it contains all key entrepreneurial and business aspects and therefore provides a holistic and complex experience. (For further information, see www.business-simulation.net.)

Our data stem from participants of seminars using all the TOPSIM versions. In a pre-testing phase we drew up a two-page, mainly Likert-scale-based questionnaire, according to state-of-the-art data collection. After a few minor changes, the data collection could start in entrepreneurship seminars for entrepreneurs presented by the Hans-Lindner-Institut, a foundation for fostering entrepreneurship, and for business and other students at six universities. The questionnaire asks the participants' perception of the simulation game seminar and can, therefore, provide information only on perceived learning effects, not on objective ones. Testing for objective learning effects requires detailed knowledge tests before and after the simulation, which necessarily narrows the subject of the study and the data collection, respectively. As the available research on the kind of knowledge gained in entrepreneurship simulation game seminars is scarce, we decided on the more exploratory design, which relies on perceptions, but allows data collection on a broader range. In order to guarantee a maximum of reliability, all lecturers involved in the data collection ensured strict anonymity.

A further problem discussed in the simulation game literature concerning reliability is the halo effect, which postulates a relationship between simulation performance of the participant and his/her game evaluation. However, Washbush and Gosen (2001) present evidence against this effect. Our decision to ensure strict anonymity in the data collection process in order to get truthful answers unfortunately prevents us from testing the existence of such an effect in our own data. Nevertheless, although our design may not allow us to test for the halo effect, it is apt to minimize any such effect through the production of more truthful answers.

The use of modern econometric methods shows that the results are robust. First, the number of cases allows us to move away from still heavily discussed methods of multiple imputation of missing values. That leaves us with 846 complete student cases for multivariate analysis. Missing values in the different learning effects variables were examined

for selection effects by the Heckman (1979) procedure and can be ignored. Therefore, we ran an analysis of variance, but on account of the unbalanced data and heterogeneity of variance, we ran the robust version available in Stata 8. In the following section we present a descriptive analysis of the structure of participants as well as multivariate evaluation results.

Characteristics of participants and perceived learning effects
The structure of our dataset is as follows: 21.6 percent of the participants are entrepreneurs, a further 32.8 percent are generally interested in start-ups and the seminar was compulsory for another 42.1 percent. The rest did not disclose the motivation behind their participation or they chose the response field 'other'. Entrepreneurs are defined as people who have recently started their own business (5.8 percent) or are in their business-planning process (15.7 percent). The categories 'generally interested' and 'compulsory' consist of students. We naturally get a majority of students, as the seminar is included in the curriculum, whereas seminars for entrepreneurs do not take place with as much regularity. For the following analysis of perceived learning effects of students of different university disciplines, we excluded entrepreneurs from our dataset; they will figure in another paper.

The students' mean age was 24 because the seminar is mainly aimed at the graduating class of a year. Entrepreneurship still seems to be a topic dominated by men, as the majority (61.3 percent) of our participants were male. Some 45.8 percent of the participating students claim to have entrepreneurs in their family. This could have given them the opportunity to collect some practical experience or know-how about managing a business.

In splitting up our dataset by the present subject of study of the participating students, we get three main subgroups. With 406 participants, business school students make up the biggest group. Second come 298 participants studying natural sciences or engineering and finally, we have data from 142 students of the liberal arts including those pursuing teaching certification. The general characteristics of these subgroups of students do not differ substantially from the above-mentioned means for all students, except for the following criteria: natural science students are mostly male (87.9 percent) and tend to waive business lectures, as most of them, 60.4 percent, took part in the entrepreneurship simulation seminar only because it was compulsory. In contrast, 65.0 percent of arts students took part because of a genuine interest in the subject; those who admitted to being forced into the seminar account for only 35.0 percent. Arts students tend to be female (62.7 percent), whereas the gender ratio is nearly even in business schools (47.5 percent male). The following finding is also interesting: those with entrepreneurs in their family tend to enroll in the business schools of their universities. Almost half (46.9 percent) of the business school students claim to have entrepreneurs in their family, whereas students of the natural sciences and arts claim this in only 37.2 and 40.9 percent of the cases, respectively.

In order to judge the perceived learning effects properly, we also collected data on the participants' business education background. On average, 43.2 percent indicate their prior knowledge of business issues as 'good' or even 'very good'. However, an analysis of the subgroups shows a very different picture: whereas two-thirds (64.2 percent) of the business school students indicate their prior knowledge of business issues as good or very

Table 13.1   Percentage of agreement with the different learning effects

Percentage of agreement	Business		Natural sciences		Liberal arts		Anova
	Male	Female	Male	Female	Male	Female	
Overview	90.2	85.9	82.1	80.6	83.0	89.9	
Teamwork	83.4	85.1	78.4	76.5	75.9	84.3	**
Entrep. thinking & action	82.8	83.9	78.0	73.5	76.7	92.3	
Interdisciplinary interrelationships	67.2	82.3	56.4	59.4	66.1	64.8	
Practical exercise	69.8	70.8	47.1	38.2	64.4	71.9	***
Economic interrelationships	81.9	81.1	75.8	58.8	81.7	84.6	
Management	70.1	64.8	66.9	66.7	71.7	68.1	
Economic understanding	77.0	69.9	67.9	61.8	75.0	75.8	
Problems of starting up	81.4	79.6	77.7	79.4	69.0	85.6	
Targets in business	61.9	57.7	57.3	43.8	59.3	58.4	
Controlling	66.5	62.3	63.7	52.9	75.0	67.8	*
Strategy	78.8	76.3	80.2	91.2	81.4	79.8	***
Marketing	80.5	80.6	81.5	67.6	67.9	83.5	
Business plan	69.8	74.9	70.8	64.7	78.3	75.8	*
Understanding investors	63.4	54.6	61.8	38.2	49.1	55.6	**
Information overload	61.0	70.2	59.3	69.2	66.0	66.7	
Mean by sex	74.1	73.8	69.1	63.9	71.3	75.3	
Mean	73.9		68.5		73.8		
n	193	213	262	36	53	89	

Note: * 10% significance; ** 5% significance; *** 1% significance.

good, this ratio goes down to a mere 16.0 and 12.0 percent for natural sciences and the arts, respectively. Therefore, the majority of non-business school participants need the simulation seminar for building up general business knowledge before they can profit from the most important methodological virtue of the seminar, that is, the complex experience of discerning an entrepreneurial opportunity and seeing the interdependencies of key variables at work.

Now we have established the background of our simulation participants, we can turn to the perceived learning effects. We asked participants to state whether the seminar enhanced their knowledge in the entrepreneurial education subjects of business-plan writing and special problems of starting up, strategy, finance and investor relations, controlling and marketing. In addition, we wanted to know whether participants felt better able to understand complex business and interdisciplinary interrelationships, entrepreneurial decision making, and management after taking part in the simulation seminar (see Table 13.1). As learning and the choice of the subject of study at university is a gender-specific phenomenon, we show the learning effects for each sex separately.

There is much agreement (categories 'totally agree' and 'mostly agree') for all tested perceived learning effects, both for knowledge content (second group of variables in Table 13.1) as well as for the complex, higher-order training objectives (first group in Table 13.1). Among the respondents, 73.9 percent of business students, and 73.8 percent of arts students, agreed on average to the existence of all the above-mentioned perceived

learning effects. In the natural sciences, slightly fewer students (on average 68.5 percent) report perceived learning effects. It is remarkable that two-thirds of the natural science students learned some entrepreneurial content and skills despite the fact that the majority had been forced to take the seminar. We can, therefore, state that the theoretically postulated learning process for knowledge content as such, as well as understanding of complex interrelationships and entrepreneurial decision making, can be achieved by simulation game seminars according to participant perception (H1). But this is not to say that students of the different groups learn the same way. However, it is necessary at this point to stress that we measure subjectively perceived learning effects, that is, change rates of abilities, so that business as well as non-business students can report equal learning effects and have abilities at different levels.

Looking in more detail at Table 13.1, the picture differentiates. The means by discipline and sex are still on a high level and for business students practically identical, but in the non-business disciplines, sex plays a role. Interestingly, in natural sciences males showed higher mean learning effects from the simulation, whereas in the arts it was the females who reported higher mean effects. The sex of the student alone is therefore not a sufficient predictor for subjective learning in a simulation game seminar.

The most important perceived learning effects of the simulation also vary by student discipline and sex, at least in the non-business disciplines, whereas all business students produced the same hierarchy of the three most important learning effects. The most clearly perceived learning effect of business students was to get an overview of what is involved in starting a business. In second place for the business students comes the teamwork experience and in third place the opportunity to practice entrepreneurial thinking and action. For the non-business students, only the ranking of the overview variable remains the same, and only for male respondents. The most important perceived learning effect for female arts students was the practical experience of entrepreneurial thinking and action, whereas for female science students, strategy learning was most important. But getting an overview over starting up a business comes in second place for all female non-business students. In third place for the female scientists is the perceived learning about problems of start-ups and for the female arts students learning about economic interrelationships. This latter effect is in second place for male arts students, whereas learning about strategy is third, which is also true for the male scientists, who put perceived learning about marketing in second place. Summing up these results, we can state that students from all disciplines appreciate getting an overview through the simulation. All business students especially liked the teamworking and entrepreneurial thinking experience, whereas all the arts students perceived high learning effects in economic interrelationships and all future scientists learned much about strategy.

With the overview variables generally ranked highest, it is, therefore, fairly safe to conclude that the entrepreneurship simulation seminar sensitizes the vast majority of participants (over 80 percent) to the professional alternative of starting up a business, and makes them somewhat familiar with its contingencies. Further, frequently perceived learning effects by all students are a better understanding of economic interrelationships and in the area of entrepreneurial content the problems of starting up, business-plan writing, strategy and marketing. Therefore, the simulation can indeed serve as a crash course for entrepreneurial content as well as for complex interrelationships.

Considering the different subgroups of students, the main question is whether there are learning objectives for which there is a significant difference in the results. In interpreting the percentages of agreement in Table 13.1, it is important to note that differences in percentages between the different groups of students still contain the effects of other factors, such as an entrepreneurial family background, level of prior business knowledge and voluntary participation as proxy for initial interest in the subject. Therefore, for each learning objective mentioned in the table, we drew up a multivariate analysis of variance model to test for the influence of the main subject of study on the different perceived learning effects, further controlling for the effects of the control variables as well as for the effect of the sex of the student. The significance of the effect of university discipline on perceived learning is shown for each of the 16 anova models in Table 13.1 on the 10, 5 and 1 percent levels and which are marked by one, two or three stars. For most learning objectives, university discipline is not significant. This implies that taking into account the effect of the control variables, mainly voluntary participation and prior knowledge, the perceived learning experience of students of various fields does not differ. In their subjective opinion, participating engineers learned as much about business interrelationships, entrepreneurial management or marketing as business and arts students, although these effects are relative. The analysis of variance models for the different perceived learning effects can be seen in more detail in Table 13A.1 in the appendix, which reports the mean sum of squares for each factor and its significance on the 10, 5 and 1 percent levels. The control variable with the biggest effects is voluntary participation, which indicates higher interest in the seminar. Second comes the level of prior business knowledge and third, gender of the participant. Females tend to report higher perceived learning effects. An entrepreneurial family background does not show any significant effect on perceived learning of entrepreneurial content and thinking.

Considering those learning objectives, which show significant differences in learning results across student groups, the initial interesting result concerns the first half of the analyzed variables measuring complex, higher-order effects. Significant differences in perceived learning can be found only with somewhat methodological variables, that is, teamwork and practical exercise. The latter is especially influenced by the opinion of natural scientists who obviously would not classify the computer simulation seminar as practical experience. All the other complex learning objectives such as overview, entrepreneurial thinking and action, interrelationships or management issues can be achieved without significant difference for all kinds of students via simulation games. H2 has, therefore, to be rejected, as there is no significant advantage of business school students in this area.

Taking a closer look at the entrepreneurial content variables (lower half of Table 13.1), the picture changes. More perceived learning objectives are significant and differ noticeably across student groups. The content variables reflect basic entrepreneurship and business knowledge, and we observe slightly lower perceived learning effects reported by business students as hypothesized in H3, as these students should already have gained much of this knowledge. Surprisingly, the perceived learning results also differ between the two groups of non-business students, that is, the natural scientists and the arts students. Again, controlling for voluntary participation, an entrepreneurial family background, gender and prior knowledge in the various anova models, the significant effects of discipline become apparent in Table 13.1. Liberal arts students show the significantly highest perceived learning effects of all groups in business-plan writing and controlling issues, whereas when it comes to investors, the natural scientists have the better perceived learning results of the two non-business groups of students. H3 is therefore true only for the perceived learning results in strategy, which might be a more unexpected aspect of entrepreneurial activity than, for example, marketing for the non-business students. This would explain the significance in different perceived learning. Interestingly, for all the other entrepreneurial content variables H3 has to be rejected, either because there is a significant difference in learning for the two groups of non-business students, or because there is no difference in subjective learning effects between business and non-business students.

The interesting result is twofold for the content variables: concerning the problems of start-ups, targets in business, marketing and information processing, the simulation can generate equally high perceived learning effects for students of all disciplines. These learning objectives have in common that they are seldom the subject of practical projects or any other application-oriented method of teaching, so there is a lot to learn for all groups of students. On the other hand, the result in the perceived learning objectives of controlling, business-plan writing and investors differs across groups of students. This may be due to different methodologies and different mindsets evolving from studies in natural sciences and the liberal arts. The creativity and ambiguity tolerance needed to draw up a business plan on the basis of a perceived opportunity, might be characteristics developed rather in studying arts than in sciences, so arts students may be more apt to gain knowledge in this field, whereas scientists get acquainted with the problem of funding relatively soon in their studies, so they are probably more sensitized to the need of understanding investors. But although there are more significant differences in perceived learning results concerning the content variables, it is still important to note that perceived learning effects can be observed with all participants, and also on high levels.

Conclusion
Considering all our results and drawing on our experience as simulation lecturers, we can recommend simulation game seminars for entrepreneurship education in and out of business schools. With our dataset of 846 simulation participants, we could show that participants undergo a subjective learning process as they learn new entrepreneurial content as well as complex entrepreneurial thinking. This is true both for students of business schools who can build on prior knowledge *and* for non-business school students such as future natural scientists or liberal arts students. With regard to the levels of reported learning, complex learning effects such as understanding of entrepreneurial interrelationships or entrepreneurial thinking and action can be generated for all participating groups of students on the same high level, whereas with regard to general entrepreneurial content, the perceived learning levels remain high, but show significant differences for the analyzed groups of students. The simulation can, therefore, be used for gaining deeper insight as well as a motivating crash course on basic entrepreneurial issues and an overview of the field. Non-business school students can, in this way, be sensitized to the whole entrepreneurial field of action. This knowledge helps to establish simulation game seminars in non-business disciplines along with the compact time frame of the simulation seminar, which takes up only one weekend. An advantage of the block-seminar is that it does not detract students from their main subject or mix up established time schedules during the working week in the non-business departments. Therefore,

entrepreneurship simulations are easily acceptable from a standpoint of practicability, even in non-business disciplines, and can be recommended to the students by the faculty. Entrepreneurship simulation game seminars constitute a valuable and motivating teaching method for university-wide entrepreneurship education.

Notes

*   We are much indebted to the Hans-Lindner-Institute (www.hans-lindner-institut.de), the foundation for fostering entrepreneurship of the family Lindner and the Lindner group, Arnstorf, Germany, for their valuable support for this research.
1.   The study took place at six different universities in South Germany (University of Passau, University of Regensburg, Universities of Applied Sciences in Deggendorf, Landshut, Regensburg and Amberg-Weiden) and at the Hans Linder Institut.

References

Argyris, C. and D. Schön (1996), *Organizational Learning II: Theory, Method, and Practice*, Reading, MA: Addison-Wesley.
Bransford, J.D., A.L. Brown and R.R. Cocking (2000), *How People Learn: Brain, Mind, Experience, and School*, Washington, DC: National Academies Press.
Feinstein, A.H. and H.M. Cannon (2002), 'Constructs of simulation evaluation', *Simulation and Gaming*, **33** (4), 425–40.
Feldman, H.D. (1995), 'Computer-based simulation games: a viable educational technique for entrepreneurship classes?', *Simulation and Gaming*, **26** (3), 346–60.
Gee, J.P. (2003), *What Video Games Have to Teach Us about Learning and Literacy*, New York: Palgrave Macmillan.
Heckman, J. (1979), 'Sample selection bias as a specification error', *Econometrica*, **47**, 153–61.
Keys, B. and J. Wolfe (1990), 'The role of management games and simulations in education and research', *Journal of Management*, **16**, 307–36.
Klabbers, J.H.G. (1999), 'Three easy pieces', in D. Saunders and J. Severn (eds), *The International Simulation and Gaming Research Yearbook 7*, London: Kogan Page, pp. 16–33.
Klandt, H. and C. Volkmann (2006), 'Development and prospects of academic entrepreneurship education in Germany', *Higher Education in Europe*, **31** (2), 195–208.
Kriz, W. and J. Hense (2004), 'Evaluation of the EU-project "SIMGAME" in business education', in International Simulation and Gaming Association (ed.), *Bridging the Gap: Transforming Knowledge into Action through Gaming and Simulation*, Munich: SAGSAGA, pp. 352–63.
Li, E.Y. and A.S. Baillie (1993), 'Mixing case method with business games: student evaluations', *Simulation and Gaming*, **24** (3), 336–55.
Piaget, J. (1950), *The Psychology of Intelligence*, New York: Routledge.
Ronstadt, R. (1987), 'The educated entrepreneurs: a new era of entrepreneurial education evolves', in C.A. Kent (ed.), *Entrepreneurship Education*, New York: Quorum Books, pp. 69–88.
Sexton, D.L. and N.B. Upton (1987), 'Evaluation of an innovative approach to teaching entrepreneurship', *Journal of Small Business Management*, **25** (1), 35–43.
Solomon, G.T. and L.W. Fernald (1991), 'Trends in small business management and entrepreneurship education in the United States', *Entrepreneurship Theory and Practice*, **15** (3), 25–39.
Timmons, J. (1990), *New Venture Creation: Entrepreneurship in the 1990's*, Homewood, IL Irwin.
Tompson, G.H. and H.B. Tompson (1995), 'Using simulations for group projects in business school education', *Journal of Education for Business*, **71** (2), 97–102.
Venkataraman, S. (2004), 'Regional transformation through technological entrepreneurship', *Journal of Business Venturing*, **19** (1), 153–67.
Washbush, J. and J. Gosen (2001), 'An exploration of game-derived learning in total enterprise simulations', *Simulation and Gaming*, **32** (3), 281–96.
West, G.P. (2007), 'Collective cognition: when entrepreneurial teams, not individuals, make decisions', *Entrepreneurship Theory and Practice*, **31** (1), 77–102.
West, G.P. and E.V. Wilson (1995), 'A simulation of strategic decision making in situational stereotype conditions for entrepreneurial companies', *Simulation and Gaming*, **26** (3), 307–27.
Whitebread, D. (1997), 'Developing children's problem-solving: the educational uses of adventure games', in A. McFarlane (ed.), *Information Technology and Authentic Learning*, London: Routledge, pp. 13–37.
Wideman, H., A. Owston, C. Brown, A. Kushniruk, F. Ho and K. Pitts (2007), 'Unpacking the potential of educational gaming: a new tool for gaming research', *Simulation and Gaming*, **38** (1), 10–30.

Wolfe, J. (1976), 'The effects and effectiveness of simulations in business policy teaching applications', *Academy of Management Review*, **1**, 47–56.
Wolfe, J. (1997), 'The effectiveness of business game in strategic management course work', *Simulation and Gaming*, **28** (4), 360–76.
Wolfe, J. and M. Chanin (1993), 'The integration of functional and strategic management skills in a business game learning environment', *Simulation and Gaming*, **24**, 34–46.

Appendix 13A

Table 13A.1   Analysis of variance for the different perceived learning effects – report of mean sum of squares for each factor

Mean sum of squares	Discipline	Voluntary	Prior knowledge	Sex	Family	Model
Overview	0.03	12.57***	0.32	0.06	0.45	2.43***
Teamwork	2.01**	4.27***	2.94***	1.60*	0.00	2.03***
Entrep. thinking & action	0.14	8.20***	0.39	1.04*	0.40	1.90***
Interdisciplinary interrelationships	0.35	4.02***	1.34**	2.55***	0.01	2.47***
Practical exercise	5.11***	10.78***	2.82***	1.81**	0.37	6.02***
Entrepreneurial interrelationships	0.88	4.55***	0.65	0.90	0.02	1.57***
Management	1.03	8.10***	1.27**	1.45*	0.58	2.03***
Economic understanding	0.83	4.93***	1.36***	0.17	0.46	1.52***
Problems of starting up	0.54	5.34***	1.17**	0.51	0.03	1.32***
Targets in business	0.29	4.96***	1.12**	1.47*	0.08	1.52***
Controlling	1.55*	7.65***	1.59**	0.29	0.01	2.07***
Strategy	2.59***	7.21***	1.46**	0.73	0.14	1.78***
Marketing	0.65	3.68***	0.58	0.66	0.11	.89*
Business plan	1.79*	4.35***	2.03***	1.41	0.51	1.97***
Understanding investors	2.09**	7.74***	1.14*	0.69	0.05	1.87***
Information overload	0.27	5.53***	0.32	1.39*	0.37	1.54***

Note: * 10% significance; ** 5% significance; *** 1% significance.

14 Intersecting entrepreneurship and law: an experiential learning exchange

Matthew M. Mars and Sherry Hoskinson

Introduction

Entrepreneurship is considered to be one of the fastest-growing fields of study within the American higher education system (Katz, 2003, p. 284; Kuratko, 2006, p. 484). The growth of entrepreneurship education has not been contained within schools of business. Specifically, entrepreneurial curricula have been formally introduced into technical fields such as engineering, biosciences, optical sciences, as well as into the more liberal arts-oriented disciplines that include history, sociology and the fine arts (Hynes, 1996, p. 11; Katz, 2003, p. 295; Mars, 2007, p. 43). As a result, new entrepreneurship courses, minors and less structured certificates have woven entrepreneurial principles and philosophies into the disciplinary fabric of higher education.

This chapter focuses on an experiential learning model for connecting entrepreneurship students with law students within a clinical setting. Specifically, we describe the inaugural year of an entrepreneurship/law exchange at the University of Arizona, Tucson, AZ. This exchange joined entrepreneurship students in the McGuire Center for Entrepreneurship and law students in the James E. Rogers College of Law for the purpose of developing strong entrepreneurial and legal skill sets through the direct application of classroom knowledge to simulated 'real-world' problems. Our discussion of this exchange includes the direct reports of the students and instructors, as well as an analysis of the method's strengths and weaknesses. Also, the discussion includes how the exchange was designed to reflect the entrepreneurial and legal conditions of the current knowledge economy. Lastly, suggestions for replicating the exchange in ways specific to the science and technology fields, as well as the liberal arts are offered.

Background and related literature

Contemporary economic conditions have made it necessary for entrepreneurs who are seeking competitive advantages within the marketplace to be highly attentive to the means and methods for protecting and managing their intellectual properties (for example, Kwan and Lai, 2003, p. 854; Landjouw and Schankerman, 2004, p. 45). The highly competitive nature of the so-called 'knowledge economy' is in large part the result of both globalization and the explosion and rapid obsolescence of commercially relevant innovations (Powell and Snellman, 2004, p. 201). In order to capitalize on emerging market opportunities, now more than ever entrepreneurs need to be highly knowledgeable in areas of intellectual property protection and the legal implications of venture opportunities.

The innovations that drive the knowledge economy are largely generated through the application of hard skills inherent in scientific and technical fields of study. However, softer skills centered on interpersonal communication, collaboration, creativity and strategic networks are also critical to the dissemination and commercialization of knowledge. Audretsch (2007, p. 91) stated:

> Perhaps the most important realization about the knowledge economy is that it is about a lot more that just knowledge, especially technical and scientific knowledge. Rather, so called softer skills and capacities, for example, creativity, the ability to communicate and emotional intelligence, may all be a part of what economists have labeled knowledge.

The creation and delivery of cross-disciplinary models of entrepreneurship education help to foster the development of these softer skills that are too often overlooked within the knowledge economy.

Schramm (2006, p. 121) identified higher education as an essential variable in the nation's formula for retaining its position as a global economic and political power. Colleges and universities have historically been and continue to be central repositories of knowledge and intellectual capital. The social and economic values of such resources are believed to be realized through entrepreneurial pathways that move innovations out of the academy and into the private marketplace. Entrepreneurship education is one such entrepreneurial pathway, which has in recent years been enhanced through trends such as cross-disciplinary collaborations and the increased agency of student entrepreneurs (Mars et al., 2008).

The cross-disciplinary expansion of entrepreneurship education has spawned learning environments that are diverse in participation and topic. Pedagogic approaches that include entrepreneurial theory, principles and practices are being integrated into a wide variety of curricula relevant to an equally diverse number of technical, economic and social problems (Mars, 2007, p. 43). For instance, entrepreneurial principles and applications have been integrated into hard sciences and engineering curricula (Creed et al., 2002; p. 185). Also, contributors to the Spring 2005 edition of *Peer Review*, which is titled 'Liberal Education and the Entrepreneurial Spirit', identified entrepreneurship education as a viable mechanism for promoting leadership, civic engagement and innovative problem solving within and across the liberal arts curricula.

Despite the significant movement to institutionalize entrepreneurship education across the curricula of colleges and universities, not all applicable disciplinary fields have been effectively involved as platforms for entrepreneurial learning. One such undertreated disciplinary intersection is that of entrepreneurship and law. Accordingly, this chapter further encourages the institution-wide scope of entrepreneurship education by documenting and describing a learning exchange that occurred between students studying entrepreneurship in the McGuire Center for Entrepreneurship and those pursing a law degree through the James E. Rogers College of Law at the University of Arizona. On the one hand, the entrepreneurship students had a wide variety of entrepreneurial interests that spanned the technological, environmental and socially oriented fields. On the other, the law students had interests in legal areas such as intellectual property protection and management, taxation and contractual agreements.

The learning exchange we discuss in this chapter centered on the transactions between aspiring entrepreneurs and emerging lawyers within a simulated market setting. The entrepreneurship students primarily benefited from the exchange through the development of a more crystallized understanding of the legal complexities associated with

Concrete Experience:
Participating in academic exercises that
intersect entrepreneurship and law

Active Experimentation:
Developing entrepreneurial strategies and
legal strategies based on exchange interactions

Reflective Observation:
Immersion in entrepreneurial-like and
legal-like environments

Abstract Conceptualization:
Applying experience to venture plan
development processes, entrepreneurial
law principles, and entrepreneurship and
legal coursework

Source: Based on Kolb's experiential learning cycle (1984).

Figure 14.1   Entrepreneurship/law student experiential cycle

launching market ventures within the knowledge economy. The law students gained the opportunity to build skills in providing legal guidance to entrepreneurs in areas such as corporate tax, intellectual property management and protection, securities and business formation. Also, students on both sides of the exchange were exposed to disciplinary and professional cultures that would otherwise not have been included in their educational experiences.

Theoretical framework and method
The learning exchange discussed in this chapter was grounded in experiential learning theory. Experiential learning theory (ELT) originated through the work of Dewey (1938) and Piaget (1952) and was developed into a comprehensive learning framework by David A. Kolb (1984). Kolb articulated experiential learning as a diverse process that occurs at the various intersections of knowledge and experience, as well as through observation, reflection and action. This process involves four modes of learning, normally grouped into two sets of two, which together engage learners in exercises that transform experiences into meaningful knowledge. The first set of modes in the experiential learning cycle, Concrete Experience and Abstract Conceptualization, address how individuals gain experience. The Concrete Experience mode accounts for the means by which individuals acquire new experiences through tangible interactions. The Abstract Conceptualization mode is specific to the ways in which individuals gain and store experiences through methodical and analytical processes. The second set of modes, Reflective Observation and Active Experimentation, address how individuals transform experiences into knowledge. The Reflective Observation mode involves transforming experience into knowledge through observation and internal reflection. The Active Experimentation mode centers on hands-on experimental approaches to determining meaning from experiences. Together the four modes create a learning cycle that describes how experimentation and processing transform experiences into meaningful and internalized knowledge (see Figure 14.1).

The selection of ELT as the principal framework used in designing and implementing the entrepreneurship–law exchange was supported by existing literature. Jones and English (2004, p. 416) described entrepreneurship as a field of study anchored in the principles of experiential learning. Honig (2004, p. 263) underscored the effectiveness of experiential learning in providing entrepreneurship students with the skills needed to respond to the often fluid and unpredictable market conditions that are inherent in entrepreneurial environments. Experiential learning models have also been indicated to be effective strategies used by law schools (MacFarlane, 1992, p. 293). Considering that ELT provided the theoretical framework for developing the entrepreneurship/law exchange, this chapter contributes to the preceding literature.

The qualitative data used to explore the outcomes of the first year of the exchange were collected through individual interviews, small focus groups with students and instructors and observations of student interactions. The interviews and focus groups consisted of open-ended questions designed to capture the experiences of the students and faculty who participated in the inaugural exchange. The questions asked during individual interviews prompted students to reflect and report on how the experiences gained (or not) through the exchange resulted in the transformation of previously acquired information into meaningful knowledge. Also, by observing student exchanges the evident learning resulting from the exchange could be recorded. The collected data were analyzed using a coding structure developed according to the modes of ELT and the goals of the exchange.

The case

Exchange design and structure
One side of the entrepreneurship/law exchange consisted of undergraduate and graduate entrepreneurship students with diverse academic backgrounds that included business, life sciences, medicine, engineering, social sciences, humanities and optics. On the other side of the exchange were third-year law students interested in areas of law that are highly relevant to entrepreneurship, such as intellectual property rights, taxation, contractual agreements and business formation. The law students were selected for the exchange during the end of their second year of law school, at which time they were completing a practicum specific to the legal dimensions of entrepreneurship. This practicum was a prerequisite for participating in the entrepreneurship/law exchange. The students on both sides of the exchange were introduced to each other during the semester prior to the beginning of the exchange through an orientation hosted by the entrepreneurship center.

The entrepreneurship student teams entered into the exchange with an identified venture concept. More specifically, each team had identified a venture concept through a series of feasibility studies conducted over the summer break under the guidance of the mentors-in-residence. The feasibility studies provided preliminary validation that each of the selected venture concepts involved potentially viable economic opportunities based on criteria specific to innovation, scalability and sustainability. Thus, the entrepreneurship students were engaged in the entrepreneurial curriculum in advance of formal interactions with the law students.

Consistent with the premises of ELT, the entrepreneurship/law exchange depended on students' application of knowledge gained through traditional instructional activities. During the exchange the entrepreneurship students were also completing one venture development seminar and two lecture-based courses specific to venture finance and the marketing of innovation. The venture development seminar was the first of a two-part experiential sequence that led the students through the venture creation process. This experiential seminar sequence was taught by mentors-in-residence. These mentors all had significant experience in leading entrepreneurial ventures and were engaged in the program on a full-time, in-residence basis. The finance and marketing courses were taught by faculty within each of the respective departments and were theoretical and technical in design and delivery. Therefore, the entrepreneurship students gained a diverse set of knowledge through both classroom and seminar settings and under the guidance of experienced entrepreneurs turned instructors/mentors as well as more traditional professors.

The law students entered into the exchange with some background in the intersection of entrepreneurship and law. In addition to having completed law courses specific to intellectual property rights protection and management, the participating students were required to complete a law practicum specific to the entrepreneurial process during the semester prior to the exchange. This practicum provided an integrated framework for addressing the legal issues that arose during the new venture creation process. This course was led by three tenured professors of law and included presentations by attorneys experienced in providing legal counsel to entrepreneurs. The course was grounded in the principles of corporate, tax, contractual and entrepreneurship law, as well as intellectual property rights protection and management. Therefore, the law students brought to the exchange some general knowledge of entrepreneurial law, which was refined and internalized through the interactions with entrepreneurship students.

The second practicum, which took the form of a mock law firm and anchored one end of the entrepreneurship/law exchange, provided the students with opportunities to exercise their knowledge in a clinical setting. This practicum was led by an experienced practitioner of entrepreneurship law with input from the three law professors who led the first practicum. The opportunity to execute knowledge gained through earlier coursework and training allowed the law students to see themselves as lawyers and to experience practicing law in a simulated professional environment. The instructor of the second practicum, who was also a prominent practicing attorney, described the value of the entrepreneurship/law exchanges as follows:

> Practicing law is no different than any other skill; there's only so much you can get from the books. At some point the training wheels have to come off. Above all else, the law students are learning how to communicate with non-lawyers. They have to deal with real, not hypothetical, fact situations. They process what they've heard from their 'clients' with what they've learned from their law professors. Finally they communicate complex and confusing concepts in a practical and understandable way to people without their training. Communicating legal knowledge to law professors and other law students is one thing; applying that knowledge and communicating it to those without legal training *is the key to the successful practice of law*. This experience will help prepare the law students to interact and communicate effectively with their future clients.

The learning environment

The entrepreneurship/law exchange occurred in the entrepreneurship center. The building that housed the center resembled the innovative business environments that symbolized the knowledge economy. There were several high-tech laboratories and numerous classrooms bearing the names of well-known corporate sponsors. The entrepreneurship center reflected an entrepreneurial work environment with a student laboratory containing informal and formal meeting spaces, eight technical work stations and an often constant flow of entrepreneurship student traffic and activity. This environment was far different from the more reserved climate common to the law school and thus introduced the law students to the conditions within which they might eventually be practicing law. Although the formal exchange took place in the entrepreneurship center, the entrepreneurship students did sometimes meet with the law students in the law school in order to access legal reference materials. In comparison to the entrepreneurship center, the law school reflected the structure and formalities associated with the law profession. Thus, the entrepreneurship students gained exposure to an environment that reflected the more concrete and objective legal components of the entrepreneurial process.

The distinctions between the physical climates of the entrepreneurship center and the law college were important nuances to the experiential nature of the exchange model. However, learning environments were important for reasons beyond physical location and conditions. Human contact and interpersonal communications provided equally important experiences by which entrepreneurship and law students could further develop skill sets essential to success in the knowledge economy. In discussing the importance of direct communication to the process of advancing innovations within the knowledge economy, Audretsch stated 'knowledge is vague, difficult to codify, and often only serendipitously recognized' (2007, p. 94). Further, the degree to which one can acquire and capitalize on knowledge in the new economy is highly dependent on human networks. In the context of the entrepreneurship/law exchange, the participating students were introduced to alternative academic/professional cultures and provided opportunities to codify existing and new knowledge into applicable and highly strategic skill sets.

The entrepreneurship curriculum is organized around the following sequential phases of entrepreneurial development: idea formulation, validation, the development of strategies, business-plan authorship and the refining of fluency, funding, and application. Included in the entrepreneurship curriculum is the importance of a well-developed legal strategy for the contemporary entrepreneurial process, especially in the areas of intellectual property protection and management. The entrepreneurship mentors-in-residence are equipped to introduce the legal issues that inform venture creation, which beyond intellectual property, include contracts, issues of liability, taxation and organization formation. However, providing entrepreneurship students with a working knowledge of such areas of entrepreneurship law is beyond their capacities. The mentors reported the entrepreneurship law exchange had in its earliest stages been effective in providing the entrepreneurship students with a more comprehensive understanding of and experience in working through the legal aspects of forming and advancing an entrepreneurial venture. One mentor stated:

> I can teach the [entrepreneurship] students what important legal issues need to be accounted for when pursuing an entrepreneurial venture. The law students are able to take the entrepreneurship students deeper into the technical workings of entrepreneurship law, which provides my [entrepreneurship] students with a much better understanding of when and how to gain legal guidance.

The benefits of the exchange were not lost on the entrepreneurship students. In talking with a focus group consisting of five entrepreneurship students who had actively engaged the services of the mock law firm, all reported having gained a more concrete grasp of the legal considerations required in a well-designed entrepreneurial strategy. While the students reported that they had gained a familiarity with the primary principles of entrepreneurship law through entrepreneurship classes, they also reported that they had gained from the law students a significantly greater understanding of how to apply this knowledge during the entrepreneurial process. For instance, one entrepreneurship student stated, 'I knew intellectual property needed to be protected through patents or copyrights, but I had no clue on how to do this. The law students provided a great overview of the steps needed to be taken in order to protect your invention. I get it now'. Another student stated, 'While the law students are not providing us counsel, they did recommend several points we should think about related to liability. We now know what steps to take to protect ourselves in case someone is hurt when using our product'. These remarks indicated that students were able to codify information gained through the classroom into meaningful and applicable knowledge using the experiential exchange process.

Outcomes and considerations
As has been highlighted by Audretsch (2007, p. 65), the knowledge economy is a complex global, social structure. Also, Hitt et al. (2001, p. 480) argued the importance to entrepreneurs of capturing competitive advantage within this new economy. Lessons specific to strategic and calculated risk taking within this climate were integrated into the McGuire entrepreneurship curriculum, which includes both classroom and 'hands-on' activities. As already stated, however, the technical and most detailed aspects of entrepreneurial law are beyond the entrepreneurship instructors' expertise. Although some students had in the past independently sought counsel from practicing attorneys, the results of such efforts had been inconsistent, sometimes costly and often not in alignment with the learning objectives of the entrepreneurship program. The past lack of comprehensive legal guidance often resulted in significant costs to the entrepreneurship students. These costs have been most often incurred by student teams seeking to launch their ventures following the completion of the entrepreneurship program. For example, some student teams have had to re-incorporate due to problematic contractual agreements or have lost position in emergent ventures because of flawed memoranda of understanding with third parties.

The entrepreneurship/law exchange showed in its earliest stages to be an innovative and effective approach to providing entrepreneurship students with more comprehensive learning experiences specific to the legal aspects of the new venture creation. First, the law students provided the entrepreneurship students with more thorough legal input specific to such technical principles and practices as the execution of memoranda of understanding and non-disclosure agreements, the formalization of legally recognized businesses and the negotiation of buyouts and exit strategies. Second, flexibility allowed the law students to be highly responsive to the fluid needs of the entrepreneurship students. Third, the close supervision and guidance of the law students by both the law professors and the practicing attorney that guided the mock law firm practicum increased the quality and sophistication of the legal strategies developed through the exchange. Therefore, the entrepreneurship students were given the opportunity to formulate more comprehensive and technically sound legal frameworks for their venture development plans.

The law students did not lend their burgeoning expertise without any returns. The returns these students realized in exchange for their input and guidance were not monetary, but rather were the experiences gained in addressing the needs common to entrepreneurs seeking success in the knowledge economy. The knowledge economy is far more entrepreneurial in nature than the previous managerial economy (Audretsch, 2007, p. 16). Thus, the law students gained valuable insights relevant to the knowledge economy by having participated in the exchange. In the context of experiential learning, the exchange provided the law students with opportunities to construct tangible meanings for classroom knowledge specific to the intersections of law, intellectual property and venture creation within a simulated entrepreneurial environment.

As beneficial as the exchange was to both sides, the fact remains that all the participants were students, not fully educated practitioners. Consequently, limitations were expected and therefore anchored in the experiential learning objectives of the exchange. For instance, the entrepreneurship students were not fully capable of adequately researching the potential legal issues facing their developing entrepreneurial ventures prior to meeting with the law students. Accordingly, these students were required to prepare agendas and questions under the guidance of the mentors-in-residence in advance of each meeting with the law students. The mentors reviewed the agendas not only to ensure that due diligence on the part of the entrepreneurship students had taken place, but also to assist the students in refining the questions in order to make each exchange as productive and beneficial as possible for both the entrepreneurship and the law students. Further, the mentors were able to demonstrate to students the value of not only understanding the primary principles of entrepreneurship law, but also how to best leverage this knowledge. Beyond providing substance to classroom lessons, the preparation also better mirrored the actual transactions between entrepreneurs and attorneys within the marketplace, where contact time equates to billable services.

On the opposite side of the exchange, the law students were also limited by minimal experience within a clinical setting. Specifically, the law students were often so conservative that discussion stalled at the most standard issues related to intellectual property rights, contractual agreement and organizational structure issues. As a result, the ability to discuss potential legal strategies and unconsidered options was constrained. In the context of experiential learning, this limitation was to be expected and represented an ideal learning opportunity for the law students. Very close supervision and coaching from the law instructional team was therefore provided. This support encouraged the law students to stretch beyond their comfort zones and to begin to practice their legal knowledge and developing skills in ways that more closely resemble the activities of an attorney working with entrepreneurs within the 'live' marketplace.

Consistent with the premises of ELT, the exchange model was initially designed with an awareness of the need for close supervision and significant contact time between the students on both sides of the exchange and the instruction teams on both side of the exchange. However, the limitations resulting from the students' lack of experience in applying entrepreneurial and legal knowledge to projects proved that more supervision and contact time than what was initially planned for was needed. The strategy being developed for upcoming exchanges is to recruit a team of academics and professionals to enhance the interactions between the entrepreneurship and law students and the overall experiential value of the exchange. These facilitators will consist of academics within the business and law schools with expertise in entrepreneurship and/or business law, as well as local attorneys and entrepreneurs willing to volunteer time with the students participating in the exchange.

Beyond providing more supervision over the student exchanges, the expansion of professional input from experts in the areas of entrepreneurship and law will allow for a more thorough exploration of the complex challenges associated with launching new ventures in the knowledge economy. For example, the delineation and management of intellectual property rights is a fluid rather than linear process that often requires sophisticated patent searches, advanced contractual agreements and corresponding memoranda of understanding, and firm negotiation strategies. In the McGuire program, entrepreneurship students have historically been confronted by barriers associated with unexpected third parties with partial rights to intellectual property once thought to be exclusively owned by either the university or an identified external third party. By adding a layer of professional guidance and sophistication to the exchange, both the entrepreneurship and the law students will be better equipped to engage in more sophisticated and in-depth explorations of the complex and often otherwise unanticipated legal issues that are inherent in knowledge-based entrepreneurship.

The increases in instructional support require an increase in human capital, which poses a potential barrier based on resource constraints commonly found within colleges and universities. There exists precedent for this strategy in the McGuire Center's technology mentor program, which consists of one engineer and two trained scientists who receive minimal compensation to assist entrepreneurship students in evaluating the scientific and technological validity of concepts and inventions being considered as the platforms for entrepreneurial ventures. The technology mentor program has been highly effective in providing entrepreneurship students with valuable scientific and technological input during the process of validating the conceptual integrity and practical utility of emerging scientific and technological concepts. This model will be used as the template for building a low-cost, high-quality, expanded professional support system for the entrepreneurship/law exchange.

The entrepreneurship/law exchange inherently attempts to bridge two very different academic and ultimately professional fields. On the one side of the exchange, entrepreneurship students are being trained and socialized to move ideas and concepts forward quickly in order to capitalize on market opportunities. In this regard, entrepreneurship students are taught the value in being nimble and are encouraged to face risks and uncertainties using strategic, but timely methods. On the other side of the exchange, the law students are being trained and socialized to be methodical and cautious in how they approach problems. In this regard, law students are taught the value of taking the needed amount of time to mitigate rather than minimize risks and uncertainties. Therefore, there is an inherent push and pull between the entrepreneurship and law students. Although the resulting tensions create frustration among students on both sides of the exchange, the differences in disciplinary/professional approaches to problems provide the students with a very valuable learning experience. Specifically, the ability to adapt to alternative approaches and varying professional environments is a critical component of the entrepreneurial process.

In order to better highlight the academic underpinning of the exchange, the formal administrative framework has been strengthened. First, clearly articulated agreements between all parties (the business and law schools, instructors and mentors, and students) have been established. These agreements further clarify that the interactions between the entrepreneurship and law students are academic exercises only and not to be taken as legally binding services. Further, the entrepreneurship students sign statements agreeing that if their team decides to move forward in launching their venture into the market, outside legal advice from licensed practitioners must be sought. In other words, the information and advice provided by the law students during learning exchanges will not be used as actual legal counsel, thereby removing any potential liability on the part of the law students should the entrepreneurship students engage in actual market activities. On the other side of the exchange, law students are now required to enter into non-disclosure agreements that prevent the unauthorized use of the ideas of the entrepreneurship students. One underlying lesson in regard to replicating this exchange is that well-articulated agreements of limitations should be established prior to implementing a similar model. By doing so, students, instructors, and other academic and professional support staff will be able to engage in the experiential learning exchange without excessive liability constraints.

Broader applications

The entrepreneurship/law exchange is one narrow application of an innovative entrepreneurship education delivery method. As has been indicated throughout this chapter, entrepreneurship is a 'hands-on' process that makes experiential learning particularly effective in educating aspiring entrepreneurs. Entrepreneurship is a cross-disciplinary field of study at many colleges and universities (Katz, 2003, p. 295; Mars, 2007, p. 43). Despite the diverse nature of entrepreneurship education, there remain voids in content that represent missed learning opportunities for students outside of entrepreneurship education. In the context of the example provided, the law students participating in the entrepreneurship/law exchange are not likely to be interested in pursuing an entrepreneurial venture. However, the law students' interests in practicing law specific to intellectual property and new venture creation fits well with the needs of the students studying entrepreneurship. In addition to developing and refining professional skill sets, students on both sides of the exchange are encouraged to codify knowledge in ways meaningful to themselves as soon-to-be learned professionals.

Graduate students in the science and technology fields are increasingly socialized toward careers in private industry (Slaughter et al., 2002, p. 283), which translates to an increase in the number of highly trained graduates interested in applying their technical and scientific training in the private sector. Entrepreneurship students seeking to leverage the potential value of scientific and technical innovations within the knowledge economy often require expert guidance in determining the functional validity of high-tech concepts. One way to provide entrepreneurship students with opportunities to develop an appreciation for and a background in working with scientists is through the creation of mock scientific advisory boards comprising students with advanced training in areas such as biotechnology, life sciences, engineering and optical sciences. A mock scientific advisory board holds the potential of providing entrepreneurship students with valuable insights into the scientific and/or technical integrity of a concept while providing science and technology students with equally valuable experiences that simulate professional scientific and technical consultation.

Finally, the model offers potential value to disciplinary fields within the liberal arts that are not typically seen as aligned with entrepreneurial principles and philosophies. For instance, an exchange model that links entrepreneurship students with students in the arts and sciences who are interested in creating social change and promoting social justice would likely produce meaningful learning outcomes for students on both sides of the exchange. In such an exchange model, entrepreneurship students would be encouraged to build and expand their entrepreneurial skills by providing guidance to emerging social entrepreneurs. Also, these students would have the opportunity to develop a more holistic understanding of and appreciation for the role that entrepreneurship plays in improving societal conditions. Concurrently, students in the arts and sciences would be exposed to the efficacy of entrepreneurship as a vehicle for social change and thereby be introduced to potentially useful entrepreneurial strategies for driving the creation and success of new social ventures.

Conclusion

In short, the entrepreneurship/law exchange represents a fresh approach to delivering entrepreneurship education to students located outside of the management fields. While more subtle than traditional offerings involving elective courses, certificates, minors, and secondary majors, exchange models represent strong experiential learning platforms for entrepreneurship students, those with a strong interest in supporting entrepreneurs through guidance and consultation and students seeking to enhance their skills and effectiveness through methods and frameworks outside of their primary fields. We have demonstrated the principles of experiential exchange using the developing entrepreneurship/law exchange at the University of Arizona, but have extended its potential application to simulated scientific and technical advisory board models and learning models that match entrepreneurship students with students, pursuing degrees in liberal arts. Finally, by arguing the value of cross-disciplinary entrepreneurship exchange models, we have helped further position university-wide entrepreneurship education in the context of the knowledge economy, which is a perspective that holds value for all students, regardless of disciplinary fields of study.

References

Audretsch, D.B. (2007), *The Entrepreneurial Society*, New York: Oxford University Press.

Creed, C.J., Suuberg, E.M. and Crawford, G.P. (2002), 'Engineering entrepreneurship: an example of a paradigm shift in engineering education', *Journal of Engineering Education*, April, 185–95.

Dewey, J. (1938), *Experience and Education*, New York: Macmillan.

Hitt, M.A., Ireland, R.D., Camp, S.M. and Sexton, D.L. (2001), 'Strategic entrepreneurship: entrepreneurial strategies for wealth creation', *Strategic Management Journal*, **22** (6–7), 479–91.

Honig, B. (2004), 'Entrepreneurship education: toward a model of contingency-based business planning', *Academy of Management Learning and Education*, 3 (3), 258–73.

Hynes, B. (1996), 'Entrepreneurship education and training: introducing entrepreneurship into non-business disciplines', *Journal of European Industrial Training*, **20** (8), 10–17.

Jones, C. and English, J. (2004), 'A contemporary approach to entrepreneurship education', *Education + Training*, **46** (8/9), 416–23.

Katz, J.A. (2003), 'The chronology and intellectual trajectory of American entrepreneurship education 1876–1999', *Journal of Business Venturing*, **18**, 283–300.

Kolb, D.A. (1984), *Experiential Learning: Experience as the Source of Learning and Development*, Englewood Cliffs, NJ: Prentice-Hall.

Kuratko, D.F. (2006), 'A tribute to 50 years of excellence in entrepreneurship and small business', *Journal of Small Business Management*, **44** (3), 483–93.

Kwan, Y.K. and Lai, E.L.C. (2003), 'Intellectual property rights protection and endogenous economic growth', *Journal of Economic Dynamics and Control*, **27**, 853–73.

Lanjouw, J.O. and Schankerman, M. (2004), 'Protecting intellectual property rights: are small firms handicapped?', *Journal of Law and Economics*, **47**, 45–74.

MacFarlane, J. (1992), 'Look before you leap: knowledge and learning in legal skills education', *Journal of Law and Society*, **19** (3), 293–319.

Mars, M.M. (2007), 'The diverse agendas of faculty within an institutionalized model of entrepreneurship education', *Journal of Entrepreneurship Education*, **10**, 43–62.

Mars, M.M., Slaughter, S. and Rhoades, G. (2008), 'The state-sponsored student entrepreneur', *Journal of Higher Education*, **79** (6), 638–70.

McGuire Center for Entrepreneurship (2007), 'Entrepreneurship. From idea to reality', http://entrepreneurship.arizona.edu, August 3, 2007.

Piaget, J. (1952), *The Origins of Intelligence in Children*, New York: International University Press.

Powell, W.W. and Snellman, K. (2004), 'The knowledge economy', *Annual Review of Sociology*, **30**, 199–220.

Schramm, C.J. (2006), *The Entrepreneurial Imperative: How America's Economic Miracle Will Reshape the World (and Change Your Life)*, New York: HarperCollins.

Slaughter, S., Campbell, T., Holleman, M. and Morgan, E. (2002), 'The "traffic" in graduate students: graduate students as tokens of exchange between academe and industry', *Science, Technology, and Human Values*, **27** (2), 282–312.

15 Assessing the impact of entrepreneurship education: a methodology and three experiments from French engineering schools

Alain Fayolle* and Benoît Gailly

Introduction

Entrepreneurship has become an important economic and social phenomenon as well as a popular research subject. Throughout the world, student interest in entrepreneurship as a career choice is growing (Brenner et al., 1991; Hart and Harrison, 1992; Fleming, 1994; Kolvereid, 1996a), while interest in traditional professional employment in big business is gradually declining (Kolvereid, 1996b). Entrepreneurship has also become both an academic and a teaching field, considering the rapidly increasing number of universities worldwide that offer entrepreneurship programs and courses. However, some pedagogical and practical challenges remain regarding the design, implementation and evaluation of those programs.

In this context, the aim of this research is to contribute to a better understanding of the role of entrepreneurship as a teaching field, in particular in the non-business context. As the number of entrepreneurship education programs (EEPs) grows across universities and other educational institutions, and as public and private resources allocated to those programs become significant, it becomes critical to better understand the impact and the effectiveness of those programs. This is particularly the case in non-business educational environments, where entrepreneurship might not have the same legitimacy as it does within business schools and must therefore compete for resources and/or suitable slots in the programs offered.

Our current scientific knowledge regarding the impact of EEPs is so far of little help to teachers and other stakeholders involved. Not much is known regarding the actual impact of entrepreneurship programs. How do they affect the future behavior of the participants? How do they affect their perceptions, values and attitudes? Is the impact achieved significant in light of the resources mobilized? Are different programs generating a different impact?

The first challenge faced by researchers tackling those questions is the wide heterogeneity of EEPs. Some programs focus on awareness and exposure to entrepreneurship situations and aim at increasing the number of students considering entrepreneurship as a potentially attractive career path. Other EEPs focus more explicitly on specific skills and knowledge related to the entrepreneurship process itself (Johannisson, 1991). The latter typically tackle issues related in particular to the 'know-why' (antecedents, mitigating factors and motivations of entrepreneurship), the 'know-what' (the key steps to launch a new business), the 'know-how' (the key success factors of entrepreneurship), the 'know-who' (the valuable contacts and networks) and/or the 'know-when' (when is it the right time for somebody to embrace an entrepreneurship career?).

The second challenge relates to the choice of adequate indicators[1] (what do we measure?) and to the timing of the measurements. Indeed, not every participant in an EEP can be expected to start a business on the first day after graduation, in particular when considering participants in non-business programs. The measurements of the impact of a program should therefore in theory include delayed effects. But as time passes it becomes more and more difficult to extract the impact of an EEP from other factors such as the environment, specific events, or the emergence of a business opportunity. Examples of indicators used include direct microeconomic impact measures such as the number of new businesses launched or the number of jobs created. Other more indirect indicators include the entrepreneurial mindset of the students or their intention to create a business in the future. Those indicators suffer, however, from the delayed effect bias mentioned above, as it is difficult to establish a clear link between a pedagogical feature and a subsequent entrepreneurial action. Finally, other factors such as the nature of the audience, the institutional context or the local culture might also affect the impact of an EEP.

Those factors highlight the need to define and develop a common conceptual framework regarding the assessment, comparison and ultimately the improvement of EEPs. This framework should include clear indicators to characterize and assess various types of EEPs as well as effective and validated measurement protocols. In particular, several authors stress the need to develop new types of evaluation criteria and indicators (Hytti and Kuopusjärvi, 2004; Moro et al., 2004). Those indicators might relate to the level of knowledge and skills acquired, or to the ability to master specific tools and concepts, as is the case for many education programs outside the field of entrepreneurship. Other classic criteria such as students' level of motivation and awareness could also be considered as relevant indicators, as well as class participation and regular attendance.

Observations such as these motivated the launch in 2004 of a research initiative dedicated to the development of a new methodology to assess the impact and effectiveness of EEPs, through measures of the evolution of participants' attitude, perceptions and intention regarding entrepreneurship. We shall outline here the main characteristics of this methodology, as well as discuss its application to three EEPs offered to non-business students. The next sections present the theoretical framework used, followed by the presentation of the three experiments and a discussion of the results and their implications.

The evaluation of EEPs
Various researchers have already attempted to assess empirically the impact of EEPs on their participants, controlling for the personal and environmental factors that might influence their orientations and behaviors (Lüthje and Franke, 2003). In particular, researchers have demonstrated that a favorable teaching environment might improve the way students consider entrepreneurship as a career option. Johannisson (1991) and Autio et al. (1997) underscore the impact of students' perceptions of entrepreneurship, along with resources and other support mechanisms available in the university environment, on students' attitudes towards entrepreneurial careers. Other research has shown the importance of the social status of entrepreneurial activities and situations (Begley et al., 1997) and the statistical link between the level of entrepreneurial intention and the number of management courses taken by students enrolled in other programs (Chen et al., 1998).

On the other hand, EEPs have been shown to influence both the current behavior and the future intentions of their participants (Kolvereid and Moen, 1997; Tkachev and

Kolvereid, 1999; Fayolle, 2002), with significant differences observed between students who had taken entrepreneurship courses and those who had not. Noel (2001) looked specifically at the impact of entrepreneurship training on the development of entrepreneurial intention and the perception of self-efficacy. The students in this sample had all taken an entrepreneurship education program and were graduates in entrepreneurship, management or another discipline. Noel's findings at least partially confirmed the assumption that the entrepreneurship graduates were more likely to launch businesses and had a higher level of intention and a more developed perception of self-efficacy than other students. Other researchers have tried to explain the relationship between entrepreneurship programs and individual characteristics, such as need for achievement and locus of control (Hansemark, 1998) or the perception of self-efficacy (Ehrlich et al., 2000). They found that entrepreneurship education had a positive impact, enhancing these characteristics and the likelihood of entrepreneurial action at some point in the future.

Several researchers have attempted to identify whether specific educational variables (course content, teaching methods, teacher profile, resources and support, and so on) might significantly influence the outcome of a program in terms of attitudes, values or knowledge. For example, Varela and Jimenez (2001), in a longitudinal study, chose groups of students from five programs in three universities in Colombia. They found that the highest entrepreneurship rates were achieved in the universities that had invested the most in entrepreneurship guidance and training for their students. Dilts and Fowler (1999) attempted to show that certain teaching methods (internships and field learning) were more successful than others at preparing students for an entrepreneurial career. Finally Lüthje and Franke (2003) discussed the importance of certain contextual factors within the university environment that hinder or facilitate the access of technical students to entrepreneurial behavior. Their findings confirm those of Fayolle (1996) and Autio et al. (1997), which were obtained using comparable samples.

A methodology to assess EEPs

Our methodology is based upon the theory of planned behavior (TPB, Ajzen, 1991, 2002), which is an extension of the theory of reasoned action (Ajzen and Fishbein, 1980), including the factor of 'perceived behavioral control'. The central factor of this social psychological theory is the individual's intention to perform a given behavior. Intention is the cognitive representation of a person's readiness to perform a given behavior and is considered to be the immediate antecedent of any voluntary behavior. Assessing the level of intention regarding a behavior is therefore an indirect way to assess the future likelihood of the behavior in question. The fundamental claim of the TPB is that the intention to perform a given behavior is the result of three conceptual determinants: the attitude toward the behavior, subjective norms and perceived behavioral control. We now detail those three factors and illustrate them in the entrepreneurial context.

First, the attitude toward a behavior is the degree to which a person has a favorable or unfavorable evaluation or appraisal of the behavior in question (Ajzen, 1991): 'Do I perceive that this would be a good thing to do?'. When new issues arise requiring an evaluative response, people can draw on relevant information (beliefs) stored in memories. Because each of these beliefs carries evaluative implications, attitudes are automatically formed. In the entrepreneurial context, the intention of launching a new business will be influenced by how personal values and attitudes have been shaped over time.

Those values and attitudes can be influenced by positive and negative experiences, personal or with one's close relatives. The professional, teaching and social environment of the person, as well as his/her exposure to awareness-raising initiatives or events are also likely to affect his/her attitudes toward entrepreneurial behavior.

Second, subjective norms are perceived social pressures to perform or not to perform the behavior (ibid.). In other words, they are the person's perception of the opinions that important others hold regarding the behavior. 'Would people important to me consider this action as a good move?'. How relatives, colleagues or friends consider a behavior will affect how a person will consider it. For example, in France the failure of a company is often negatively perceived, whereas in the United States a person can often undergo several failures and still undertake new attempts at creating a successful business. These cultural differences would be represented in the person's set of subjective norms.

Finally, the perceived behavioral control is the perceived ease or difficulty of performing a behavior (ibid.): 'Could I do it if I wanted to?'. This concept was introduced into the TPB to accommodate the non-volitional elements inherent, at least potentially, in all behaviors (Ajzen, 2002). In the context of entrepreneurship it relates to the perceived ease of launching a new business (such as the technical competencies required, the financial risks, the administrative burden and so on) and one's assessment of his/her resources and abilities. Krueger and Dickson (1994) highlighted that an increase of perceived behavioral control regarding a new venture increases the perception of business opportunity. For example, a few years ago during the 'dot-com bubble', launching a successful business was perceived as relatively easy, which led many people to try.

In summary, one's intention to launch a new business is driven by the level of internal and external desirability of that behavior (attitudes and subjective norms) and its perceived feasibility (behavioral control). EEPs can potentially influence both the desirability and feasibility of an entrepreneurial behavior and their impact can therefore be assessed through an evaluation of the change in those factors resulting from a student's attending the EEP.

In this model (see Figure 15.1) the independent variables are the characteristics of the EEP that is assessed. They can be related either to the level of commitment of a student or to more specific parameters such as the characteristics of the audience, the objective of the EEP, its content (Gibb, 1988; Wyckham, 1989; Gasse, 1992; Ghosh and Block, 1993), or the teaching approaches mobilized or the institutional settings (Safavian-Martinon, 1998). The dependent variables are the antecedents to the entrepreneurial behavior as defined by Ajzen, which are the attitude, the subjective norms, the perceived behavioral control and the level of intention itself. Those dependent variables can be measured individually before and after participating in an EEP and observed variations can then be linked with the independent variables discussed above.

In summary, the core of our approach is to measure whether the level of attitude, subjective norms, perceived behavioral control or intention regarding the entrepreneurial behavior is significantly lower/higher after attending an EEP, and how those differences correlate with the characteristics of the EEP. The main strength and key feature of this approach is that we do not attempt to directly measure the entrepreneurial behavior itself. Indeed, as discussed above, that behavior is multidimensional, can suffer delays and can be influenced by environmental factors or personal choices. It is, therefore, quite difficult to characterize and measure in a systematic way. By contrast, the key factors of

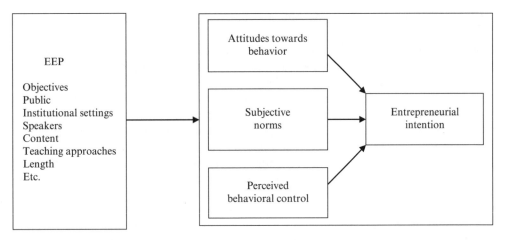

Figure 15.1   EEP assessment model

Ajzen's model can be measured at various points in time through validated question-naires (Kolvereid, 1996b) and correlated with some or all of the independent variables considered. This allows comparisons among the impact of various programs. It can also be used to improve the design of EEPs by analyzing how specific changes of pedagogical approach affect the impact in terms of entrepreneurial intention. Specific research questions that can be addressed therefore include:

- Do EEPs significantly affect participants' attitudes regarding the entrepreneurial behavior? What about their intention?
- How is the impact of an EEP affected by the characteristics of the audience, such as participants' previous exposure to entrepreneurship?
- How is the impact of an EEP affected by changes in the design of the program (objectives, teaching approaches and so on)?
- How is the impact of an EEP related to its content, in particular regarding the five levels of learning identified by Johannisson (1991): know-why, know-what, know-how, know-who and know-when?

In the next section we shall discuss how the method presented above has been applied to test some of those research questions in the case of three EEPs offered to French engineering students.

Experiments

Context of the experiments
We applied the assessment approach presented above to three EEPs aimed at French technology and engineering students, offered by three postgraduate schools in Grenoble, Lyon and Limoges. The three EEPs were all 'awareness' programs, as they shared the same objective of increasing the number of students considering entrepreneurship as a potentially attractive career path.

On the other hand, the three EEPs differed significantly in terms of pedagogical approach:

- The Grenoble EEP was a one-day program using traditional teaching methods delivered by a single professor. It was attended by a homogeneous group of 20 young engineers (only males) who were on average 22 years old and of whom 19 were French.
- The Limoges EEP was a seven-month program using participative teaching methods ('learning by doing') supported by a multidisciplinary team of academics, entrepreneurs and experts. It was attended by a homogeneous group of 43 technology students (three females, 40 males) who were on average 24 years old and all of whom were French. It included a final examination.
- The Lyon EEP was a three-day program using teamwork and case studies (evaluation of potential new business opportunities) supported by a multidisciplinary team of academics, entrepreneurs and experts. It was attended by a homogeneous group of 144 young engineers (10 females, 134 males) who were on average 23 years old and 90 percent of whom were French.

The three groups of students were given questionnaires to fill in before and/or after they attended the EEP. Those questionnaires included 47 Likert-scaled items related to the parameters of Ajzen's intention model (attitudes towards behavior, subjective norms, perceived behavioral control and intention) and 23 questions related to the students' background (age, gender, entrepreneurial experience and so on). The questionnaire for the measurement of the parameters of Ajzen's intention model was derived from the questionnaires developed and validated by Kolvereid (1996b). Each item was scaled from 1 to 7 and different model parameters were measured as the average score of the corresponding set of items. It should be noted that because of the very small number of females in each group, and because of the small number of non-French participants, neither sex of the participant nor country of origin could be built into the statistical design.

The three experiments specifically addressed three research questions, the results for which are presented in the next section. The three questions are:

1. What is the impact of the EEP on the level of entrepreneurial intention?
2. Is the impact of the EEP influenced by previous exposure to entrepreneurship?
3. Is the impact of the EEP influenced by the initial level of intention?

Note that for practical reasons the questionnaire was only partially administered after the Grenoble program and was not administered before the Limoges program. The data gathered in these illustrative cases are therefore incomplete. The setting of those cases also prevented the administration of the questionnaires to a control group of students, which might be useful when considering EEPs that continue for several weeks or months. Nevertheless, we believe that the experiments still provide interesting results, which are presented below.

Results

With regard to the first research question mentioned above, Table 15.1 presents the results available regarding the average level of intention and its antecedents (on a scale from 1 to 7) for the three groups of students, respectively, at the start and/or immediately after each program was completed. The observed differences are in brackets and significant

Table 15.1   Average level of entrepreneurial intention and its antecedents

	Grenoble (*n* = 20)	Limoges (*n* = 43)	Lyon (*n* = 144)	Lyon (correlations)
Initial values				
Attitudes	4.49	n.a.	5.01	0.37**
Subjective norms	4.12	n.a.	3.69	0.55**
Control	3.41	n.a.	3.86	0.34**
Intention	2.94	n.a.	3.90	–
Final values				
Attitudes	n.a.	4.6	5.00 (–0.01)	0.42**
Subjective norms	n.a.	4.2	3.67 (–0.02)	0.60**
Control	3.73 (+0.32*)	4.3	3.95 (+0.09)	0.40**
Intention	3.58 (+0.64*)	4.2	3.97 (+0.07)	–

*Note: *$p < 0.05$, **$p < 0.01$.

differences have been identified using a means comparison *t*-test comparing 'before' and 'after' average results. For the Lyon program, the correlation between the antecedents of the intention and the intention itself (in line with Ajzen's model) is also presented.

The results indicate a positive impact for the Grenoble EEP. For the Lyon EEP there was also an apparent increase in the correlations between the intention and its antecedents, indicating that as a consequence of the EEP the entrepreneurial intention of the students could be better aligned with their attitudes, norms and perceptions.

Furthermore, the final values of the Limoges students were higher than the final values of the other two programs, although they targeted similar groups of students. One potential explanation is the length of the EEP, which is substantially longer for the Limoges program, as well as the teaching approach adopted (participative learning with a relatively small group of students, followed by a formal examination). We were not able to test the persistence of this impact (through later measures of intention) although we expect it to be higher for the longer Limoges program.

Hence although the cases presented above should be considered mainly as illustrative, they highlight how the proposed approach can be used to assess the impact of an EEP on participants' attitudes regarding the entrepreneurial behavior and/or their intention.

With regard to our second research question, the impact of the characteristics of the audience and in particular of the previous exposure of the participants to entrepreneurship, we tested on the group of students who attended the Lyon program how the impact of the EEP was influenced by the previous exposure of students to factors that are known to influence the level of entrepreneurial intention:

- the presence of entrepreneurs among one's close relatives;
- the previous involvement in the launch or management of student associations;
- a long stay abroad (cultural, professional and geographic mobility); and
- a previous participation in an EEP.

We tested the influence of these factors through mean comparison (*t*-test) and correlations. Table 15.2 details the average impact of each of the four factors, respectively, on

Table 15.2   Impact of student characteristics (Lyon group, n = 144)

Factor	Share of students (%)	Impact on initial intention	Impact on change in intention
Entrepreneurs among relatives	63	+0.38	+0.16
Student association	54	+0.37	+0.06
Stay abroad	47	+0.08	+0.01
Previous EEP	23	+0.48	−0.02

the initial intention and on the variations of the intention resulting from that EEP. The values in the two last columns indicate the average difference between students having the characteristic considered and the rest of the sample, each characteristic being tested independently.

Although the subsets of students considered were too small to extract highly significant results and test the impact of correlations between those factors,[2] the results indicate that previous entrepreneurial exposure might affect the initial level of intention (which is consistent with the fact that those factors are known to influence the level of entrepreneurial intention). Indeed, students involved in the launch or management of student associations or living abroad for a long time face situations similar to entrepreneurial contexts. Among engineering students, those two types of exposure are strongly correlated with the ultimate launch or buyout of a venture (Fayolle, 1996).

Previous entrepreneurial exposure might also affect the variation of the intention resulting from an EEP, in particular for students having entrepreneurs among their close relatives (with $p = 0.2$ in this case). To belong to a family of entrepreneurs is indeed the most quoted factor in the literature as influencing entrepreneurial intention, since being exposed in day-to-day life to entrepreneurs feeds an entrepreneurial mindset. Anecdotal evidence suggests that a large majority of students applying for elective EEPs do indeed have entrepreneurs among their relatives (63 percent in the Lyon case).

Although the results presented above are not significant and should be further investigated before firm conclusions are drawn, they illustrate how the proposed approach can be used to test the influence of some characteristics of the audience, in particular previous exposure to entrepreneurship, on the impact of an EEP.

We investigated further the influence of the initial level of entrepreneurial intention upon the effect of the EEP, in the Lyon case. Indeed, this initial level should provide a good measure of the students' previous entrepreneurial exposure and therefore of their sensitivity to awareness initiatives. This 'direct' measure should provide more accurate results than the 'indirect' measures of measuring the individual factors presented above. As an illustration, the presence of an entrepreneur among one's family (the first factor measured above) does not indicate whether that entrepreneur was perceived as successful and therefore whether he or she had a positive or negative impact on the initial level of intention. Measuring the initial intention directly should therefore provide more accurate results.

Table 15.3 presents the average variation of intention and its antecedents for the whole group of students and for four subsets corresponding to successive quartiles of initial intention (from the lowest to the highest). The probability mentioned refers to the subsamples that differ significantly.

Table 15.3   Impact of the EEP for various levels of initial intention

Sample	n	Initial intention	Average impact of the EEP			
			Attitudes	Norms	Control	Intention
All students	144	3.90	0.00	0.02	0.09**	0.06
First quartile	36	2.39	0.00	−0.08	0.11	0.25**
Second quartile	36	3.39	0.09	0.05	0.19**	0.27*
Third quartile	36	4.29	−0.05	−0.01	0.03	0.09
Fourth quartile	36	5.56	−0.07	−0.04	0.06	−0.36***

Note: $* p < 0.10$, $** p < 0.05$, $*** p < 0.01$.

The results highlight that the change in intention resulting from the EEP is signifi-cantly positive for the students with the lowest level of initial intention (first two quar-tiles, respectively, +0.25 and +0.27), which were the students with the lowest level of previous entrepreneurial exposure. By contrast, the variation of intention resulting from the EEP is strongly negative for the students with the highest level of initial intention (last quartile, −0.36). Note that this result cannot be interpreted as simply a regression toward the mean as the average intentions of the first and fourth quartiles remain signifi-cantly different after the EEP ($p < 0.001$).[3]

Hence in this specific case our results indicate that the initial level of intention of a student appears to significantly affect the impact of an EEP on this student. Those results can be compared with the results from the Grenoble sample (Table 15.1), which had both a low level of initial intention (2.94) and a significant positive increase resulting from the EEP (+0.64).

Conclusions

The objectives of this chapter were (i) to stress the importance of assessing EEP, in particular when they are targeted at non-business students, (ii) to propose an original method to assess the impact of EEP and to highlight a range of research questions that could be addressed and (iii) to illustrate this method through experimentation on three EEPs aimed at French non-business students.

The first observation is that the proposed method allows one to empirically measure the short-term impact of the EEPs considered.

The second is that the impact observed appears to be influenced by some of the char-acteristics of the audience. In particular, for the Lyon program there was a strong and negative link between the initial level of intention of the students and the effect of the EEP on their intention.

One interpretation of those findings is that awareness programs such as the three EEPs analyzed above might generate a 'catch-up' or 'alignment' effect. Students with a low initial level of entrepreneurial intention (because they have experienced low, no or negative exposure to entrepreneurship) appear to be strongly and positively affected by the program and somewhat catch up with the rest of the group. By contrast, the effect of awareness EEPs on students with a high initial level of intention (high and positive previous exposure) appears to be insignificant or even negative, as they consider more seriously what entrepreneurship could mean for them. This interpretation is reinforced by the observation that the correlation between the entrepreneurial intention and its antecedents (Table 15.1) appears to be reinforced by the program.

Considering that entrepreneurship education programs targeted at non-business students are often electives and that a large share of students applying for those electives have previous exposure to entrepreneurship, this calls for more exploration of the relevance of the programs for those students and therefore of the resources allocated to them. Not only are such awareness programs potentially targeting the wrong people, but their impact might even for some students be counterproductive with respect to the initial objectives of such programs, which was to increase the number of students considering entrepreneurship as a potentially attractive career path.

The results, which obviously need to be tested further, indicate, for example, that multiplying the number of such awareness programs might not always be an effective way to increase the number of entrepreneurs.

The method we propose is therefore relevant not only for researchers interested in the questions raised above, but also for practitioners aiming at designing, implementing and evaluating innovative pedagogical approaches in order to improve the effectiveness of EEPs and the allocation of the limited resources available to entrepreneurship education. Potential improvements that should be investigated might include a better selection of students (which for some institutions might be quite revolutionary) as well as an adaptation of the pedagogical approaches to their initial level of entrepreneurial intention. Designing EEPs that have the right effect on the right people could therefore become more of a science and less of a craft, and be subject to rigorous evaluation approaches. This concerns not only the academics and the program managers, but all the stakeholders who support, facilitate or finance EEPs and obviously, also ultimately the students who attend the programs and want to achieve their personal and professional objectives.

Concerning more specifically the research implications, these preliminary results lead us to ask some new and important research questions. For example, depending on the type of EEP, are there some ways and tools for selecting non-business students and orientating them with an appropriate EEP that fits their profile and background? In some cases, EEPs aiming to give a first awareness of entrepreneurship might not be effective for certain types of students. Further research along these lines could improve our understanding about these issues. In addition, we are far from having a good knowledge about the influence of the main factors playing a role within an EEP. Further research would allow us to verify specific relations between pedagogical and educational variables and perceived behavioral control. Among others, our research model could be improved by including new independent variables influencing one or more of Ajzen's antecedents.

Notes

*   I would like to thank my colleague Frank Janssen who presented our paper at the Cross Campus Entrepreneurship Education Conference organized on November 8–10, 2007, by Wake Forest University. Unfortunately, I could not attend due to my father's poor health.
1.   As rightly pointed out by one of the reviewers, this is particularly an issue when using those indicators to rank educational institutions, as is now common in the popular press.
2.   'Entrepreneur among relatives' is significantly correlated with 'Student association' (0.18, $p < 0.01$) and 'Previous EEP' (0.20, $p < 0.01$). All other correlations are lower than 9 percent and not significant ($p > 0.10$).

3. The standard error of the average intentions actually increase only marginally, from 0.07 to 0.11 for the first quartile and from 0.09 to 0.14 for the fourth quartile.

References

Ajzen, I. (1991), 'The theory of planned behavior', *Organizational Behavior and Human Decision Processes*, **50**, 179–211.

Ajzen, I. (2002), 'Perceived behavioral control, self-efficacy, locus of control, and the theory of planned behavior', *Journal of Applied Social Psychology*, **32**, 1–20.

Ajzen, I. and Fishbein, M. (1980), *Understanding Attitudes and Predicting Social Behavior*, Englewood Cliffs, NJ: Prentice-Hall.

Autio, E., Keeley, R.H., Klofsten, M. and Ulfstedt, T. (1997), 'Entrepreneurial intent among students: testing an intent model in Asia, Scandinavia and USA', *Frontiers of Entrepreneurship Research*, Babson Conference Proceedings, Babson Park, Wellesley, MA, www.babson.edu/entrep/fer.

Begley, T.M., Tan, W.L., Larasati, A.B., Rab, A., Zamora, E. and Nanayakkara, G. (1997), 'The relationship between socio-cultural dimensions and interest in starting a business: a multi-country study', *Frontiers of Entrepreneurship Research*, Babson Conference Proceedings, Babson Park, Wellesley, MA, www.babson.edu/entrep/fer.

Brenner, O.C., Pringle, C.D. and Greenhaus, J.H. (1991), 'Perceived fulfillment of organizational employment versus entrepreneurship: work values and career intentions of business college graduates', *Journal of Small Business Management*, **29** (3), 62–74.

Chen, C.C., Greene, P.G. and Crick, A. (1998), 'Does entrepreneurial self-efficacy distinguish entrepreneurs from managers?', *Journal of Business Venturing*, **13** (4), 295–316.

Dilts, J.C. and Fowler, S.M. (1999), 'Internships: preparing students for an entrepreneurial career', *Journal of Business and Entrepreneurship*, **11** (1), 51–63.

Ehrlich, S.B., De Noble, A.F., Jung, D. and Pearson, D. (2000), 'The impact of entrepreneurship training programs on an individual's entrepreneurial self-efficacy', *Frontiers of Entrepreneurship Research*, Babson Conference Proceedings, Babson Park, Wellesley, MA, www.babson.edu/entrep/fer.

Fayolle, A. (1996), 'Contribution à l'étude des comportements entrepreneuriaux des ingénieurs français', PhD thesis, Université Jean Moulin de Lyon.

Fayolle, A. (2002), 'Les déterminants de l'acte entrepreneurial chez les étudiants et les jeunes diplômés de l'enseignement supérieur français', *Revue Gestion 2000*, no. 4, 61–77.

Fleming, P. (1994),. 'The role of structured interventions in shaping graduate entrepreneurship', *Irish Business and Administrative Research*, **15**, 146–57.

Gasse, Y. (1992), 'Pour une éducation plus entrepreneuriale. Quelques voies et moyens', Education Entrepreneurship Workshop, Centre d'Entrepreneuriat du cœur du Québec, Trois-Rivières, May.

Ghosh, A. and Block, Z. (1993), 'Audiences for entrepreneurship education: characteristics and needs', in F. Hoy, T. Monroy and J. Reichert (eds) *The Art and Science of Entrepreneurship Education*, vol. 1, Berea, OH: Project for Excellence in Entrepreneurship Education, pp. 65–82.

Gibb, A.A. (1988), 'Stimulating new business development', in A.A. Gibb, *Stimulating Entrepreneurship and New Business Development*, Geneva: Interman International Labor Office, pp. 47–60.

Hansemark, O.C. (1998), 'The effects of an entrepreneurship program on need for achievement and locus of control of reinforcement', *International Journal of Entrepreneurial Behavior and Research*, **4** (1), 28–50.

Hart, M. and Harrison, R. (1992), 'Encouraging enterprise in Northern Ireland: constraints and opportunities', *Irish Business and Administrative Research*, **13**, 104–16.

Hytti, U. and Kuopusjärvi, P. (2004), *Evaluating and Measuring Entrepreneurship and Enterprise Education: Methods, Tools and Practices*, Turku: Small Business Institute.

Johannisson, B. (1991), 'University training for entrepreneurship: a Swedish approach', *Entrepreneurship and Regional Development*, **3** (1), 67–82.

Kolvereid, L. (1996a), 'Organizational employment versus self-employment: reasons for career choice intentions', *Entrepreneurship Theory and Practice*, **20** (3), 23–31.

Kolvereid, L. (1996b), 'Prediction of employment status choice intentions', *Entrepreneurship Theory and Practice*, **20** (3), 45–57.

Kolvereid, L. and Moen, O. (1997), 'Entrepreneurship among business graduates: does a major in entrepreneurship make a difference?', *Journal of European Industrial Training*, **21**, (4), 154–60.

Krueger, N. and Dickson, P.R. (1994), 'How believing in ourselves increases risk taking: perceived self-efficacy and opportunity recognition', *Decision Sciences*, **25** (3), 385–400.

Lüthje, C. and Franke, N. (2003), 'The making of an entrepreneur: testing a model of entrepreneurial intent among engineering students at MIT', *R&D Management*, **33** (2), 135–47.

Moro, D., Poli, A. and Bernardi, C. (2004), 'Training the future entrepreneur', *International Journal of Entrepreneurship and Small Business*, **1** (1/2), 192–205.

Noel, T.W. (2001), 'Effects of entrepreneurial education on intent to open a business', *Frontiers of Entrepreneurship Research*, Babson Conference Proceedings, Babson Park, Wellesley, MA, www.babson.edu/entrep/fer.

Safavian-Martinon, M. (1998), 'Le lien entre le diplôme et la logique d'acteur relative à la carrière: une explication du rôle du diplôme dans la carrière des jeunes cadres issus des grandes écoles de gestion', PhD thesis, Université Paris I Pantheon-Sarbonne.

Tkachev, A. and Kolvereid, L. (1999), 'Self-employment intentions among Russian students', *Entrepreneurship and Regional Development*, **11** (3), 269–80.

Varela, R. and Jimenez, J.E. (2001), 'The effect of entrepreneurship education in the universities of Cali', *Frontiers of Entrepreneurship Research*, Babson Conference Proceedings, Babson Park, Wellesley, MA, www.babson.edu/entrep/fer.

Wyckham, R.G. (1989), 'Measuring the effects of entrepreneurial education programs: Canada and Latin America', in G. Robert, W. Wyckham and C. Wedley (eds), *Educating the Entrepreneurs*, Faculty of Administration, Simon Fraser University, Burnaby, British Columbia, pp. 1–16.

16 Leadership studies, civic engagement and entrepreneurship: exploring synergies on the practical side of liberal education

Samuel M. Hines, Jr

> A liberal arts education might be viewed as a metaphor for entrepreneurship. The humanities suggest that the entrepreneur is an artist. History might see entrepreneurs as the true revolutionaries of technological, economic, and social change. A liberal arts education is rich in metaphors that are capable of capturing the multifaceted life of an entrepreneur. A course in film or the theatre might suggest that the entrepreneur is a stage or film director, while a course in physical education might reveal the entrepreneur as a coach. . . . Undergraduate entrepreneurship education should not be viewed as a narrow careerist pursuit, but as giving new life to the traditions of a liberal arts education.
>
> (Ray, 1990: 80)

Introduction

The topics identified in the title of this chapter are not typically linked together in the academy. Liberal education and service learning may seem to go naturally together, but leadership and entrepreneurship are less obviously linked to the first two topics. This chapter shows how several prominent lines of scholarly inquiry into leadership and entrepreneurship, currently popular academic and student affairs programming in civic engagement, and the venerable goal of liberal education relate to one another in a number of ways. Moreover, we shall argue that they offer real potential for synergies that can contribute to the creation of innovative colleges, cultures, and curricula. Furthermore, leadership studies, student-oriented programs for responsible civic engagement and service learning, and research on and programs in entrepreneurship actually can provide a nexus for new initiatives that will enrich both liberal education and the study and practice of entrepreneurship. A related argument is that the current environment for higher education requires that colleges and universities become more entrepreneurial in their operation, given the limited resources and numerous challenges these institutions face in the twenty-first century. (See Breneman, 1993; Engell and Dangerfield, 2005; Zemsky et al., 2005; Hines, 2008; and the pages of every issue of the *Chronicle of Higher Education* for documentation of the fiscal crisis in higher education.) This condition of financial peril is important because it provides a stimulating context for the synergistic effects of linking these various strands of activity within the academy.

The following assumptions underlie my analysis. First, entrepreneurship is a legitimate area of scholarly inquiry and curricular component for the entire university, not only departments, schools and colleges of business. When one considers how much the following attributes – so often associated with liberal education – are equally identified with entrepreneurship, leadership and civic engagement, then it is easy to see how the curricular cross-fertilization that courses on entrepreneurship in a variety of departments and schools can add to the campus dialogue about liberal education:

- critical thinking skills;
- holistic and contextual thinking;
- ethical and moral responsibility;
- active learning;
- peer to peer/group learning and collective endeavor;
- development of personal authenticity and character; and
- vision and strategic perspective.

Second, the fundamental elements of a liberal education are essential to the development of an 'entrepreneurial mindset' and to the development of leaders in all fields of endeavor. The importance to both entrepreneurs and leaders of a mindset that is forward looking, holistic, synthetic, strategic and visionary may seem obvious to many, but it is important to stress how different this is from a more traditional managerial, administrative, tactical type of 'leader'. Part of this difference is captured well in Burns's (1978, 2003) distinction between 'transformational' and 'transactional' leaders. In one important article, Hitt et al. (2002) have explored the new mindset that is required of entrepreneurs to enable them to succeed in a highly fluid, rapidly changing, hyper-competitive environment in which conditions of uncertainty prevail. They also emphasize the critical importance of strategic thinking. Anyone in a responsible leadership position in any sector of society is increasingly aware of how essential strategic thinking is to survival, adaptive capacity and success.

And third, both the study of entrepreneurship and the goal of liberal education can derive mutual benefit from curricular and extra-curricular initiatives intended to develop students' potential for leadership through service learning and civic engagement (as well, of course, as internship experiences). The growth across campuses in the number of students who are actively engaged in their local community and throughout the world in some cases is impressive. The expansion of curricular and extra-curricular programs that put students into the world as active learners and participants as interns, relief workers, participant observers, and volunteers in all capacities is indicative of how much more civic engagement is going on in our colleges and universities.

I shall begin by briefly defining the key concepts in the title of this chapter (liberal education, leadership, civic engagement, and entrepreneurship) and elaborating on their common elements and points of connectivity. Then I shall review some of the activities and programs that have grown up around these ideas and make a case for the synergies that can arise. Finally, we shall consider some of the opportunities presented by entrepreneurial universities in the quest for support for higher education in general and liberal education in particular.

Liberal education
The concept of liberal education as defined by a distinct general education core curriculum dates to the establishment of the first private liberal arts colleges in the United States during the colonial period and the early eighteenth century. These early colleges were deeply committed to the preparation of moral, civic-minded citizens. Of course, the curriculum of those institutions was based upon the classical *artes liberales* that included the *quadrivium* (arithmetic, geometry, astronomy, and music) and the *trivium* (grammar, logic, and rhetoric). Indeed, one can easily trace the origins of liberal education to

ancient Greece (Rothblatt, 2003). As Rothblatt notes, there is no easily identifiable essence to liberal education: 'The inevitable conclusion is that the telltale identifying marks of a liberal education are the manner in which a subject is taught or learned, the spirit in which it is offered, and the attitudes that may just result from teaching and learning' (p. 15). He offers the following definition: 'Liberal education offers the intellectual and emotional basis on which is constructed a capacity to make decisions. It is the means by which men and women have sought to interpret the world or take a comprehensive view of it' (p. 15). He also quotes Leon Botstein, president of Bard College as saying that liberal education is 'a sense of value that is beyond material gain, beyond wealth and fame and power. It is about the way you conduct your life both as a private individual and as a citizen' (p. 15). We might also consider a slightly different and important definition offered by the conservative political philosopher, Leo Strauss, in his well-known commencement address, 'What is Liberal Education?' (cited in Schaub, 2002: 53):

- Liberal education is the necessary endeavor to found an aristocracy within democratic mass society.
- Liberal education consists in reminding oneself of human excellence, of human greatness.
- Liberal education consists in listening to the conversation among the greatest minds.
- Liberal education supplies us with experience in things beautiful.

For Strauss, as for many earlier advocates of liberal education, this type of education was only for a minority of learners whose families had the means to provide for their higher education and who had the intellectual preparation and ability to engage the classics. This reality has changed, and many colleges and universities committed to liberal education are equally committed to access and equity and believe fervently that all students can benefit from a liberal education. This is explicitly the case for the 25 institutions that belong to the Council of Public Liberal Arts Colleges.[1]

Drawing upon a large number of sources, we can offer the following description of the ideal 'liberally educated student of the twenty-first century': The liberally educated person is open-minded, tolerant, intellectually curious, courageous, self-actualizing (with the capacity for attaining personal growth and physical and mental health and spiritual well-being), and a lifelong learner. He or she values: education for its own sake, the natural world, the rights of other individuals, the richness of diverse cultures and peoples, the need for community, and respect for the common good. The liberally educated person is actively engaged as a learner and a citizen with his or her world in all of its complexity, diversity, and dynamism. He or she is characterized by an attitude of openness and curiosity, and seeks to make a positive contribution to the future of humankind.

A liberal education should develop such skills as: oral, written and nonverbal communication (including foreign languages); scientific methods and quantitative methodologies; research and technical capacities; ethical, critical, logical, analytic, and synthetic thinking and problem solving; interpersonal and leadership capabilities, and an aesthetic sense. Along with these skills it is expected that students will acquire substantive knowledge that is historical, philosophical, mathematical, scientific, cultural, literary, political, social and economic in content. By making it possible for students to acquire these skills, a liberal education proves itself to be the most practical of all educations because it prepares students to deal with change and with the new. As the CEO of Xerox recently observed:

> In such a world there is only one constant: change. And the only education that prepares us for change is a liberal education. In periods of change, narrow specialization condemns us to inflexibility – precisely what we do not need. We need the flexible intellectual tools to be problem solvers, to be able to continue learning over time. [I]t is not simply what you know that counts, but the ability to use what you know. In this way knowledge is power – the ability to use specialized knowledge as you adapt to new requirements. (Ramaley and Leskes et al., 2002: 28)

Above all, as proponents of liberal education we seek to instill in our students a desire to learn – to seek actively new ways of knowing and new knowledge. Over the course of their lives they should strive to integrate their skills and substantive knowledge and use that knowledge for the betterment of humankind and the stewardship of the natural world.

Ramaley and Leskes et al. define the best education for the twenty-first century as:

> based on a liberal education that produces an individual who is intentional about learning and life, empowered, informed, and responsible. To achieve these goals, liberal education will need to change in two major ways from its earlier incarnations. First, it must define itself as the best and most practical form of learning for a changing world and then strive to meet that standard. Second, it needs to become available to all students, not simply the self-selected and 'comparatively privileged' group of the past. (Ibid.: 25)

Although there are a great many definitions of liberal education beyond those mentioned above, we shall use the one provided in the well-received report by the Association of American Colleges and Universities (AAC&U), 'Greater Expectations: A New Vision for Learning as a Nation Goes to College' (Ramaley and Leskes et al., 2002). There, liberal education is defined as:

> A philosophy of education that empowers individuals, liberates the mind from ignorance, and cultivates social responsibility. Characterized by challenging encounters with important issues, and more a way of studying than specific content, liberal education can occur at all types of colleges and universities. (Ibid.: 25)

A key component of liberal education is general education, '[t]he part of a liberal education curriculum shared by all students. It provides broad exposure to multiple disciplines and forms the basis for developing important intellectual and civic capacities' (ibid.: 25). The idea that liberal education is empowering, liberating, and moral leads to the realization that the desired and intended outcome of a liberal education is an individual who is free, principled, capable of independent thinking and learning, reflective, and informed by a set of values that support the idea that knowledge is desirable for its own sake and that the individual has social responsibilities in an increasingly complex, diverse world.

Current thinking on liberal education, as reflected in all of AAC&U's publications and advocated in Ramaley and Leskes et al., places increased emphasis on the importance of liberal education for life, work, and stewardship. Some defenders of liberal education who still embrace the earlier vision of a classical liberal education are reluctant to embrace the idea that the liberal arts are of practical value. While any advocate of liberal education ought to defend the proposition that the pursuit of knowledge is worthwhile for its own sake and does not have to be of any other value, increasingly it is important to engage students, parents, and the general public in a dialogue that reveals the relevance and power of liberal education. Liberal education in the twenty-first century is, I would argue, essential to our ability as a species to achieve peace and prosperity and to provide the stewardship that the world needs. Liberal education helps the student learner become actively engaged in responding to the issues of our age and helps that independent learner to acquire the intellectual competencies and skills that are and will be most in demand. Because liberal education is committed to breadth (general education) and depth (the major) and engages the student with historical, philosophical, scientific, quantitative, and rhetorical methodologies while challenging the student to improve written and oral communication skills, that education is the best preparation possible for responsible citizenship and leadership. Ramaley and Leskes et al. remind us:

> Liberal education for the new century looks beyond the campus to the issues of society and the workplace. It aims to produce global thinkers. Quality liberal education prepares students for active participation in the private and public sectors, in diverse democracy, and in an even more diverse global community. (Ibid.: 25)

In discussing liberal education in comparative and historical contexts, Sheldon Rothblatt observes that one of the traditions of liberal education has been leadership: 'As one of the oldest traditions of liberal education, preparation for political leadership dates back to the Greeks and is connected to holism and character formation' (2003: 28). Let me now turn to the subject of leadership.

Leadership
The study of leadership has seen tremendous growth in recent years in the field of business and in the emerging interdisciplinary field of leadership itself. In addition, work in social psychology and organization theory and behavior has continued to contribute to our understanding of human motivation, leadership and followership roles, and the relation of leadership to organization culture, particularly in decision making, strategic thinking, innovation, and visioning. The University of Richmond (Richmond, VA), one of the first universities to establish a formal program in leadership studies, now has a thriving Jepson School of Leadership Studies that has offered an interdisciplinary bachelor's degree in leadership for over 10 years. Faculties at Richmond are in the process of exploring additional relationships between the School of Leadership Studies and the School of Business. The subject of leadership has long been embedded in curricula in history, political science, international studies, and business. And, as noted above in the section on liberal education, leadership has been linked with liberal education since ancient Greece.

Although largely embedded in these respective curricula, 'leadership' has begun to be treated as a separate subject in its own right. The *Journal of Leadership Studies* and the *Leadership Quarterly*, for example, have become primary sources of current research in this new field. In business administration, older, more established journals (for example, the *Harvard Business Review* and the *Journal of Management*) routinely publish articles dealing with the subject of leadership, as do publications of the Academy of Management.

The study of leadership has progressed from initially being focused upon the traits of leaders, to the examination of leadership behavior, and finally, to the development of contingency theories of leadership that recognize that leadership is, ultimately, contextual or situational. Another significant trend in leadership studies has been the realization that the primary situation of all leadership is to be found in the interrelationship between leaders and followers. At the federal service academies and The Citadel, all of which are committed to the core curricular elements associated with liberal education, leadership is infused throughout the curriculum and the extra-curriculum. At The Citadel, we have developed a comprehensive, integrated four-year leadership development model that prepares the cadet to take on greater responsibilities and challenges in a structured environment that builds on leadership experience beginning with 'followership' in the first year through peer mentoring as a sophomore, small unit leadership as a junior and organization leadership as a senior. The goal is the development of principled leaders in all walks of life. The leadership studies minor includes courses from the School of Business that include the study of leadership, management, and entrepreneurship.

Popular books on the leadership secrets or principles of such diverse figures as Attila the Hun, Colin Powell, Machiavelli, Mother Teresa, Abraham Lincoln, Moses, George Washington, and others abound, not to mention innumerable books on leadership and management.[2] Perhaps the most influential thinker writing on leadership today (with appropriate kudos to Peter Drucker's and John Gardner's numerous contributions) is the political scientist, James MacGregor Burns. This is especially the case because of his elaboration of the concept of 'transforming leadership' with its emphasis on vision and the pursuit of improvements in society. Indeed, 'visioning' has become a dominant theme in work on leadership. In his first study of leadership, Burns distinguished 'transactional leadership' (read management/administration) from 'transformational leadership'. In his subsequent treatment of transforming leadership, Burns (2003) went on to examine numerous cases of transforming leaders who had been inventive, had shown initiative, and who had literally transformed whatever enterprise they were engaged in. In particular, he focused on 'creative leadership':

> At its simplest, creative leadership begins when a person imagines a state of affairs not presently existing. This initial creative insight or spark is elaborated into a broader vision of change, possible ways of accomplishing it are conceived, and – in a fateful act of leadership – the vision is communicated to others. Because most ideas of significant change make some persons followers and others opponents, conflict arises. It is such conflicts that supply powerful motivation for transforming leadership and followership, fusing them into a dynamic force in pursuit of change. (p. 153)

We can, of course, cite many examples of leaders and entrepreneurs who have done exactly what Burns describes. Let me cite one example: Ewing Marion Kauffman. Kauffman's experience as a salesman, working entirely on commission, was that his boss failed to appreciate his contribution and in doing so showed a failure to appreciate the value of his workers. When the president became concerned that Kauffman's incredible success as a salesman had resulted in his making a salary greater than the president, he cut Kauffman's territory out of spite. Kauffman promptly quit and started his own company (Marion Laboratories) founded on a different vision:

> I based the company on a vision of what it would be. When we hired employees, they were referred to as 'associates,' and they shared in the success of the company. Once again, the two principles that have guided my entire career, which were based on my experience working for that very first pharmaceutical company, are these: 'Those who produce should share in the profits,' and 'Treat others as you would be treated'. (Kauffman, cited in Bolman and Deal, 1997: 117)

Thus Kauffman became one of the early champions of a leadership style that Bolman and Deal describe as a 'human resources' style. These pathbreaking leaders are engaged in the pursuit of a vision – a goal or set of goals that motivates them – and they in turn motivate others to embrace that vision.[3] Burns (2003) goes on to argue that as interesting as the individualist interpretations of the origins of creativity, what is even more important is the creation of cultures that engender creativity. Because leadership is situational and contingent, fostering cultures of innovation is a particularly important goal of leaders (entrepreneurs) who understand the challenges of constant change. The successful leader knows that his or her organization must be capable of adapting, and therefore, it must be a 'learning organization' (Senge, 1990).

Building cultures of innovation and learning organizations requires a kind of leadership and followership that is capable of thinking holistically, systematically, and humanistically, and that is characterized by a continuous renewal of the founding vision, the core values, and the mission of the organization as understood in the context of a complex environment. As Edgar H. Schein, professor of management at the Sloan School of Management at MIT, has argued, this kind of leadership requires that the leader be an 'animator' (a source of energy), a creator of culture, a sustainer of culture, and a change agent (Schein, 1996). He goes on to say:

> Once an organization has the potential to live and survive, the entrepreneur's beliefs, values, and basic assumptions are transferred to the mental models of the subordinates. This process of building culture occurs in three ways: (1) the entrepreneurs only hire and keep subordinates who think and feel the way they do, (2) they indoctrinate and socialize subordinates to their way of thinking and feeling, and (3) their own behavior is a role model that encourages subordinates to identify with them and thereby internalize their beliefs, values, and assumptions. (p. 61)

But Schein also observes that organizations can develop dysfunctional cultures. The successful leader/entrepreneur must therefore be capable of being a leader of change. This requires 'a true understanding of cultural dynamics and the properties of their own organizational culture' (ibid.: 64).

Finally, Schein (p. 67) lists the following characteristics of leaders of the future:

- Extraordinary levels of perception and insight into the realities of the world and into themselves.
- Extraordinary levels of motivation to enable them to go through the inevitable pain of learning and change, especially in a world with looser boundaries, in which loyalties become more difficult to define.
- The emotional strength to manage their own and others' anxiety as learning and change become more and more a way of life.
- New skills in analyzing cultural assumptions, identifying functional and dysfunctional assumptions, and evolving processes that enlarge the culture by building on its strengths and functional elements.
- The willingness and ability to involve others and elicit their participation, because tasks will be too complex and information too widely distributed for leaders to solve problems on their own.
- The willingness and ability to share power and control according to people's knowledge and skills, that is, to permit and encourage leadership to flourish throughout the organization.

Elsewhere in the study of leadership one finds an emerging literature that explores 'authentic leadership'. The work of Terry (1993) in public administration explores this view of the courageously ethical leader in a way that parallels Burns's work on the transforming leader. Among those writing in the field of management, Walumbwa et al. (2008) have developed a view of authentic leadership that combines the individual psychological capacities of the leader with the advantage of a positive ethical climate, thus creating the potential for a self-developmental framework for leaders and followers in pursuit of mutually beneficial goals. The similarities among these various strains of leadership studies discussed above and the overlapping interest of students of entrepreneurship and advocates of liberal education in preparing leaders and followers to actively engage around goals and issues that are of value to society (whether meeting an economic, social, cultural, or political need), takes us back to the fundamental value of a liberal education for anyone aspiring to leadership or entrepreneurship.

The real value of a liberal education can be found in the way in which liberally educated leaders can draw upon the breadth and depth of that education to have that true understanding of themselves, of cultural dynamics, and of the nature of the complex environment in which the organization is embedded. A liberal education that takes seriously the need for students to engage with their communities, to bridge the gap from campus to community, and to become responsible citizens while still students, will provide the experiences and the experiential learning that prepares them to be effective leaders for change and to become future entrepreneurs. The liberally educated citizen of the twenty-first century, far more than the narrowly trained specialist, will be well prepared to demonstrate the characteristics that Schein believes will be needed in the future.

An example of how this kind of education prepares students for the future can be found in the College of Charleston's major in international business. Students are required to take a full complement of business and economics courses appropriate for a program in international business. But, in keeping with the commitment to liberal education, they must also complete a third year of foreign language study (building upon the general education requirement of two years of foreign language study) and study in one of our regional or area studies programs (African Studies, Asian Studies, European Studies, Latin American and Caribbean Studies) where they take interdisciplinary courses and courses in anthropology, sociology, history, political science and literature. They also have numerous opportunities for study abroad and for internships abroad. Similarly, our foreign language majors can minor in language and international business. The College of Charleston's foreign language programs have been transformed to go beyond grammar and literature to include courses in civilization and culture as well as specialized courses in German for Business, for example. Students may even take some business courses in a foreign language (for example, LeMarketing – Marketing in French). This approach to the study of international business provides the contextuality that is so very much needed for successful business ventures in today's global economy.

Civic engagement

One of the most powerful developments in liberal education in recent years, from the standpoint of experiential learning and applied liberal learning, has been the emergence of a renewed commitment to service learning and civic engagement on campuses across the country (for an overview of these developments, see Ehrlich, 2000; Schneider, 2000). This constitutes a renewal because the earliest liberal arts colleges were intended to prepare a highly selective student body for responsible social roles in their communities.

Although a consistent goal of liberal education, this goal had become increasingly submerged and implicit over the years. As indicated in AAC&U's 'Greater Expectations' document, responsible citizenship in the twenty-first century is now one of the foremost goals of liberal education. One of the most visible examples of this is the organization, Campus Compact,[4] which currently boasts 100 member institutions with a wide and growing array of programs designed to facilitate the involvement of undergraduates in a number of experiences in their communities including internships, volunteer projects, undergraduate research on social and community issues, and increased work–study experiences. The publication of Campus Compact, *The Campus Compact Reader*, contains example after example of the way its member institutions have effectively engaged their students in their communities. The AAC&U, the leading higher education organization promoting liberal education, alone has produced numerous publications and initiated several programs designed to help colleges and universities increase their commitment to and sustain these largely extra-curricular programs that help link liberal education to citizenship and work, and to encourage experiential learning and applied research through faculty/student/community partnerships.[5] One of the best examples of this kind of institution is Portland State University which is a model of the engaged, urban university that builds on a general education foundation in the liberal arts and extends to a plethora of programs designed to immerse students in their community in mutually beneficial ways.[6]

As more liberal arts colleges and universities encourage this kind of engagement, students will become better informed about the many challenges we face in society, and they will understand why new ideas, new techniques and technologies, and new solutions are called for. Some of them will encounter outstanding leaders and others will encounter bad leaders. They will work in organizations that have dysfunctional cultures and in ones that are learning organizations. When coupled with the empowering liberal education they are receiving on campus, these off-campus, extra-curricular learning experiences will prepare them well to take on responsibilities of leadership and to become the entrepreneurs we need.

Entrepreneurship
To gain an understanding of the current status of entrepreneurship education, one need only go to the Ewing Marion Kauffman Foundation web page[7] to find several papers in the section devoted to entrepreneurship education. In a series of reports that can be downloaded, the tremendous growth in programs, centers, and curricula devoted to the study and practice of entrepreneurship is thoroughly documented. A summary statement on the Kauffman's College Entrepreneurship first web page reads:

> Fifteen years ago, entrepreneurship courses could only be found in a handful of schools in the United States. Today, more than 2,000 colleges and universities offer some form of entrepreneurship training – a trend that started in the early 1990s and continues to flourish. Interest in entrepreneurship education has spread to non-business disciplines, where students in engineering, life sciences and liberal arts are interested in becoming entrepreneurs.

This is indeed a dramatic increase in programs and curricula devoted to the exploration of entrepreneurship (see also Fairweather, 1988; Slaughter and Leslie, 1997; and Clark, 1998). Although liberal arts is mentioned in the Kauffman documents, the reality is that outside of engineering and the life sciences among non-business programs, relatively few institutions that are committed to liberal education have participated in this dramatic trend in higher education. If entrepreneurship education is to realize its full potential, this last group – the liberal arts – must be drawn into the dialogue about how to foster entrepreneurial life on those campuses that are committed to providing liberal education.

Leaving aside the real possibility that some schools and colleges of business have wanted to keep entrepreneurship to themselves, I would hazard that the primary reason for the neglect of entrepreneurship in predominantly liberal arts institutions has involved some combination of the following: (i) a perceived incongruity in the goals of the two endeavors; (ii) ignorance on the part of each about the other; and (iii) a lack of specific programming and funding designed to explore the points of intersection between the two endeavors. The now well-established initiative by the Kauffman Foundation to reach out to arts and sciences colleges in universities has already begun to address the last of these obstacles to cross-fertilization. Efforts to engage faculty from predominantly liberal arts institutions and the leading higher education organization in support of liberal education, AAC&U, through a consortium and AAC&U-sponsored workshops (Hines, 2005) hopefully will begin to remove the other two obstacles, at least for the participating institutions.

As noted in the Kauffman reports, while there is evidence of exploration of entrepreneurship education outside schools and colleges of business, there is almost no evidence presented of entrepreneurship and the liberal arts, although recent Kauffman Foundation grants to universities is an attempt to correct this deficiency. This is in stark contrast to the perspective provided by Ray (1990) in his article 'Liberal arts for entrepreneurs' as evidenced by the quotations from his article cited at the beginning of this chapter. Ray argues:

> The core learning relevant for an entrepreneurial life and career may not be found in a separate discipline; it may involve refocusing, rearranging, and clarifying many of the things done in a typical liberal arts college or in the undergraduate offerings of any university. In fact, liberal arts colleges may have an advantage in entrepreneurship education because they are not oriented to preparing individuals to become employees either in terms of skills or temperament. Entrepreneurship education should not be viewed as some mechanistic or technocratic process but as a holistic and integrative process which ultimately liberates people from employee status. (p. 80)

I wholeheartedly agree with his assessment.

I shall not review the origins and current meanings of entrepreneurship – a brief review can be found in Dees's (1998) 'The meaning of social entrepreneurship'. The concept of social entrepreneurship, however, deserves some attention in as much as it resonates so well with the goals of liberal education. Dees defines social entrepreneurship as follows (Dees et al., 2002: 5):

Social entrepreneurs play the role of change agents in the social sector by:

- Adopting a mission to create and sustain social value (not just private value).
- Recognizing and relentlessly pursuing new opportunities to serve that mission.
- Engaging in a process of continuous innovation, adaptation, and learning.
- Acting boldly without being limited by resources currently in hand.
- Exhibiting a heightened sense of accountability to the constituencies served and for the outcomes created.

Because liberal education is committed to educating for responsible citizenship, there is a special affinity between liberal education and social entrepreneurship. The last of Dees's aspects of social entrepreneurship speaks especially to this desired outcome of a liberal education and represents a powerful point of connection between liberal and entrepreneurial educational goals. As the former CEO of General Motors, Roger Smith, concludes in his article 'The liberal arts and the art of management': 'The ultimate impact of the liberal arts on the art of management, then, is a major contribution to the evolution of an ethical and humanistic capitalism – a system that stimulates innovation, fosters excellence, enriches society, and dignifies work' (Smith, 1987: 33). For Peter Drucker the very concept of entrepreneurship should really be subsumed under the rubric of 'innovation'. Like the other students of leadership I have cited (Burns, Schein, Nanus, Yukl), Drucker sees 'a commitment to the systematic practice of innovation' (2002: 95) as the trait that is common to all entrepreneurs. He says that what defines entrepreneurs is a particular sort of activity associated with their enterprises: 'At the heart of that activity is innovation: the effort to create purposeful, focused change in an enterprise's economic or social potential' (p. 96).

Creating the synergies we need for innovation
As Ray (1990) has argued, the liberal arts college or university offers the opportunity for a holistic educational experience that is well suited to the needs of the potential entrepreneur, primarily because the would-be entrepreneur needs to encounter a wide variety of perspectives, paradigms of inquiry, ethical norms, and the critical thinking and communication skills normally associated with the 'liberally educated student'. Rather than being 'trained', the potential entrepreneur needs to experience the various disciplinary and interdisciplinary perspectives found in the general education component of a liberal education. In addition, the contemporary liberal arts college is committed to the preparation of responsible citizens who will take their place in an increasingly complex and diverse world. Most liberal arts colleges are deeply committed to interdisciplinary, intercultural, and international education in its various manifestations. Proponents of liberal education are equally dedicated to providing students with the opportunity to become independent, active learners capable of charting their own course over a lifetime and engaged in an ongoing process of learning. The ideal liberal arts education models a process of continuous adaptation and innovation that is manifest in one's personal and professional life. Thus liberal education really is, as Dennis Ray contends, a 'metaphor for entrepreneurship'.

The concept of synergy is relatively well known in business education. An extremely popular book, Stephen R. Covey's *The 7 Habits of Highly Effective People* lists 'Synergize' as the sixth habit. Covey defines synergy as principle that the whole is greater than the sum of its parts: 'It means that the relationship which the parts have to each other is a part in and of itself. It is not the only part, but the most catalytic, the most empowering, the most unifying, and the most exciting part' (Covey, 1989: 263). Synergistic outcomes, according to Covey, maximize trust and cooperation to achieve win/win solutions. Corning has written extensively about the power of synergy and the role of synergy in evolution – both natural and social (Corning, 1983, 2003; Corning and Corning, 1986).[8] After noting that synergy comes from the Greek *synergos*, meaning 'working together' or (literally) 'cooperating', Corning defines synergy as 'the combined, or cooperative, effects produced by the relationships among various forces, particles, elements, parts, or individuals in a given context – effects that are not otherwise possible' (2003: 3).

We have been talking about liberal education, leadership, entrepreneurship, and civic engagement. Each of these subjects can be pursued on its own. But when we pursue them together, we recognize that although they are distinct, they also can be combined into a synergistic experience for students, faculty, and administrators, and the community to produce powerful results that are greater than the sum of the parts. The leadership we need to achieve this is a different type of leadership. Capra sees this as leadership that

> consists in facilitating the emergence of novelty. This means creating conditions rather than giving directions, and using the power of authority to empower others. . . . Being a leader means creating a vision; it means going where nobody has gone before. It also means enabling the community as a whole to create something new. Facilitating emergence means facilitating creativity. (2002: 122)

This is the kind of academic leadership and entrepreneurship that we need to create new synergies between the discrete areas we have been discussing. At one level, the level of the curriculum, there are exciting possibilities for exploring leadership and entrepreneurship in combination with civic engagement and informed by liberal education. Leadership programs for students, when combined with curricula that focus upon leadership and entrepreneurship and coupled with extra-curricular programs that engage students with their communities can produce liberally educated social entrepreneurs who are committed to solving social problems through innovative solutions that are empowering and produce value-added outcomes that are mutually beneficial. It is even the case that these synergies can transform the very institutions that make them possible and re-create them as engaged universities, linked to their communities, economies, and governments and non-profit organizations at all levels.

Making colleges entrepreneurial, learning organizations
An oft ignored benefit of introducing a culture of innovation into the academic mix of a liberal arts college (or any university) is the prospect of creating a leadership team within the institution that is committed to building a more entrepreneurial organization – one that sustains innovative practices and evolves into a true 'learning organization', following the model described in Peter Senge's (1990) *The Fifth Discipline: The Art and Practice of the Learning Organization*. Colleges and universities today face enormous challenges as they seek to sustain their venerable missions while increasingly being responsive to ever-greater demands that are placed upon them. And they are required to do so with increasingly less support from federal and state governments. Both public and private institutions are now in keen competition for philanthropic support and grants, and are actively exploring ways of generating revenues that have not been pursued heretofore. Just to underscore this point in the public sector of higher education in South Carolina, the College of Charleston's budget in 1973 was 68 percent state appropriated funds. In 2007, that percentage has dropped to 18 percent. Weekly, the *Chronicle of Higher Education* documents the anticipated budget cuts that are coming for the 2008–09 academic year. In March, both Kentucky and Florida were highlighted in the *Chronicle* as facing serious budget cuts. South Carolina is anticipating a significant budget reduction as the projected state revenue projections predict a $150 million

shortfall. To say that today's colleges and universities are financially challenged is a gross understatement.

Burton R. Clark, an eminent student and scholar of higher education practice, was funded by the Mellon Foundation and the Spencer Educational Foundation to study best practices in innovation at five European universities that are engaged in risk-taking, entrepreneurial strategies to address the problems referred to above. His study, *Creating Entrepreneurial Universities* (Clark, 1998) is well worth reading. I shall cite only one example to give the flavor of how these five universities have broken with tradition and embraced entrepreneurship. Warwick University in the United Kingdom had cut its budget to the quick and did not have the option of increasing its tuition to help meet its financial needs. The university leadership made a different choice:

> What Warwick turned to instead was an earning scheme within which various parts of the university – some old, some new – could be permanently put in a posture of paying for themselves and generating an annual surplus that could be used by the entire university. The idea became 'an earned income policy. . . .' The idea of earned income was given organizational footing as it developed hand in hand with the creation and growth of a number of units at Warwick that were to compose an enlarged developmental periphery. Foremost in its unusual nature as well as its contribution to earned income has been the Warwick Manufacturing Group (WMG), set up in 1980 and directed ever since by a charismatic professor, Kumar Bhattacharyya, in the university's engineering department . . . (Ibid.: 17)

Clark goes on to describe a hugely successful conference center, and science park, and to review leadership and management practices that have made these ventures successful. And then he discusses what, for our purposes, may be the most interesting aspect of this 'earned income policy' – *the stimulated academic heartland*:

> Entrepreneurship has not been left to a few subject areas such as engineering and business, and only to a managerial group dedicated to earning income, but has come to characterize virtually all academic fields. Four features reveal much about the involvement of core academic units: the melding of periphery into the core; the extensive building of research centers under departments; the construction of a university-wide graduate school; and the introduction of an imaginative and highly attractive research fellowship scheme that reached across the campus. (p. 27)

He goes on to describe initiatives in the social sciences, humanities and the arts:

> The entrepreneurial spirit shows through in these departments and centers. For example: the head of theatre studies, professor David Thomas, reported in interview that he was a 'happy opportunist' who came to Warwick because it 'had an entrepreneurial feel about it.' He takes experimental performances – undergraduates may be included – out to international festivals and audiences, raising money as he goes, while training 'cultural administrators' in advanced programs in a 'research-led department.' With self-funding courses, the department is basically self-supporting: it 'washes its own face'. (p. 28)

Other examples exist at the four other universities Clark studied.

The key point I want to make is that there are all kinds of synergies that arise as liberal education contributes to the shaping of the entrepreneurial mind and spirit through its courses of study. The entrepreneurial spirit of students, faculty and administrators in turn leads to innovative practices and an entrepreneurial culture for the entire institution.

Such mutually beneficial reciprocities bring new possibilities for liberal and professional education simultaneously. Barriers to collaborative teaching, research, and community service are broken down as teams of students and faculty engage in risk-taking behaviors grounded in their educational experiences that literally transform the university.

The tipping point for liberal education and entrepreneurship

Gladwell's (2002) *The Tipping Point: How Little Things Can Make a Big Difference* has attracted a great deal of attention. The back cover of the book explains: 'The tipping point is that magic moment when an idea, trend, or social behavior crosses a threshold, tips, and spreads like wildfire'. Gladwell gives numerous examples of this phenomenon. What is striking is that we are possibly at 'the tipping point' for the synergistic possibilities for a collaboration between liberal education and entrepreneurship. Gladwell cites three different agents of change that he believes account for tipping points. First, what he calls 'The Law of the Few' (Messengers) refers to the incredible influence that some extremely well-connected and interconnected individuals can have in spreading everything from disease to the purchase of Hush Puppy shoes. Second, he refers to 'The Stickiness Factor', which pertains to the way in which some ideas (Message) 'stick' more than others. That is to say, the content of the message matters, but the way you package it really matters. Finally he speaks of 'The Power of Context: Parts 1 and 2', which means that: (i) trends are 'sensitive to the conditions and circumstances of the times and places in which they occur' (p. 139); and (ii) that groups play a critical role in social trends (or epidemics).

If you think about the current state of readiness (for tipping) of entrepreneurship studies, leadership studies, civic engagement projects on campuses, and the liberal education agenda of the New Academy as envisioned by AAC&U, and you add to that rich context the message from the Kauffman Foundation and the institutional leadership of the authors in this volume along with others who are championing projects on their respective campuses, it seems to me that we are meeting the criteria described by Gladwell for a tipping point. In referring to the Law of the Few, Gladwell labels one type of connected individual the 'maven'. Maven is from the Yiddish and means someone who is a storehouse of knowledge. Mavens are often an important source of the information that is crucial to the message and to the understanding of context. We are today helping to identify who among us and those who are not with us who are 'mavens' or are 'connectors' and can help pique the interest of academic leaders in liberal education in the potential benefit of linking entrepreneurship and liberal education together for the benefit of our students. We have an opportunity through a consortium of institutions interested in developing this 'synergy for innovation' to support one another in our endeavors while producing model curricula, syllabuses, and programs to further a shared agenda. Peter Bernstein in his recent work, *Against the Gods: The Remarkable Story of Risk*, reminds us that 'the revolutionary idea that defines the boundary between modern times and the past is the mastery of risk: the notion that the future is more than a whim of the gods and that men and women are not passive before nature' (1998: 1). As a political theorist, I am ever mindful of Machiavelli's (Ledeen, 1999) discussion of the interplay of *virtu* on the part of the Prince and *fortuna* – the winds of chance that makes the removal of risk impossible. That aside, I do believe that we should risk creating a consortium of predominantly liberal arts and sciences colleges and universities that are committed to exploring the many possibilities of linking entrepreneurship with liberal education through a variety of means.

Building campuses, cultures and curricula for innovation

I have tried to show ways in which the study of leadership and entrepreneurship and the 'best practice' of civic engagement are potentially linked in important ways. I have also tried to show how linking the liberal arts with business education in the exploration of the entrepreneurial spirit or mindset can be mutually beneficial to both academic endeavors. Indeed, I believe such collaborations can definitely lead to new synergies that can help today's liberal arts colleges and universities improve their situation relative to the challenges they face from forces in their environments. By building 'entrepreneurial campuses' committed to experimentation, risk taking, and entrepreneurial ventures, colleges potentially can increase their range of choices and strategic options as they navigate to avoid potentially mission-threatening resource shortfalls. As Burton Clark has shown in his study of five European universities and as we know from initiatives taken at a number of American universities (for example, Stanford, Harvard, Portland State University, Hampshire College, Syracuse University and others) there are many opportunities for both profitable ventures and for 'social entrepreneurship' directed toward solving social problems and meeting consumer/constituent demand. All of these initiatives can help students draw upon their liberal education as they become involved with their communities and as they seek to chart their individual career paths. While there are few causal explanations that show conclusively that the synergies created will result in positive outcomes for the universities or for the students, there is a lot of evidence of the success of entrepreneurship programs in business and there is growing evidence that disciplines, interdisciplines and programs other than business can usefully promote the study of leadership and entrepreneurship by students and implement programs of civic engagement (in particular internships) that draw heavily upon the former courses of study. Such efforts to bridge the liberal arts and the professions, far from threatening either, can serve to create new, exciting partnerships and interdisciplinary paths of inquiry and service learning that will repay the effort for all involved. The liberal arts, long venerated, have a great deal to offer to students seeking to gain a more holistic perspective and to cultivate the life of the mind in the service of chosen career objectives.

In closing, I want to cite the remarks of Alan Greenspan, former Chairman of the Federal Reserve Board. In an address at the International Understanding Award Dinner of the Institute of International Education in New York, Greenspan underscored the crucial role of liberal education in relation to our economic future and to the human prospect. I believe he gets it right (Greenspan, 2003: 53):

> Creative intellectual energy . . . drives our system forward. As the conceptual inputs to the value added in our economic processes continue to grow, the ability to think abstractly will be increasingly important across a broad range of professions. Critical awareness and the abilities to hypothesize, to interpret, and to communicate are essential elements of successful innovation in a conceptual – based economy. [E]ven without hard indisputable evidence, a remarkable and broad presumption is that the ability to think conceptually is fostered through exposure to philosophy, literature, music, art, and languages. So-called liberal education is presumed to spawn a great understanding of all aspects of living – an essential ingredient to broaden one's worldview. . . . Most conceptual advances are interdisciplinary and involve synergies of different

specialties. Yet the liberal arts embody more than a means of increasing technical intellectual efficiency. They encourage the appreciation of life experiences that reach beyond material well-being and, indeed, are comparable and mutually reinforcing.

Notes

1. See www.coplac.org.
2. See Yukl (1998) for a bibliography of the latter.
3. See Nanus (1992) for a detailed discussion of visionary leadership.
4. See www.compact.org.
5. See www.aacu-edu.org/civic_engagement and see also the American Association of State Colleges and Universities' American Democracy Project at www.aascu.org/programs/adp.
6. See also the list of colleges and universities provided in Colby et al. (2003).
7. See www.kauffman.org.
8. See also the recent work of Capra (2002).

References

Bernstein, Peter (1998), *Against the Gods: The Remarkable Story of Risk*, New York: John Wiley & Sons.
Bolman, Lee G. and Terrence E. Deal (1997), *Reframing Organizations: Artistry, Choice, and Leadership*, 2nd edn, San Francisco, CA: Jossey-Bass.
Breneman, David (1993), *Higher Education: On a Collision Course with New Realities*, Washington, DC: Association of Governing Boards.
Burns, James MacGregor (1978), *Leadership*, New York: Harper & Row.
Burns, James MacGregor (2003), *Transforming Leadership*, New York: Atlantic Monthly Press.
Capra, Fritjof (2002), *The Hidden Connections: Integrating the Biological, Cognitive, and Social Dimensions of Life into a Science of Sustainability*, New York: Doubleday.
Clark, Burton (1998), *Creating Entrepreneurial Universities: Organizational Pathways of Transformation*, New York: IAU Press and Elsevier Science.
Colby, Anne, Thomas Ehrlich, Elizabeth Beaumont and Jason Stephens (2003), 'Educating undergraduates for responsible citizenship', *Change*, **35** (6): 40–48.
Corning, Peter (1983), *The Synergism Hypothesis: A Theory of Progressive Evolution*, New York: McGraw-Hill.
Corning, Peter (2003), *Nature's Magic: Synergy in Evolution and the Fate of Humankind*, Cambridge: Cambridge University Press.
Corning, Peter and Susan Corning (1986), *Winning with Synergy: How America Can Regain the Competitive Edge*, San Francisco, CA: Harper & Row.
Covey, Stephen R. (1989), *The 7 Habits of Highly Effective People: Powerful Lessons in Personal Change*, New York: Free Press.
Dees, J. Gregory (1998), 'The meaning of social entrepreneurship', www.gsb.stanford.edu/services/news/DeesSocentrepPaper.html.
Dees, J. Gregory, Melissa Taylor and Jed Emerson (2002), 'The question of scale: finding an appropriate strategy for building on your success', in J. Gregory Dees, Jed Emerson and Peter Economy (eds), *Strategic Tools for Social Entrepreneurs: Enhancing the Performance of Your Enterprising Nonprofits*, Greenwich, CT: John Wiley, pp. 235–66.
Drucker, Peter (2002), 'The discipline of innovation', *Harvard Business Review*, **80** (8): 95–102.
Ehrlich, Thomas (ed.) (2000), *Civic Responsibility and Higher Education*, Phoenix, AZ: American Council on Education/Oryx Press.
Engell, J. and A. Dangerfield (2005), *Saving Higher Education in the Age of Money*, Charlottesville, VA: University of Virginia Press.
Fairweather, James S. (1988), *Entrepreneurship and Higher Education*, Washington, DC: Association for the Study of Higher Education.
Gladwell, Malcolm (2002), *The Tipping Point: How Little Things Can Make a Big Difference*, Boston, MA: Back Bay Books/Little, Brown.
Greenspan, Alan (2003), 'Remarks on the liberal arts', *Liberal Education*, **89** (3): 52–3.
Hesselbein, Frances, Marshall Goldsmith and Richard Beckhard (eds) (1996), *The Leader of the Future*, San Francisco, CA: Jossey-Bass.
Hines, Samuel (2005), 'The practical side of liberal education: an overview of liberal education and entrepreneurship', *Peer Review*, **7** (3): 4–7.

Hines, Samuel (2008), *The Entrepreneurial University in Support of Liberal Education*, Washington, DC: Association of American Colleges and Universities.

Hitt, M.A., R.D. Ireland, S.M. Camp and D.L. Sexton (2002), *Strategic Entrepreneurship: Creating a New Mindset*, Oxford: Blackwell.

Johnston, Joseph S. Jr, Stanley Burns, David Butler, Marcie Schorr Hirsch, Thomas Jones, Alan Kantrow, Kathryn Mohrman, Roger Smith and Michael Useem (1987), *Educating Managers: Executive Effectiveness Through Liberal Learning*, San Francisco, CA: Jossey-Bass.

Ledeen, Michael A. (1999), *Machiavelli on Modern Leadership*, New York: St. Martin's, Griffin.

Nanus, Burt (1992), *Visionary Leadership*, San Francisco, CA: Jossey-Bass.

Ramaley, J. and A. Leskes et al. (2002), 'Greater Expectations: A New Vision for Learning as a Nation Goes to College', National Panel Report of the Association of American Colleges and Universities, Washington, DC: AAC&U.

Ray, Dennis (1990), 'Liberal arts for entrepreneurs', *Entrepreneurship Theory and Practice*, **15** (2): 79–93.

Rothblatt, Sheldon (2003), *The Living Arts: Comparative and Historical Reflections on Liberal Education*, Washington, DC: Association of American Colleges and Universities.

Schaub, Diana (2002), 'Can liberal education survive liberal democracy?', *Public Interest*, **147** (Spring): 45–60.

Schein, Edgar H. (1996), 'Leadership and organizational culture', in Hesselbein et al. (eds), pp. 59–69.

Schneider, Carol Geary (2000), 'Educational missions and civic responsibility: toward the engaged academy', in Ehrlich (ed.), pp. 98–123.

Senge, Peter M. (1990), *The Fifth Discipline: The Art and Practice of the Learning Organization*, New York: Doubleday.

Slaughter, Sheila and Larry L. Leslie (1997), *Academic Capitalism: Politics, Policies, and the Entrepreneurial University*, Baltimore, MD: Johns Hopkins University Press.

Smith, Roger B. (1987), 'The liberal arts and the art of management', in Johnston et al. (eds), pp. 21–33.

Terry, Robert W. (1993), *Authentic Leadership: Courage in Action*, San Francisco, CA: Jossey-Bass.

Walumbwa, F.O., B.J. Avolio, W.L. Gardner, T.S. Wernsing and S.J. Peterson (2008), 'Authentic leadership: development and validation of a theory-based measure', *Journal of Management*, **34** (1): 89–126.

Yukl, Gary (1998), *Leadership in Organizations*, 4th edn, Upper Saddle River, NJ: Prentice-Hall.

Zemsky, R., G.R. Wegner and W.F. Massy (2005), *Remaking the American University: Market-Smart and Misson-Centered*, New Brunswick, NJ: Rutgers University Press.

Index